With all our ♡ W9-ANB-892

Marketing at The
Institute

May, 1992

THE SMITHSONIAN BOOK OF BIRDS

LORDS OF THE AIR

JAKE PAGE AND EUGENE S. MORTON

Introduction by S. Dillon Ripley
Secretary Emeritus, Smithsonian Institution

SMITHSONIAN BOOKS
WASHINGTON, D.C.

ORION BOOKS
NEW YORK

THE SMITHSONIAN INSTITUTION
Secretary Robert McC. Adams
Assistant Secretary for Public Service
   Ralph Rinzler
Director, Smithsonian Institution Press
   Felix C. Lowe

SMITHSONIAN BOOKS
Editor-in-Chief Patricia Gallagher
Administrative Assistant Anne P. Naruta
Senior Editor Alexis Doster III
Editors Amy Donovan, Joe Goodwin
Research Bryan D. Kennedy
Copy Editor Elizabeth Dahlslien
Acting Senior Picture Editor
   Frances C. Rowsell
Picture Editor R. Jenny Takacs
Picture Research Paula Ballo-Dailey,
   Carrie E. Bruns, Ann Monroe Jacobs
Picture Assistant Sebastian C. Hayman
Production Editor Patricia Upchurch
Production Assistant Martha Sewall
Business Manager Stephen J. Bergstrom
Marketing Director Gail Grella
Marketing Manager Barbara Erlandson
Product Specialist John Salisbury
Design The Watermark Design Office
Typography Harlowe Typography, Inc.
Separations The Lanman Companies
Printing Ringier America

Distributed to the trade by Orion Books, a
division of Crown Publishers, 201 East 50th
Street, New York, NY 10022. Orion is a
trademark of Crown Publishers, Inc.
ISBN 0-517-57407-1 (Orion Books)

Library of Congress Cataloging-in
Publication Data

Page, Jake.
   Lords of the air : the Smithsonian book
of birds / Jake Page and Eugene S. Morton ;
introduction by S. Dillon Ripley.
      p.   cm.
   Includes index.
   ISBN 0-89599-024-5 (alk. paper) :
   1. Birds.   I. Morton, Eugene S.   II.
Title. QL673.P33   1989
   598—dc20   89-600208

Manufactured in the United States
of America

First Edition
10   9   8   7   6   5   4   3   2   1

Page 1: sedge wren, Muscatatuck National Wildlife Refuge, Indiana; pages 2-3: microscopic view of peacock feather; pages 4-5: overlapping breast feathers of a ring-necked pheasant; pages 6-7: exquisite "eye" in a peacock's tail feather; page 11: young American coot, Whitford Lake, Alberta.

CONTENTS

For us humans, birds occupy a unique place in the world of nature. Like us, they have a keen sense of color that is not shared by other highly developed classes of animals, such as, in general, mammals. The reason for this heightened sense of color may lie in the fact that birds can fly and, as masters of the air, are transported into another dimension from which mammals, along with reptiles and the rest of the more highly integrated animals, to a large extent are excluded. Crocodiles, for example, cannot fly, even though their heart construction brings them close to birds in some ways. Nor do many reptiles, as far as we know, possess the ability to see color. And yet color rules the bird kingdom almost throughout, and is often shown to its best advantage in the elaborate rituals brought on by the need for most bird species to seek out mates in a highly competitive atmosphere.

Thus, color and visual acuity, which go together and are closely linked to flight, are predominant in birds, and make them perhaps more subject to the development of a kind of kinship, on the one hand, and of great fascination to us humans on the other. Birds are not essentially likable in their habits: some people are frightened of crowds of birds and find their presence menacing. The shrill noise of certain birds is obnoxious to some people, and yet the beautiful songs of birds, mostly undertaken for mating or territorial purposes, have been an inspiration to countless poets and writers. It is obvious that birds are attractive and noticeable, have a highly personal relationship to humans, stimulate interest and, indeed, beyond interest, enjoyment and sometimes passion. At the same time, being of a different taxonomic class from ourselves, birds are objects of continuing scientific study.

Almost from its beginnings, the Smithsonian Institution has been a center for the scientific study of birds, originally describing the state of nature in our new nation and now perhaps warning us of the decline of our environment. Not many months after the formation of the Institution in 1846, our first Secretary, Joseph Henry, received a letter from Spencer Fullerton Baird, a young man who had written to request a job as Henry's assistant. At the time, the great task of describing and understanding the resources of the United States territories was paramount. Descriptive and nomenclatural biology was a high priority even to an outstanding physicist such as Joseph Henry. How was it possible otherwise that in 1850 Henry should designate this young upstart as Assistant Secretary? Baird was approximately half Henry's age (27 as against 53), and thus must have seemed even to Henry a somewhat callow young man, possessed helplessly with the collecting mania, especially for objects of natural history. Could he be suitably trained in all aspects of science as curator of a National Museum-to-be? That must have seemed a question that the physicist was not entirely anxious to address. Nonetheless, Baird packed up and came down from Carlisle, Pennsylvania, with two freight cars loaded with the fruits of his collecting talents: 4,000 bird skins, several thousand eggs and nests, 500 glass jars, barrels, kegs, and tin vessels of reptiles and fishes, 600 skulls and skeletons, and a liberal assortment of bird, mammal, frog, and toad embryos, not to mention a wealth of fossil bones dug up in caves from Pennsylvania and Virginia, all to be deposited in the Smithsonian Building, or "Castle," to enlarge enormously the nucleus of natural history collections.

Over the years, Spencer Baird proved himself to be perhaps the most assiduous collector of natural history specimens that the United States has ever seen. Furthermore, he recognized the unique opportunity for the study of natural history that the many expeditions then setting out to explore the West offered. Accordingly, he saw to it that naturalists—some of whom he himself trained and outfitted—accompanied the government survey teams and collected for the Smithsonian.

Baird also saw the importance of the donation of specimens, and he corresponded with people all over the world, stimulating and

One of about 55 species of often brilliantly colored wood warblers that breed in North America, a palm warbler pulls at a vine-entwined reed in Florida's Everglades National Park. Summer denizens of sphagnum bogs in the northern United States and Canada, palm warblers winter as far south as the West Indies and Honduras.

guiding collectors-and friends-to-be. These ranged from anonymous forwarders of dead garter snakes and damaged luna moths, as one chronicler of the Smithsonian, Geoffrey Hellman, has written, to major collectors of specimens and skins and skulls. In some cases, as Hellman observed, when the collectors' "ardor flagged," Baird exhorted them to continue. "Never fear the non-acceptability of anything you may send," he wrote in 1853 to Alexander Winchell, head of the Mesopotamia Female Seminary of Eutaw, Alabama, who, while sending him 650 species of southern birds, insects, and plants, had complained that Secretary Henry seemed to wish to discourage such contributions. "It is true, Prof. Henry is opposed to indiscriminate collections; so'm I," Baird replied, "but our idea is a complete North American collection at least."

The final 20-odd years of Secretary Henry's reign marked the development and recognition of Spencer Baird as the outstanding naturalist of the United States. As Assistant Secretary of the Institution, he was preeminent in setting up the plans for the construction of a second building, now called the Arts and Industries Building, as an addition to the U.S. National Museum and as an exhibit hall not only for specimens but also for the treasures donated to the Institution after the great 1876 Exposition, which celebrated the nation's 100th birthday. Altogether, Baird was an extraordinary and complementary assistant to Henry and indeed performed ably as his successor.

Not surprisingly, Baird developed an important school of followers in natural history, particularly in ornithology. In collaboration with his highly respected colleagues Thomas Brewer and Robert Ridgway, Baird prepared the definitive *A History of North American Birds*. He later went on to head the U.S. Commission of Fish and Fisheries, in addition to broadening his own specialties in zoology, and succeeded in laying the foundation for the Woods Hole Oceanographic Institute as well as many other important societies. Certainly Baird deserved his selection as the second Secretary in 1878, and certainly

Passionate naturalist and collector Spencer Fullerton Baird, seen at right with wife, Mary, and daughter, Lucy, came to the Smithsonian as Assistant Secretary in 1850. Bird skins opposite, including the now-extinct Carolina parakeet (third from top), are a small sampling of his contribution. Arriving at the Smithsonian at the time the federal government's exploration of the West was surging, Baird promoted the collection of flora and fauna on these expeditions. Below, a 19th-century lithograph depicts a researcher working with bird specimens in the Smithsonian's Castle.

he played his part in reaffirming the almost incomparable role of the Institution in natural science.

Baird was followed by a succession of Secretaries who, though eminent in their own fields, were not naturalists. Then, in 1944, astrophysicist and fifth Secretary Charles G. Abbot was succeeded by ornithologist Alexander Wetmore. Wetmore had served as Assistant Secretary of the Institution and as director of its National Museum since 1925. His appointment, as Smithsonian observer Paul Oehser has noted, "in several ways marked a milestone in Smithsonian history. [It] came in 1944 in the closing days of World War II, which meant that the Institution could resume its peacetime programs."

As a young man at the University of Kansas, Wetmore had been concerned with the U.S. Biological Survey and with state studies of birds. Until the end of his career he persisted in publishing a multitude of reports on American bird fauna, both recent and paleontological and, in his time, was this country's most prominent avian paleontologist. It has, in fact, been a tradition of the Institution (now kept up by curator Storrs Olson) that the paleontological history of birds is more actively pursued at the Smithsonian than anywhere else in the United States.

Much beloved as a president of the American Ornithologists' Union and the secretary general of the American Scientific Congress, which met in Washington in 1937, Wetmore participated in both the technical and organizational affairs of the world of natural history, as well as in the dawning of international wildlife protection. As had Baird, he became the preeminent American ornithologist of his time, thus balancing the succession of physicists represented by Henry, Samuel P. Langley, and Abbot. Through his popular writings and his outstanding scientific work he enriched the study of birds by both amateur and

Walter A. Weber's painting of a Tacarcuna wood quail, opposite, introduces Part 1 of The Birds of the Republic of Panamá, *a four-volume work by preeminent ornithologist and fifth Secretary of the Smithsonian Alexander Wetmore. Right, a young Alexander Wetmore examines a blue jay around 1902. Wetmore would go on to become one of the world's most respected ornithologists, publishing hundreds of scientific works and describing some 189 previously unknown species and subspecies of birds. He served as Secretary of the Smithsonian from 1945-52.*

It was during Alexander Wetmore's tenure as Secretary of the Smithsonian that the Institution became the administrator of Barro Colorado, a 4,000-acre island in a lake created during the construction of the Panama Canal. The rich flora and fauna of this island reserve continue to afford scientists a unique opportunity for tropical study. Opposite, lianas stream down from a lofty Ceiba pentandra, one of Barro Colorado's largest species of trees. Below left, a toad blends in with the leaf litter on the forest floor, though not nearly as well as the nesting pauraque, left. Numbers on a helicopter damselfly, below right, identify it to researchers.

professional. It is difficult, thinking back, to recall anyone so universally respected and beloved in his field.

During Wetmore's tenure the Smithsonian became the administrator of the biological study being conducted on Barro Colorado, a 4,000-acre island created by damming the Chagres River during the construction of the Panama Canal. While distant from Washington, Barro Colorado Island has served over the years as perhaps the hallmark of the dawning of the environmental age for Americans. Situated in Gatun Lake in the Panama Canal about midway through the Isthmus and covered with tropical rain forest, it is the only such holding under the American flag, and the richness of its flora and fauna has afforded the opportunity for studies marking the commencement of modern-day tropical ecological research. Here was performed the first long-term study of succession in tropical-forest growth, and the understanding derived from this and many other research projects has helped to foster in Americans a renewed interest in tropical study.

It would seem that the alternate cycles of field biology and physics have ushered in a new era of broader understanding in which almost all the aspects of scientific research come together. Today, at the Smithsonian and elsewhere, ornithology plays a signal role in biology in its history of development through ethology, and field studies offer a new understanding of the major problems facing the world. As the eighth Secretary of the Smithsonian, I had the good fortune to travel extensively in the tropics, primarily in the Old World, but in the New World as well, and, as an ornithologist, I derive much food for thought and inspiration in the field of ecological understanding of long-term environmental change.

At present, the world is on the brink of another era of exploration in which we will study environmental degradation, for indeed the planet as a whole is beginning to suffer, with many overt signs of overpopulation and overdevelopment. My own research over the years has served to give me a heightened

Secretary of the Smithsonian from 1964-84, ornithologist S. Dillon Ripley holds Canada goslings at his waterfowl sanctuary in Litchfield, Connecticut, right. Continuing in the tradition of 19th-century Secretary Spencer Baird, who along with colleagues Thomas Brewer and Robert Ridgway published the multi-volume The History of North American Birds, *including the woodpecker plate below, Ripley collaborated with the late Sálim Ali to write the 10-volume* Handbook of the Birds of India and Pakistan. *A sarus crane, opposite, the largest of its family, attends its chick in a northern Indian wetland.*

awareness of and concern for many aspects of physical phenomena. It is curious indeed to contemplate the future of field biology today as the health of the planet declines. Perhaps greater than any other event and of more significance to the economy of the world's peoples will be the discovery in the next few years of what the future holds for us. Famine, disease, lack of water, and the multiplication of other severe hardships could well be the result of our present course, and it is only to be hoped that the economic and political interests of the world's nations will help to synthesize a pattern for the future that can ensure the continued maintenance of civilization. How enigmatic and provocative such a picture can be! The future is, as always, unknown, but the results of field biology may well provide many of the clues to our unlocking of the secrets of the future.

Certainly, the world of birds offers one of the clearest indications of the importance of field biology. For these purposes, knowledge of the distribution of birds and of their life histories plays a vitally important role in our understanding of the present status of the environment. I myself find that the presence or absence of birds is as significant a test of our nation's health as almost any other. In years to come we shall realize that the state of this country is defined in ways that we are still discovering—in the state of our birds, ebbing and flowing across the land.

Nesting in marshes and on ponds throughout much of North America, pied-billed grebes, left, often carry their precocial young on their backs for early glides over the water. Right, symbol of Athena, the Greek goddess of wisdom and the arts, an owl graces an ancient Greek coin from about 390 B.C., and lives on also as a symbol of the Smithsonian.

Mankind is a singing species. A plausible case could be made that our earliest ancestors crossed the subtle threshold into humanity when they learned to sing, to take rhythmic and melodious note of the things in their world, the better to remember and pass the information along. It is also plausible that one of the things early people sang about was birds, those other singing creatures. Certainly they memorialized birds in their early paintings and engravings in the caves and grottoes of Europe (though nowhere near as much as they did mammals). Images of birds—owls, cranes, eagles, ravens—have also been found etched into Paleolithic bone tools.

Can anyone think that it was much later that the universal dream of free flight became recurrent—the certain sensation of soaring through the air, arms outstretched, the wind in your face, the deft maneuver with hand or wrist to veer off or pull out of a power dive? How long could it have been before the eagle became one of the shaman's totems, the

Preceding pages: The embodiment of avian power and grace, mighty trumpeter swans splash into the air from a lake at Jackson Hole, Wyoming. Deep-voiced trumpeters may spread their wings six feet, and weigh nearly 30 pounds.

Dreams of flight reach deep into the human past: enigmatic Ice Age images of a bird and perhaps a bird-headed human, above, adorn a wall in France's Lascaux Cave. The "Winged Victory" or "Nike of Samothrace," opposite, from about 200 B.C., portrays the Greek goddess of victory. Left, realizing the ancient myth of the flight of Daedalus and his son, Icarus, from Crete, Greek cyclist Kanellos Kanellopoulos pedal-piloted the human-powered aircraft Daedalus *72 miles from Crete to the Aegean isle of Santorin in 1988. The 112-foot-wingspan, 68.5-pound* Daedalus *was designed and built by a team from the Massachusetts Institute of Technology.*

incomparable feather an item of adornment that additionally conveyed the magical power of flight to one's prayers?

There were other tenants of the air, to be sure—insects, bats—all highly noticeable, but nothing to equal the split-second violence of a falcon diving, the irritable congregation of vultures at a potential source of carrion, the symmetrical V of geese in flight, the ghostly night passage of an owl, the imperious dignity of cranes, or the miracle of birdsong in the morning.

Humanity's vital connection with birds—as food, competitor, guide, symbol, and ambition—is surely as old as our species: it is no surprise that landfall's proximity was signaled to Noah by that superior flier, the dove.

It was another dove that helped the Hopi Indians, then dwelling in an earlier world under the ground, to locate their fourth and present world in the arid highlands of Arizona. And it was a mockingbird, named *yawapa*, who greeted them upon their arrival and, always the polyglot, bestowed on them and the other tribes their various languages. Golden eagles still sit on the rooftops in Hopi villages watching the rain ceremonies, themselves messengers to the spirits.

Throughout the North American continent, once-migrant tribes of people took note of the eagle, soaring upward in greater and greater circles to a vanishing point in the clouds. They associated it with thunder, lightning, and rain, and deemed it Thunderbird. Later, Benjamin Franklin complained when the bald eagle was designated an emblem of the recently formed United States. The eagle, he found, was a sometimes scavenger, a bird of perhaps pusillanimous character. Franklin's burgomaster choice was the wild turkey, also unique to America and a practical bird, at least when it came to human intentions and desires. But Franklin did not sense what the Indians knew: there is nothing like the eagle— he who suffers the little birds to sing.

Of course, there is nothing ignoble about a turkey—though it has become a term of ridicule. Some American Indians today like to sport a T-shirt that expresses their gratitude that Columbus set sail for India, not Turkey. There is, for that matter, nothing ignoble about any bird, for they are all expressions of life, but humans have always attributed meanings to them—meanings that the birds themselves no doubt would find surprising. We humans appear always to have been on the lookout for ways to understand ourselves and our world, and for most of our tenure here we have rarely looked at any bird—say, a crow—and simply seen a crow, one of many crows, which are themselves one of many kinds of bird. In the first place, crows and most other birds fly, and flight has meaning. The crow is black, and black means something. Feathers mean something, as do the eggs from which the crow is born. For most people throughout time, these meanings have been as real as the bird itself, and perhaps more so, since the meanings were taken to be universal and eternal.

Flight means space, light, thought, imagination. In almost every society we know of, flight has meant raising oneself up to greater heights of morality, strength, or creativity. The opposite, of course, is the descent, the fall. One scholar of symbols, Gaston Bachelard, has said that "of all metaphors, only those pertaining to height, ascent, depth, descent and fall are axiomatic. Nothing can explain them but they explain everything."

Thus the bird came early to signify the soul. The Egyptians, the Greeks, and the Romans all portrayed the soul as a bird with a human head. In a Hindu tale, an ogre explained where he kept his soul. Far away, his story went, there was a tree. "Round the tree are tigers, and bears, and scorpions and snakes; on the top of the tree is a very great fat snake. On his head is a little cage; in the cage is a bird; and my soul is in that bird." When Mohammed went to heaven he found the Tree of Life, and in the surrounding trees were uncountable birds, brightly colored and singing: the souls of the faithful.

In ancient Egypt, the feather, that quintessential feature of birdness, was one of the hieroglyphic elements that spelled such words as lightness and height. The feather symbolized not just the wind but the creator-gods, including Osiris. The quill meant the "delineator of all things." Similarly, in medieval Christianity, feathers denoted faith and contemplation; the quill, with which generations of monks copied ecclesiastical manuscripts, also meant the Word of God. Like feathers and flight, wings have been seen as analogous to spirituality, though to the Greeks they signified love and victory as well.

Noah's dove symbolized peace in this late-medieval illustration for a bestiary, left. The "Vulci Vase," right, from around 550 B.C., depicts the mythical Greek hero Hercules in his sixth Labor, as he readies his sling to drive sinister man-eating birds from Lake Stymphalis. To Egyptians of antiquity, the ibis, opposite, represented Thoth, god of wisdom.

The statue "Nike of Samothrace" may be armless, but being winged it remains victorious.

In prehistoric tombs, clay eggs were interred, evidently a symbol, or a hope, for immortality. The egg pictured floating above a mummy meant the same thing for the Egyptians, who added to its meaning the idea of potentiality, the seed of becoming. Later, the Romans buried their dead with eggs, and the Maoris of New Zealand would place a moa's egg in one hand of a deceased kinsman—until they wiped the birds out. The Egyptians, obviously aware that some secret process of life was going on inside an eggshell, took this to be proof that hidden things—what we call the occult—were real. To this day, divination by eggs, called oomancy, is practiced in many cultures, usually by letting the albumen drop into water and seeing the future in the shapes it assumes.

Not every aspect of birds was positive, however. Multiplicity—too much of a good thing—has generally struck people as negative. The great restless teeming of flocks of birds such as blackbirds, gusting up in the air like swarms of insects, noisy and apparently angry, no doubt seemed somehow ominous, just as they do today. The flocks of birds that rose up from Lake Stymphalis during the labors of Hercules represented the evil desires of humanity. Nor was flight good in every instance: the story of Icarus, whose wax wings melted when he approached too near the sun, is the archetypal reminder of the fruits of an overreaching ambition. And, of course, individual bird species have long been given a bad rap.

While Athena, the Greek goddess of

wisdom, took the owl as one of her emblems (as has the Smithsonian Institution), for the Egyptians it denoted cold, death, and night. It was when owls were active that the sun itself was dead, passing through the sea of darkness. For the Romans as well, the owl was an ill omen, its hooting—or worse, its appearance in the house or courtyard— presaging death. An owl screeched before Julius Caesar's murder. For most American Indian tribes, the owl forecasts a death, though the Pawnees believe that owls are a protection against the night. A number of African tribes connect owls with the evil-doings of sorcerers, and the Book of Leviticus includes owls among the unclean birds that must not be eaten.

Another unclean bird is the raven, which has often been regarded unfavorably in the annals of human myth and symbol. For many, the raven is another omen of death, or pestilence; for some it transports the souls of the damned. The Devil himself reportedly has appeared as a raven, which is also a symbol of the enemy in Russian legend. On the other hand, in ancient Greece the raven was a bird of prophecy and was held sacred by Apollo . . . until the raven, then a white bird, became the messenger of bad news. Apollo's lover, Coronis, had run off with a mortal, and the white raven reported her faithlessness to the god. In a rage, he condemned the messenger to be evermore black.

Among the Indians of the Pacific Northwest, where the bird's evident intelligence and mischievousness are well noted, the raven is something of a cultural hero. Raven, it is told, extracted man out of a clamshell, stole fire and the sun, and provided humanity with these gifts, along with water and the other animals. He created the features of the Earth—mountains, rivers, and the like—and remains a clever trickster to this day, always deceptively on the lookout for food, in one story having dived deep into the water to steal a halibut from a fisherman's hook.

Among some Indians, the role of Raven is played by the crow, its cousin, a creator and civilizer, a messenger whose black plumage is associated with the beginning of things. In Christian symbolism, the crow bespoke solitude; in ancient China, a three-legged image of a crow represented yang, or the active life of the emperor.

For most of our history we have made the most of birds—and almost universally in our own behalf. Though unquestionably now the most powerful force on the planet, we clearly arose from some state of terror. We learned to run on two legs, but for a long time we were the hunted, only later becoming accomplished hunters ourselves. First, though, we had to become athletes capable of fleeing, then maybe of learning to wing a bird with a rock or getting up the courage to chase a flock of vultures from some other animal's prey. We emerged from what may have been a classic case of

insecurity: only such origins could explain why we have always used the creatures around us as clues to our identity, our place in nature.

We ate them, and still do. But as we ate, we believed that we could thus garner some of their unique powers, and so they became—universally and specifically—symbols for what we hoped and dreamed and imagined, part of our moral landscape. Nor is this necessarily just ancient history and the untamed fairy tales of so-called primitive society. Jungian psychology takes note of the flight of birds in our dreams, seeing it as symbolic, now and ever since the earliest human dreaming, of a state of becoming—where a youth, say, is ready to take on a new role as an adult, or where a middle-aged person yearns to take on a new career, a new life. Bird flight is seen as transcendence, the suggestion being that *without* dreaming of flight one may not be ready for or capable of change. "Today," writes psychologist Joseph L. Henderson, "we could as well speak of jet planes and space rockets, for they are the physical embodiment of the same transcendent principle, freeing us at least temporarily from gravity."

Even in earlier civilizations less given to the thought processes of a scientific age, the living birds themselves in all their symbolic repertoire were not always sufficient. Mythi-

cal creatures also were invented, embodying the meanings of birds and often joining them with aspects of other animals. One such creature was the griffin, part eagle, part lion, with a serpentine tail, a generally benevolent guardian of the roads to salvation and, more mundanely, the guardian of mines and treasure, such as the Scythian gold. Of all mythic birds, none perhaps was so ripe with meaning as the phoenix—usually portrayed as the size of an eagle but with some pheasantlike features. In China, it was the emperor of birds and a symbol of the sun. But in the Levant and Europe, it took on its deepest meaning: the bird that rises from the ashes. As its death approached, the bird made a nest of wood out in the searing full sun. The nest caught fire and from the ashes a new phoenix arose. The Egyptians said this happened every 500 years, clearly a suggestion of the rise and fall of civilizations. In early Christianity, the

phoenix signified the resurrection of Christ and the survivability of the soul.

But we are also a practical, down-to-earth race, and in some cases birds are seen just as birds. Some hunters in the Appalachian backwoods still listen, without a trace of romance, for the irritated rasp of a raven and know that there are turkeys nearby. Just what it is about wild turkeys that bothers ravens the hunters do not know or care. They merely have listened and found turkeys. There are some situations where the advantages are clearly mutual. In sub-Saharan Africa, a species called the greater honeyguide has developed a reciprocal arrangement with a kind of honey badger, or ratel, and, more lately, with Homo sapiens. The bird will set up a great hue and cry, chattering noisily in a bush to get the honey badger's or the man's attention. Then it flies a short way off and chatters again, eventually leading its mammalian collabora-

Real and imagined attributes of birds have been employed throughout history as symbols of traits humans admire. Thus, the stylized raven on a ceremonial drum, opposite, from the Northwest Coast of North America may represent wisdom and strength; the eagle on the Great Seal of the United States of America, below, the might and majesty of the state; and the mythical Thunderbird of many North American Indian tribes the elegant power of the 1957 Ford Thunderbird, above.

tor up to half a mile to a hive of honeybees. The honey badger or man digs out the hive and takes the honey, and then the bird arrives to eat beeswax (which, thanks to a population of helpful bacteria in its gut, it is able to digest) and bee larvae. Two African species of the honeyguide family (aptly named the Indicatoridae), the greater and the scaly-throated, are the only known vertebrates to eat wax, and what they gain nutritionally from it remains unknown.

The honeyguides, like some cuckoos, lay their eggs to be raised in the nests of other birds, so the wax-seeking behavior is purely instinctive and not learned. And how their cooperative behavior with the ratel and then man came about remains one of the many puzzles in the study of birds. There is a belief, of course, among the African tribesmen, that, if they do not leave some honey for the honeyguide, the next time it will lead them unawares to a snake or a lion.

Generally speaking, the relationship between birds and people has been one-sided, though it can be argued that those domesticated birds that do not end up in the pot, and some birds that are taken as decorative elements and live in cages, have a longer life than would be natural, being free of predation and the need to seek food. A little tropical finch with a life expectancy of some three years in the wild may live more than a decade in an aviary.

Even before we humans learned to write, we kept birds in cages made of twigs. The first written word for bird cage was *subura*,  from the Sumerian. Myna birds and parakeets, tethered or with wings cropped, graced very ancient Indian parades. One of the founding fathers of the modern bird trade was Glaucon of Athens, who in 400 B.C. raised Asian and European songbirds for sale (two obols for a goldfinch), along with quail, cranes, and peacocks (the last costing a whopping 10,000 drachmas). Around 325 B.C., several of Alexander the Great's generals took some of the colorful parakeets of northern India back with them to Babylon and even Greece. Soon talking birds became popular in Europe, with Alexandria becoming a major bird-trading hub, among its many other cultural accomplishments. Parrots were largely for the rich—one

evidently kept a slave around to train a parrot—but any middle-class Roman could aspire to a pet raven, the price depending on the bird's linguistic talent. Pliny the Elder wrote of a man who killed a particularly loquacious raven and was promptly lynched.

One of the fabled attractions of Tenochtitlán in what is today Mexico City, when it was discovered by Hernán Cortés in 1519, was its innumerable aviaries: the city rivaled Venice in its architectural beauty, and its thousands of private gardens all were graced with cages of singing birds. When an angry Cortés returned to the city, this time bent on revenge, he destroyed its buildings, its canals, its gardens. And in a final act designed to break the will of the inhabitants, he put all the aviaries to the torch, one of the sorriest symbolic acts in the history of Western man in the New World.

The original inhabitants of the New World, so inventive when it came to domesticating plants such as corn, tomatoes, potatoes, and chili peppers, also tamed two birds for economic use—the Muscovy duck and the wild turkey. It was evidently the Chinese who domesticated the wild mallard, ancestor of most domestic ducks today, some 2,000 years ago. Far earlier, Neolithic people in Europe had tamed graylag geese, keeping them around for food and perhaps as avian watchdogs, a role they continue to play in many a farmyard, being easily disturbed by unfamiliar noises and often surprisingly aggressive. Pigeons may have been kept even earlier—another handy food source—but by the time of Alexander the Great their homing ability had been put to use in early postal services from the front lines, and they continued to play that role up through World War II. They are still used—for sport, of course—but also for delivering blood in remote parts of France. Africa produced the domestic guinea fowl, and the other domesticated birds—pheasants, peafowl, and the chicken—arose in Asia. Many birds can be tamed, it seems, but their progeny tend to be wild: each generation must be tamed anew. Only a few have been successfully domesticated for the long haul, none more important than the chicken, which is probably the bird that has had the most widespread effect on humanity. One statistic may suffice: in 1980, the citizens of Manhattan and the other bor-

昨因王母使玉姜生歡穎

Symbol of sunset and dawn, death and rebirth, the fabled phoenix of Arabia lived for 500 years, then immolated itself on a pyre. From the ashes it rose again to another 500 years of splendor. Such potent imagery traveled far, even to China, where Ch'ing Dynasty painter Hua Yen captured it in soft brush-strokes in the mid-18th century.

In addition to providing food, feathers, and symbolism, birds have also served as companions and even helpers to people. Opposite, peacocks attend an Indian princess; above, in a photograph taken by his friend Henri Cartier-Bresson, painter Henri Matisse sketches a tame dove; a medieval manuscript illumination, right, depicts a watchful goose protecting its flock from a threatening raptor.

oughs of New York City ate 126 million *dozen* eggs.

The chicken became a domesticate in Neolithic times. Archaeologists recently have radiocarbon-dated chicken bones from northeastern China and found them to be about 8,000 years old. Chickens were—and remain—a kind of pheasant, specifically descendants of an undetermined one of four tropical, forest-dwelling species of jungle fowl that live wild from India to Java. The new finds in China suggest that the chicken may have been derived from the red jungle fowl *(Gallus gallus):* certainly such warm-weather birds could not have existed in such icy climes without the help of people. They may have been transported from there, across Russia, to Europe.

That the Spanish conquistadors found chickens upon their arrival in the New World is evidence in favor of occasional Polynesian trips to Central and South America before the time of Columbus. There is a theory that the popularity of the chicken was long a result of their tendency to fight, cockfighting being one of the earliest spectator sports. But the ancient Egyptians had noted that the hen was the bird that laid once a day, and the resulting hieroglyphic also stood for fertility. In fact, the Egyptians were the first to artificially incubate chicken eggs, thus creating the first factory chicken.

Adaptable to most climates and small enough to care for relatively easily, chickens in countless breeds have spread all over the world with people, becoming probably the most widespread of any bird on Earth. In

their fighting role, they became symbols for the pugnacious, such as the Gauls and, earlier, the Greeks in their troubles with Persia. In Roman times, sacred hens were used for oracular purposes, pecking at wheat grains placed on letters in circles. Virtually everywhere, the rooster was, for obvious reasons, thought of as the herald of the day: an alarm clock when all other timepieces—such as water clocks and hourglasses—were silent. So the rooster became a natural symbol for the sun, for regeneration, and for Christ. The cock weathervanes on many New England churches are reminders of this last meaning, though it is largely forgotten by modern congregations.

The pelican, too, became a symbol for Christ because of its alleged habit of picking at its breast until it bled in order to feed the blood to its young. During medieval times, people invented a number of remarkably sophisticated things—such as the stirrup (which permitted the use of lances on horseback and may have saved Europe from the Mongols), the escapement device that made possible the mechanical clock, and what may be humanity's grandest and most soaring architecture—the great cathedrals. Yet a deep ignorance persisted then, an ignorance that to us is unimaginable, even comic. Natural histories, or bestiaries, were full of fables and the fabulous, happily coexisting with the real. Unicorns, for example, had a long zoological history, and the learned men of the Church were familiar with specimens of a northern goose brought to Europe by sailors. It was called the barnacle goose because, word had

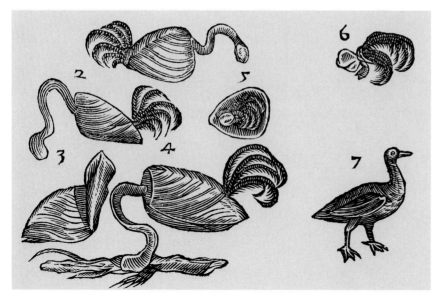

Reflecting Renaissance Europe's increasing awareness of nature, Conrad Gesner's Historiae animalium *of 1555 accurately pictured a preening grebe, above. Much later, Mark Catesby's* Natural History of Carolina, Florida, and the Bahama Islands *(1731-1743) described North American birds, including the ivory-billed woodpecker, opposite. Catesby's "goatsucker of Carolina," below, confused three similar species, the common nighthawk, the chuck-will's-widow, and probably the whippoorwill.*

it, the bird hatched from barnacles. After some deliberation, the barnacle goose was ecclesiastically declared seafood and thus could be eaten by the faithful on Fridays.

Surprising gaps abounded in peoples' understanding of nature. The sudden disappearance of swallows each autumn had long ago led to the notion that swallows hibernated each winter in the mud of ponds. It took wide-ranging seafarers, rediscovering the world, to give Europeans a clearer inkling of bird migration. It began to become clear that Aristotle and all those who had stood on his shoulders could not see far enough. With the Renaissance came the attitude of staring at the surrounding world less blinkered by old beliefs passed down as facts, and Europeans began to see the world afresh. They began to see birds as birds. St. Francis of Assisi, that quintessential model of the humble lover of nature, had in fact taken to preaching *to* the birds. In the 1500s, impelled by the new attitude and by incoming exotics from the explorers to compare with local faunas, people began to learn about birds systematically. And in this endeavor, for several centuries, art and science—those two separate cultures we fret about so—were indistinguishable. To know birds, one needed both.

The seeds of this fresh approach had already been sown—by the Holy Roman Emperor Frederick II, of all people, who, among other things, was a devotee of the ancient sport of falconry. In the 13th century he compiled *De arte venandi cum avibus (The Art of Hunting with Birds),* illustrated with woodcuts detailing the falcons and what was

known of how their bodies worked. It was falconers, of course, who knew birds best, and it was birds of prey that were favored subjects of early bird artists. In 1551 a Swiss physician, Conrad Gesner, began publishing a multivolume *Historiae animalium,* of which one volume of 800 pages and 200 illustrations was given over to the birds. In 1599, the year before Dutch opticians invented the telescope and two great astronomers, Tycho Brahe and Johann Kepler, began to collaborate in the enterprise of astronomy that itself would soon shift the Earth from the center of the universe, an Italian naturalist named Ulisse Aldrovandi published the first of his three-volume *Ornithologiae,* the first comprehensive natural history of birds in modern times. Aldrovandi set a new style, having artists accompany him on bird walks in order to sketch the subjects as they were in nature.

Bird books came to be extremely popular items. Improvements in printing by the 1700s permitted more elaborate illustration. In England, Thomas Bewick's straightforward *History of British Birds* went through six editions. On the continent, Le Comte de Buffon's natural histories were even more popular, going through a whopping 52 editions in French and 20 in other languages, replete with hand-colored engravings by a long list of artists. In the 1800s, an Englishman named John Gould emerged as one of the great bird book publishers of all time, producing volume after volume on the birds of Europe, Great Britain, Asia, America, and Australia. An artist himself, he employed many others of the best available, including his wife, Elizabeth.

Quercus, anpotius; Ilex Marilandica
Folio longo angusto Salicis: Ray: Hist:

Willow Oak.

Picus maximus rostro albo:
Largest White Bill'd Woodpecker.

T. 16.

Best remembered for his illustrated nonsense verse, 19th-century English artist Edward Lear painted his avian subjects as individuals, as is evident in this vivid portrait of a macaw from London's Zoological Gardens. Opposite, fellow Briton Elizabeth Gould pictured the extraordinary resplendent quetzal of Central America for husband John Gould's A Monograph of the Trogonidae, or family of trogons, *1835-1838.*

One artist Gould employed early on was Edward Lear, better known today for his nonsense rhymes and limericks and his drawings of dancing ravens and the Visibly Vicious Vulture. As a youth, however, Lear had taught himself both painting and ornithology. In his late teens he produced what is considered the first book (or, we might say, monograph) on a single family of birds—parrots, which he observed extensively carrying on their lively activities in the gardens of the Zoological Society of London. His paintings of these flashy birds are among the finest ever made of any bird. For a few years afterward he worked as an artist in the private menagerie of the Earl of Derby, but in 1837 he gave up birds and animals for landscape painting, and then followed his odd genius into zany verse and stories.

A gain for a minor branch of literature was a major loss to the art of birds: so skillful was Lear that he captured even the individual personalities of his parrots, giving them an unprecedented reality and liveliness. But this, it seems, was ornithological error. The purpose of zoological illustration in the West was seen to be the generalized display of a species, for reference and recognition. Perhaps because of this prosaic tradition, bird art itself rarely has achieved the status of great masterworks. Instead it is one of many genres that play a minor role, if any at all, in the curriculum of the art historian. Birds do, of course, appear here and there in the works of the grand European masters but, with rare exception, only as decorative elements or minor parts of the landscape. Sifting through the works of the major and minor artists who did devote themselves to birds, from the Renaissance on to the end of the 19th century, one is surprised by how few illustrations there are of birds doing what they are best known for: flying. In the interests of purer knowledge, birds evidently had to be de-enchanted.

Elsewhere, another artistic tradition flourished, in which birds were often essential components of high art. More than a millennium ago in China, bird painting reached a high level of achievement that continued on into the 20th century. As Robert H. Welker wrote in *Birds and Men:* "Even a casual inspection of Chinese bird painting makes one aware of its subtlety and sophistication . . . it is part of the magic that [the Chinese painter's]

MACROCERCUS ARARAUNA.

Blue & Yellow Maccaw

birds are alive, located naturally within the pattern, and existing neither as symbols nor as miniature human beings, but as the creatures they are." Writing of what he sees as "spirit" in the Chinese painters' renditions, Welker goes on to note that "the Chinese painter sees birds with sympathy and affection, as creatures neither inferior to the human being, nor bound up with human preoccupations, but rather as distinctive inhabitants of a larger world which takes in all natural things." This is all based upon a vast difference in religious outlook and philosophy between the Orient and the West, where, since the Renaissance, we have tended to cast ourselves in the role of separate observers of the details of nature rather than as participants in its grander whole.

The early settlers of America were, of course, of this latter tradition, and soon skillful artists were in the service of science. Perhaps the earliest illustrations of American birds were some watercolors done in 1585 by an artist named John White, who briefly visited the Roanoke colony. But the first serious ornithological work in America was *Natural History of Carolina, Florida and the Bahamas* by Mark Catesby, an Englishman. He set out to portray all of the birds of his chosen region, along with the rest of its natural elements; he was in fact more a botanist by training than anything else. Given such a grand scheme but also the eternal limitations of space in such publishing endeavors, he hit on an illustrative scheme that would reach great fruition only in the work of John James Audubon a century later: on one plate, Catesby would include a bird *and* a plant typically associated with it—as well as, often, an insect that particular bird might eat. In this, he may be considered the first ecological illustrator.

To produce this work, Catesby made two long trips to the Americas between 1712 and 1726, and he began to publish his two volumes in sections in 1731. His is considered a notable ornithological work in itself—large vivid plates accompanying a text comprising close observations. He would accept no common opinions about the habits of the birds he described unless they were confirmed by his own observation, and he demonstrated an admirable scientific acumen. For example, noting that the chimney swift (which he

TROGON RESPLENDENS.
Resplendent Trogon

1. *Green Heron.* 2. *Night H.* 3. *Young.* 4. *Great White H.*

61

PLATE I.

Great American Cock Male VULGO (WILD TURKEY.) *Meleagris Gallopavo.*

Often called the father of American ornithology, Alexander Wilson crammed illustrations onto the plates of his nine-volume, chronically underfunded American Ornithology, 1808-1814, opposite. Quintessential bird artist John J. Audubon portrayed that quintessentially American bird, the wild turkey, left, in one of his 435 plates of the avifauna of North America, published as The Birds of America between 1827 and 1838.

In the hands of such masters as Maryland's Madison Mitchell, above, blocks of white pine became decoys once prized by Chesapeake Bay duck hunters, now eagerly sought by collectors. To meet the demand for antiques, such as the Dudley brothers' canvasback, opposite above right, skilled counterfeiters create look-alike fakes, opposite above left.

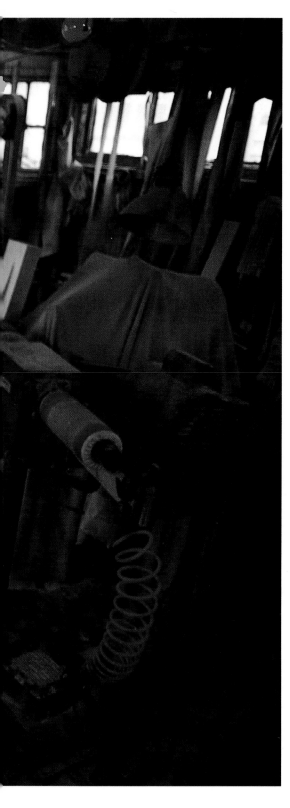

called the "American Swallow") came and went from the region seasonally just as swallows did in England, he suggested "the place they retire to from *Carolina* I think most probably *Brazil*, some part of which is in the same latitude in the southern hemisphere, as *Carolina* is in the northern." In fact, most chimney swifts winter in the Amazon Basin in Peru, just west of Catesby's reasoned guess.

In addition, Catesby had a tendency, rare in those times, to put the bird in an animated pose, giving his volumes a liveliness missing in most other such works of the time. That the poses were sometimes distorted, even inaccurate, was not taken too seriously at the time and, in fact, also foreshadowed the great Audubon. A measure of the value of Catesby's efforts is that they provided a Swedish naturalist named Carolus Linnaeus with a major part of the information on American birds that he used in one of the greatest biological efforts of history: the classification of all living organisms into a rational system—the basic system that remains in universal use today, including a standard binomial nomenclature. It gave each creature a genus and species name and then placed each genus in a family, each family in an order, and so on down the line of more and more distant relatedness.

This helpful system was largely in place when a strange immigrant from Scotland to American shores got the notion to produce a full-scale American ornithology. He was a weaver by trade, a poet by avocation. He was untrained in painting and knew next to

Conceived in the 1930s by cartoonist J.N. "Ding" Darling to aid waterfowl conservation, duck stamps, above, have become art as well as big business in their own right.

BLUE FINCHES

♀ ♂

BLUE GROSBEAK

♂ molting ♂ summer ♀

INDIGO BUNTING

♀ ♂

LAZULI BUNTING

♀ ♂

PAINTED BUNTING

The advent of good, inexpensive binoculars and, perhaps more important, the publication in 1934 of bird artist Roger Tory Peterson's A Field Guide to the Birds *revolutionized amateur ornithology. Plates in the Peterson guide, such as the one above, featured easy-to-spot "field marks" that simplified bird identification. Today, some 14 million Americans, including this spotting-scope-equipped group at Cape Ann, Massachusetts, opposite, pursue the pastime—some would say passion—of birdwatching, or "birding."*

nothing of scientific ornithology, but by 1804 Alexander Wilson had set his grand goal and proceeded to teach himself how to do it—cadging as much knowledge as he could from such naturalists as William Bartram and from various artists, including Charles Willson Peale, as well as from a talented engraver named Alexander Lawson. Despite his utterly amateur status, Wilson was a quick study. He also evidently possessed a naturally scientific mind in the sense that he understood the importance of relating American birds wherever possible, via proper nomenclature, to those of Europe and elsewhere, and in the sense of basing his illustrations and accounts ruthlessly on observation and not hearsay. His first volume appeared in 1808; the eighth and ninth appeared just after his death, in 1814—a remarkable achievement merely from the standpoint of human energy, for it was all written and painted by Wilson, who made the great bulk of the field observations, collected most of the specimens used, saw seven volumes through the press, and arranged for the sale of the entire work by subscription.

A great debunker of legend and myth, Wilson put down for good the swallow hibernation idea, as had Catesby implicitly before him, and pointed out the absurdity of the storied origin of the barnacle goose. His paintings, though clearly seen today as the work of a naive artist, were sprightly and vivid and displayed great attention to accuracy. In all, costs and space limitations permitted Wilson a total of 76 plates in the nine volumes—each being a hand-tinted copper engraving. Confined by this straitjacket, Wilson would cram a number of birds into a page, more often than not birds that were not especially closely related but nonetheless were presented in artful designs. For his prodigious effort in the last decades of his life, he is generally considered to be the father of American ornithology.

While Wilson was hard at work, another man was developing an even grander ornithological scheme, even as he was going bankrupt as a retailer in Kentucky. This was, of course, John James Audubon, of French-Caribbean origin, who took to the American land and its birds as if he and they had been created for one another. The idea was simple: to paint every bird in America life-size and as alive as possible. And of course the idea was, it would have seemed to most people, grandiose to the point of being undoable. Outside of the Oriental tradition, Audubon's *Birds of America*, published serially from 1827 to 1838, is generally considered the greatest work of bird art in history. People have quibbled with details, with individual plates, with distorted birds in poses that would have been impossible had the models not been dead and pliable. People have even pointed out the wholesale plagiarism of three of Wilson's paintings. None of this has or probably ever will bring down Audubon's monument—a single work of unrivaled energy and spirit.

Audubon also represents what might be called a turning point in the history of the association of ornithology and art. Though some of a new breed of ornithologists—including the young Spencer Baird—learned from Audubon, the science of birds was going professional. Art and science would diverge as disciplines. Even as Audubon was seeing his volumes through the press, a young naturalist named Charles Darwin was on board H.M.S. *Beagle*, finding evidence in the astonishing variety of finches on the Galápagos Islands that species become adapted to different environments and evolve into new species, thanks to a process called natural selection. The study of birds and of all of Earth's other creatures would never again be the same.

Bird art would proceed, of course. Artists like Louis Agassiz Fuertes, who were more technically competent than Audubon, would create enviable bodies of work, but none of them would produce one as artistically powerful as *Birds of America*. Hundreds of bird artists continue to work in Audubon's tradition to this day, all no doubt finding their work, as naturalist Ulisse Aldrovandi said almost 500 years ago, "accompanied with the most exquisite gratification and astonishment." But in the 20th century another form of bird art would arise that has probably done more to tie people intimately to birds than any other—the straightforward identification art developed by Roger Tory Peterson for the quick-to-use field guide. Just as the clothes designer with the most widespread influence on fashion in the last 100 years was surely the man named Levi who gave his name to denim work pants, Peterson is the artist who, with his followers and emulators, has brought

countless millions upon millions of people into the direct enjoyment of nature.

It is common—and surely accurate—today to see great difficulty ahead for birds and the rest of nature. Habitats and their denizens are disappearing at a stunning rate. Yet hope lies in several places. Attitudes—even entire philosophies—have changed rapidly at times in human history. Thanks to artists and field guides, even city dwellers who rarely see much more than pigeons retain a fondness, even a yearning, for the company of birds. The birdwatching industry is reckoned in the billions of dollars annually in this country alone. And, over the past century, ornithologists have come to understand the nature of being a bird more intimately than anyone of Audubon's time might have thought possible. We are, through science, beginning to learn to see the world through the eyes of birds—a slightly different universe from ours. In these new perceptions lies the possibility—and the hope—of the re-enchantment of birds in the mind of man. 🐦

Rare Books, Rare Birds:
Ornithology and its Illustration 1450-1900

Gallopavo Criftatus.   The Crefted Turkey Cock.

Eleazar Albin's A Natural
History of Birds *(London,
1731-38), featured this
splendid turkey cock.*

When bird illustrations first were printed in books in the late 15th century, scientific knowledge about birds was scant. Writings about birds at that time consisted of ancient Greek and Latin texts whose scientific content was distorted by medieval symbolism and religious allegory. Not surprisingly, the accompanying woodcut illustrations are typically clumsy and erroneous, showing birds that are only vaguely recognizable in form.

By the end of the next century, however, knowledge about birds had increased greatly. A new generation of students—later to be known as ornithologists—was observing birds systematically and gathering new information for the first time since Aristotle. Conrad Gesner and Ulisse Aldrovandi produced important encyclopedias of birdlife in the 16th century that served as the foundation for the development of modern ornithology.

Woodcutting reached the height of its achievement for bird illustration in the hands of Gesner's and Aldrovandi's artists. In their books, individual species, each with its distinct characteristics, were depicted for the first time. The cuts them-

*This woodcut of the fifth
day of creation appeared
in Hartmann Schedel's
Liber Chronicarum (1493).*

selves, in their detail, their effective use of black and white to indicate color and pattern, and their range of size to suggest relative sizes of species, show how much had been learned about birds.

In the 17th and 18th centuries engraving on metal plates replaced woodcutting in the printing of illustrations. The more precise line of the engraving process revealed the increased attention to detail being given to bird study. Around the same time that Carolus Linnaeus developed his system of classification the number of species known to naturalists swelled significantly; collecting bird specimens became a popular way to catalogue and classify birdlife. Le Comte de Buffon's nine-volume compilation on birds in the mid-18th century, describing the contents of the largest natural history collection in Europe at the time, attempted to capture the abundance of birdlife being revealed by explorations around the world.

Color plates and the depiction of foliage and habitat, two features of bird illustration introduced in the 18th century, became standard as the accumulated

Conrad Gesner's 16th-century Historiae animalium *featured woodcuts of individual bird species, such as the hoopoe, left. A cardinal, or "Virginian nightingale," below left, appeared in Francis Willughby's* Ornithologiae libri tres *(London, 1676). Below, Le Comte de Buffon's portrait of another "exotic," a king vulture.*

TAB. XLIIII.

Coccothraustes Indica cristata.
The Virginian Nightingale.

Great-headed Titmouse.

knowledge of ornithology demanded increasing realism in the portrayal of birds. With a change from engraving to lithography in the following century, realism in bird illustration saw its finest expression. The magnificent hand-colored lithographs of 19th-century bird books captured the dazzling plumages and exotic habitats of the species newly discovered in such distant lands as New Guinea and Australia.

Lithography, a process that involves drawing rather than cutting or engraving, also allowed bird artists to present species in more realistic behavioral displays and stances. Ornithology was losing its dependence on skins and specimens (which had resulted in awkward and unnatural postures in many earlier illustrations) and was taking a fresh look at the live bird in its natural environment.

The representation of the female and young of a species and the production of books devoted to a single family of birds are among the other contributions of 19th-century bird art. To the end of that century, a wealth of insightful and colorful bird illustrations documented the discovery of the worldwide richness and diversity of avian life.

Katherine E. Boyd is a rare-books librarian in the History of Medicine Division of the National Library of Medicine, National Institutes of Health, Bethesda, Maryland.

Above, John Latham's hand-colored etching of a "Great-headed Titmouse" from his A General History of Birds, *published between 1821 and 1828. Engravings of the legs and feet of certain water birds, right, appeared in Mathieu Jacques Brisson's six-volume* Ornithologia *(Paris, 1770-1783). A plate from Daniel Giraud Elliott's* A Monograph of the Pittadae, or family of antthrushes *(1893-95), opposite, epitomizes the richness of color and detail in late-19th-century bird illustration.*

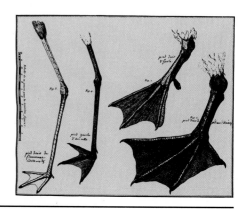

W. Hart del. et lith.

Mintern Bros. imp.

EUCICHLA BOSCHI.

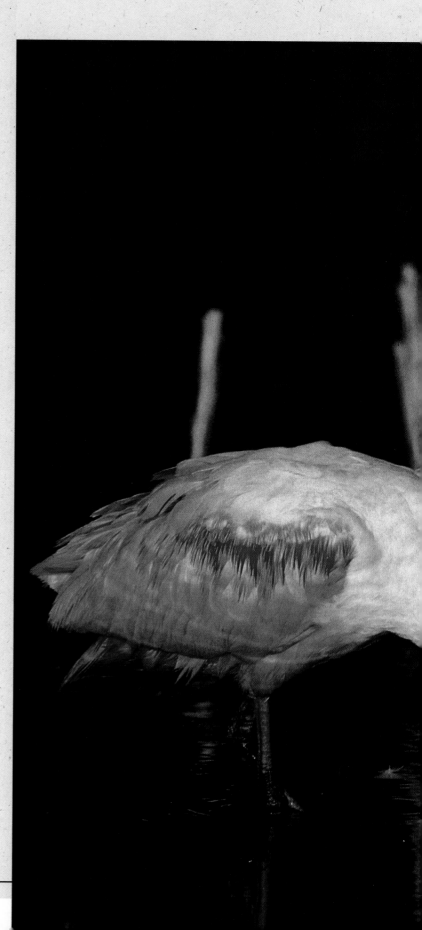

*I*n William Golding's novel *Pincher Martin*, the protagonist is a castaway whose ship has been torpedoed. Drifting at sea, he is driven to hallucinations by isolation, hunger, and thirst, and imagines himself stranded on a small, rocky island. Time slows down. Sea gulls fly around him, some approaching threateningly close. In the castaway's increasing madness, the birds go through an odd metamorphosis, becoming flying reptiles with scales, claws, and other reptilian attributes.

Pincher Martin was seeing evolution in reverse, and that, of course, is not how evolution works.

If we could speed up the entire course of evolution like a motion-picture film, the proliferation of anatomical variations would seem utterly frantic, although certain themes would calmly persist. Fossils may at times illuminate these themes for us, some representing single frames in the film of evolutionary history. Such frames, properly put in sequence, illustrate the changing of structural form. There are so many fossils, for ex-

Preceding pages: These rose-ate spoonbills of the American tropics and all other birds are almost certainly the descendants of a dinosaurian ancestor that lived perhaps 150 million years ago. Birds are, in a sense, living dinosaurs.

In an artist's recreation of a Jurassic beach scene of some 140 million years ago, pter-osaurs of the genus Rham-phorhynchus *ply the air, while tiny, chicken-sized di-nosaurs,* Compsognathus, *scamper on the sand. Feath-ered* Archaeopteryx, *the most ancient birds known, flap and glide near the water's edge. Fossils of these animals were found in Germany's Solnhofen sediments.*

ample, of the sequence from a small forest herbivore to today's horse that paleontolo-gists can observe virtually the entire process. Most of the evolutionary footage for birds is missing, but bird study has been called auspicious—a word that derives from the Latin for "bird" and "to look." And, in 1861, by one of those quirks of luck that sometimes smile on human endeavors, some Bavarian quarrymen came across a fossil of a creature that is transitional between reptile and bird.

The quarrymen were extracting a fine grade of limestone near the town of Solnhofen, near Munich—stone that had been in use since Roman times for buildings and roads but was now in demand also for the litho-graphic printing process. The limestone had been laid down layer by sedimentary layer in lagoons that date back to the late Jurassic age, some 140 million years ago, and already fossils discovered there had provided a rich picture of life in that era. It was a tropical region then, its lagoons surrounded with palmlike trees. The smallest known dinosaurs —chicken-sized *Compsognathus*—plied the shoreline; pterosaurs—flying reptiles—soared above, along with moths and flies, while jellyfish and crustaceans and mollusks fed in the waters. The quarrymen were wise to such things, and knew right away that they were on to something big when they found the fossil remains of a single flight feather— the first avian sign to come to light—with the same contours as a modern feather.

Within a month, a Frankfurt scientist, Hermann von Meyer, reported to his scien-tific colleagues that a nearby quarry had yielded a complete fossil of what its skeleton showed to be a reptile but one replete with flight feathers along its arms and its long tail. Meyer named its genus *Archaeopteryx*, mean-ing "ancient wing," and gave it a species name of *lithographica*. Charles Darwin's *On the Origin of Species* was only two years out at the time, and already controversy had begun to rage about it. Opponents, who were drawing special attention to the very dis-tance between living reptiles and birds, dis-missed this new, crow-sized fossil as a small pterosaur. Proponents triumphantly took it as the first bird.

Meanwhile, the fossil found itself in the hands of a district medical officer who specu-lated in fossils, Dr. Karl Häberlein. He allowed only a few experts to examine the fossil in order to demonstrate that it was not a fake, and then he put it up for sale. At the urging of Sir Richard Owen of the British Museum (Natural History), who did not share Charles Darwin's belief in the mechanism of natural selection, *Archaeopteryx* came to London in 1862.

Disputes about it eddied, scientists seeing in it what they needed to see. The limestone matrix included part of a skull and jaw; the jaw was toothed. Opponents said that it therefore could not be a bird. On the other hand, Thomas Henry Huxley, one of Darwin's most eminent advocates, said that it was indeed a reptilelike bird but that the head and toothed jaw belonged to another animal, a dinosaur. He drew attention to another Solnhofen find, the small dinosaur *Compsognathus*. This, Huxley said, was a birdlike reptile that sat on a plausible sequence leading to the reptilelike *bird* called *Archaeopteryx*.

In 1877, as the argument over the classification of these two fossils continued, another *Archaeopteryx* specimen emerged from a quarry about 10 miles from the site of the original finds. The skeleton of this one occurred in a natural pose with the wings extended, the arched-back head and jaws complete. Feathers were attached symmetrically to the tail, and the wings and hands bore both primary and secondary flight feathers hardly distinguishable from those of today's birds. The Germans quickly bought up this one—in fact, from Häberlein's son, also a fossil speculator. Known as the Berlin *Archaeopteryx*, the fossil is now considered one of the most important specimens in all of natural history, coming before long and to the satisfaction of most to demonstrate conclusively that birds descended from reptiles. Since then, four other *Archaeopteryx* specimens have been found, including one in 1988 that was larger—more the size of a raven than a crow.

Nonetheless, *Archaeopteryx* has continued to generate controversy. In 1985, in one particularly melodramatic instance, an Israeli physicist and electronics consultant raised a question about *Archaeopteryx* with Sir Fred Hoyle, a well-known British astronomer who often is drawn into controversial topics in other fields. Hoyle astonished paleontologists when, after examining detailed photo-

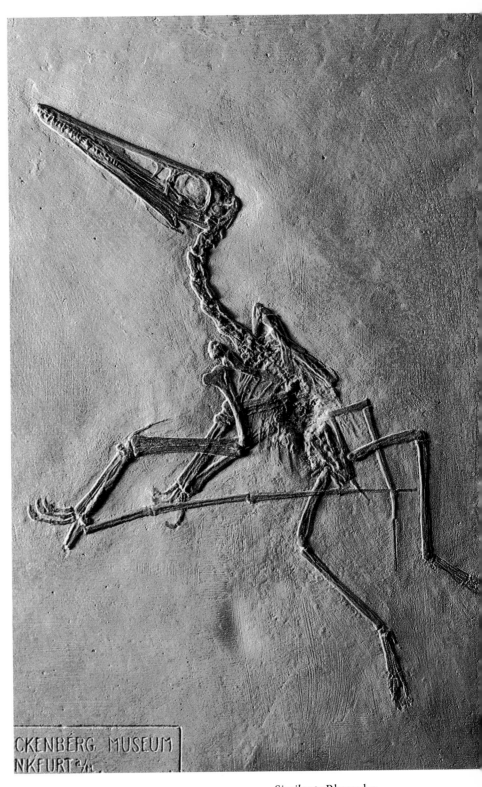

Similar to Rhamphorhynchus, *opposite,* Pterodactylus kochi *lived about 145 million years ago. The elongated third finger that supported the pterosaur's outer wing extends from the "hand" at lower left in this Smithsonian cast of the original German fossil.*

A single fossil feather discovered in Germany in 1861 provided the first hint that birds were present in the late Jurassic, about 140 million years ago. Like those of modern birds, this Archaeopteryx *feather is asymmetrical, an indication that* Archaeopteryx *could fly or glide.*

Recreated by artist Rudolf Freund, Archaeopteryx, *or "ancient wing," above, is the earliest known bird. With its teeth and other reptilian features,* Archaeopteryx *is skeletally almost indistinguishable from some small dinosaurs. Opposite, one of the most important fossils ever discovered, this* Archaeopteryx *was unearthed near Eichstatt, Germany, in 1877. Impressions of feathers extend from its forelimbs and tail, while teeth can be seen in its jaw. Experts debate whether it was capable of true, flapping flight.*

graphs of the London fossil, he called the specimen a fake. He and a few associates went on to claim that Häberlein was the hoaxer, who, having scraped away some of the matrix around the reptile's arm, had added a bit of cement and glue and pressed chicken feathers in it. They also found what they felt were discrepancies between the slab bearing the actual fossil and the counterslab, which has a mold of the fossil pressed into it.

Said a British Museum spokesman: "Codswallop . . . I don't know why people who are eminent in astronomy or physics think they can write papers about vertebrate paleontology. Perhaps it's because we all get dinosaurs in our cornflakes."

Double-checking anyway, scientists at the British Museum found that the discrepancies between the two slabs were explainable by the shifting of the fossil as it became calcified—a common occurrence in paleontological finds. More to the point, examining the specimen under ultraviolet light they found no glue but instead fine hairline cracks and inorganic bits of manganese running across the matrix, the fossil bones, *and* the feathers, proving a common and ancient origin for all.

More informed (and generally quieter) disputation has also surrounded the fossil. Some paleontologists have claimed that *Archaeopteryx* had to have been an offshoot in an avian evolution that began far earlier than in the late Jurassic. This is based in part on questions of whether the animal could actually have flown, feathers or not. It does not have the keeled breastbone of birds, to which flight muscles can adhere; instead, its collarbones are fused into a boomerang-shaped wishbone, or furcula, that is typical of modern birds and that some say was sufficient for flight muscles, while others disagree.

Another question is, assuming *Archaeopteryx* could fly or glide, how had it evolved to that point? One hypothesis is that it was an arboreal creature that began by gliding down from one tree to the base of another, like a flying squirrel, thus expanding its foraging range. Flapping the wings would have further extended the range. Or was it a creature that ran along the ground chasing insects, its feathered arms developing as a better insect trap, soon also becoming an aid to cursorial speed and eventually leading to a probably frantic flapping flight?

ROXIE LAYBOURNE, FEATHER ACE

AMY DONOVAN, EDITOR

Feather-identification wizard Roxie Laybourne stands in the foreground with but a few of the half-million bird specimens in the Smithsonian's collections. Using down plucked only from the left side of the upper breast of specimens, Roxie is developing an information bank of the microscopic characters of these small, fluffy feathers, characters that are unique to each bird family.

ROXIE LAYBOURNE, FEATHER ACE

Whether she's studying the highly magnified detail of a peregrine falcon feather on the screen of the Smithsonian's electron microscope, left, or examining a down feather with her hand lens, below, Roxie has honed her ability to identify feathers. Over the past 30 years she has used this skill to solve mysteries ranging from the identities of birds that have struck airliners to theft and even homicide.

*B*irds may have evolved feathers more than 140 million years ago, and used them to master flight, but over the past 30 years a woman named Roxie Laybourne has learned more about feathers than any bird—or any other human— could possibly know. Dropping by to see her in the Division of Birds in the Smithsonian's National Museum of Natural History, one is likely to find her on the telephone regarding a recent bird strike— a collision between a bird and an aircraft. Identifying the avian remains of these strikes is one of the areas of feather identification in which Roxie, as she is generally known, excels—often to the amazement and always to the edification of aviation officials.

Like any pro, Roxie makes it look easy. When she receives a package of bird-strike material, she washes the bird remains in a mixture of mild soap solution and warm water and dries them by gently blowing them with compressed air. She then examines them macroscopically and, if necessary, microscopically. Despite what often becomes a complex process, since each feather is, as she puts it, "custom-made," Roxie always gets her bird, and the mystery of the bird strike is solved.

Roxie has been involved with numerous other kinds of mysteries as well. In fact, for much of her career she has worked for the Division of Law Enforcement of the U.S. Fish and Wildlife Service, testifying on feather identification in a number of cases, including homicide. In her expert hands, even the tiniest bit of down left behind at the scene of a crime can become a highly incriminating piece of evidence. Roxie's prowess is also a great boon to scientists—from biologists to anthropologists—who need feathers identified.

But Roxie's first love these days is her own research. Using both the scanning and the transmission electron microscopes, she is probing the makeup of downy barbules, the smallest division of the feather. Are they composed of one cell or different cells? How are the melanin granules shaped and arranged? "The more you learn, the more questions you can ask," says Roxie. It looks as though we're going to be learning a lot more about feathers.

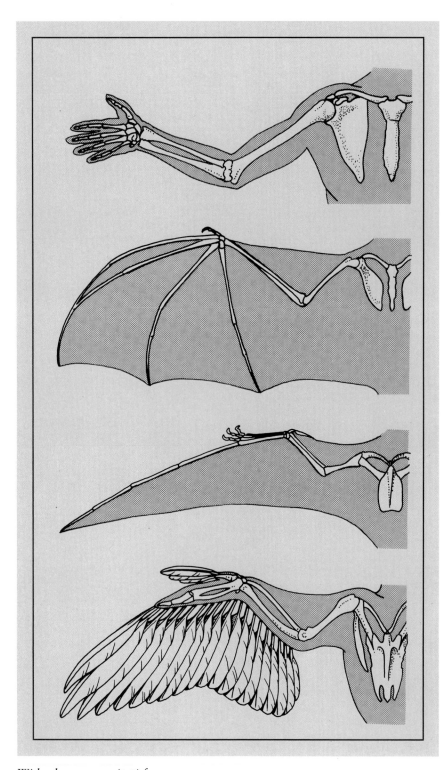

With a human arm (top) for comparison, wings of a bat, a pterosaur, and a bird show how different vertebrates have evolved structures to meet the demands of flight.

There are many considerations in this hypothesis, some of them quite technical, others argument by analogy. For example, with the possible exception of the pterosaurs, which may have begun as sea-cliff dwellers, all land vertebrates that have taken to the air, such as flying squirrels and bats, began as arboreal animals. But in all these cases, too, the aerodynamic surface has been a membrane of skin. So a great deal of the debate over *Archaeopteryx* centers on the fact that it had not only feathers, but feathers that were nearly identical to the flight feathers of today, including their asymmetry—a narrower leading edge and a wider trailing edge, the quintessential airfoil. How could feathers have come about?

Evolutionary theory precludes long-range goals or purposes. It is not allowed to think that some reptile evolved a bunch of useless enlarged scales that hung from its arms and tail *because* of a reptilian intent to turn into a bird one day. In other words, each evolutionary step along the way must confer a present advantage. Flight, even protoflight, is a matter of aerodynamics, and recently a group of scientists including an aerodynamicist and led by ornithologist Russell Balda of Northern Arizona University argued against the "tree-down" theory, saying that it does not make sense for a gliding animal to begin flapping its wings.

Specifically, a powered wing designed for flapping gets its thrust from the outer third and thus tends to be longer and thinner than the wing of a glider. An arboreal glider, they say, would waste a lot of energy by flapping, like a parrot flying with clipped wings. They cannot visualize the incremental steps of evolution bridging this gap. Other aerodynamic models demonstrate that a kind of flight called "flap-gliding"—a strong downward stroke and a slow upward stroke—

On Anacapa Island off the coast of California, prehistoric-looking brown pelican chicks display the enormous throat pouch and webbed feet typical of their species. The lineage of the family to which they belong, the Pelicaniformes, stretches back 100 million years to the time of the dinosaurs.

would have overcome such transitional difficulties; and, given the creature's incompletely developed flight musculature, such a flight mode would accord with its anatomy, though no modern bird is known to fly that way. Aerodynamic reasoning remains inconclusive.

One leading student of archaeopteryxian affairs, John Ostrom of Yale University, has proposed that rudimentary feathers might have begun first as a device for retaining bodily heat (thermoregulation) among reptiles that were developing warm-bloodedness (endothermy). There is considerable debate as to whether the dinosaurs themselves evolved endothermy; the argument is vastly complex, with vehement adherents on both sides. In any event, feathers as a thermal device would have provided an adventitious advantage of added lift for a bipedal runner, not to mention a kind of butterfly net for clasping insects, and, from there, could have developed incrementally into aerodynamically sound feathers.

Alan Feduccia of the University of North Carolina finds this hypothesis overly elaborate, agreeing with a number of other scholars that feathers can plausibly be seen to have evolved precisely as mechanisms for flight, with other advantages such as heat regulation

Little is known of bird evolution between Archaeopteryx *of the late Jurassic and* Hesperornis, *above, and* Ichthyornis, *opposite above, of the late Cretaceous. Hesperornis was a five-foot-long flightless bird that probably swam and dived for fish, seizing them in its tooth-filled jaws. Though capable of flight and somewhat smaller, today's anhingas, below, and loons probably superficially resemble* Hesperornis *in form and habit.*

being adventitious. If one begins with the notion of a highly active, arboreal reptile that leaped from branch to branch after its prey, then, as Feduccia paraphrases the work of zoologist D.B.O. Savile, "the slightest fringe of elongated scale or proto-feather along the trailing edge of the forelimb would have an immediate advantage in parachuting or jumping." And once one assumes that any further elongation of the fringe would be similarly beneficial, "the problem of accounting for the adaptiveness of stages intermediate between scales and feathers disappears."

Thus, for now at least, the "tree-down" school has it, but *Archaeopteryx's* true place in avian evolution is nonetheless by no means certain. No one is at all sure where this strange creature came from. One choice is that it evolved from a "birdlike" meat-eating dinosaur, the tiny theropod called *Compsognathus,* as Thomas Huxley first proposed back in the 19th century. Another school holds that it came from a far earlier, less specialized group of predinosaurian creatures called thecodonts, which were ancestral to both dinosaurs and birds. It seems to hang on which feature or features one chooses to emphasize. In Ostrom's view the only nondinosaurian feature of *Archaeopteryx*

was its wishbone. On the other hand, certain aspects of the modern bird's (and the modern crocodile's) inner ear seem to point to thecodonts. But then in 1982 a Cretaceous dinosaur was found in Canada's Dinosaur Provincial Park, and it had periotic sinuses—the system of chambers that brings air to the middle ear—identical to birds'. Called a *Troödon*, this dinosaur was also characterized by certain dental features that were more similar to those of early birds than to those of its descendants, the theropods.

In 1988, paleontologists unearthed a fossil not from the ground but from the collections of the Cleveland Museum of Natural History. The fossil, it turned out, represented a pygmy version of the gigantic, six-ton theropod *Tyrannosaurus rex*, which clearly was related to the *Troödon* and also had—like birds—extensive air canals in the brain case and similar ankle bones.

Seek and you shall find, and the part of the anatomy you study can lead to different reptilian analogues, perhaps ancestors, for birds. Paleontologists have found 30 features—for example, a distinct constriction between the roots and crowns of teeth—of both ancient birds and crocodilians that unite them as descendants of a common creature. Most

Ichthyornis, *above, was a tern-sized bird of about 80 million years ago; except for its toothy jaws, it resembled today's gulls and terns in most respects. Indefatigable dinosaur discoverer Othniel C. Marsh of Yale University found fossils of both* Ichthyornis *and* Hesperornis *in the Cretaceous chalk deposits of Kansas. Below, Marsh, standing at center with rifle, and his 1870 expedition pose with their stove near Bridger, Wyoming.*

of these features are to be found in the skull. Looking elsewhere, paleontologists have come up with some 39 features—such as an elongated snout and the shape of the nostrils, but mostly postcranial features—that unite birds with coelurosaurian dinosaurs. A good number of other features have to do with the hand, where the standard reptilian hand and digit bones have become reduced in number and fused, essentially creating a simpler form with fewer bones and three digits overall.

And it is in digits that some scientists see the source of the answer. Paleontologists generally have gone along with the proposition that it is the fourth and fifth digits that both the theropods and the subsequent birds lost in the process of fusion. So they call the remaining digits 1, 2, and 3. But embryologists, peering in on the stages of development of chickens and other modern creatures born of eggs, have found fairly conclusively that it is digit 1 and digit 5 that are lost. Thus they consider birds to be 2-3-4s that could not have arisen from 1-2-3s, which is what most people still believe the theropods were. Biologists presume that once you have, evolutionarily, lost your thumb and your pinky finger, none of your descendants is going to grow a thumb again and at the same time

lose the ring finger. With this issue raised, some paleontologists concluded that the theropods were 2-3-4s, too, not 1-2-3s, and the debate goes on.

At present, what exactly gave rise to birds remains up in the air, as perhaps it should, but it does seem certain that, like mammals, the birds emerged through some narrow and fortuitous evolutionary bottleneck of unquestionably reptilian nature. One tends to pull for the dinosaurs, perhaps because we all have had them along with our cornflakes.

Sitting in the evolution theater watching the fossil movie, the audience has had little by way of an avian cast of characters—and has a lot of dead time ahead. Indeed, if all we had to go on were fossils, someone slumped in his Jurassic seat watching blank frames go by could have no glimmer that, in a rousing climax, these near-birds will produce one of the most varied, most colorful, and most widespread faunas imaginable. Thanks to the antifossilization plan built into avian skeletons, what fossils do crop up over the next 80 million years or so after *Archaeopteryx* will also give the impression that birds, having painstakingly learned to fly around in the trees, however clumsily, perhaps alighting on the ground to forage from time to time, veered off abruptly for a life at sea and in many cases gave up on flight altogether.

A feather, found in Spain and determined to be contemporary with *Archaeopteryx*, shows that birds were not only Bavarian. It should be noted that, as the Jurassic Period gave way to the Cretaceous 135 million years 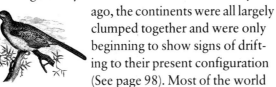 ago, the continents were all largely clumped together and were only beginning to show signs of drifting to their present configuration (See page 98). Most of the world was what we would call tropical. And many of the continental land masses were covered with vast inland seas and waterways. Even though it drowned auspiciously in a lagoon, *Archaeopteryx* was a land bird, and there must have been plenty of other land birds before long or even earlier, but what we know about birds from the Cretaceous—the next 70 million years—comes from those that inhabited marine environments . . . except for a few important instances.

In February 1988, a Spanish paleontologist announced the discovery of a fossil bird that was intermediate between *Archaeopteryx* and the birds of today. An amateur collector had discovered it in early Cretaceous sediments in Las Hoyas, Spain, and had given it to J.L. Sanz to study. A major distinguishing characteristic between birds and reptiles is the fusion of a bird's skeleton into fewer working parts. The tail vertebrae, for example, are fused and reduced into the bird's pygostyle, or "pope's nose," from which the tail feathers grow. Overall there are fewer vertebrae, and bones in the legs and wings are fewer and also in some cases fused. The separate plates of the skull typically are fused as well.

The skull was missing from the Las Hoyas find, precluding its study. The rest of the skeleton revealed a number of reptilian features still lingering on, such as its pelvis and hind limbs. But it had two evolutionary novelties that bespeak bird—a pygostyle and two strutlike bones called coracoids in its pectoral region, adapted to providing skeletal strength for the rigors of flight. The remains of a feather were found nearby.

What is striking about the find is that it was from early Cretaceous sediments. It existed only some 15 to 20 million years after *Archaeopteryx*, meaning that the demands of flight were having a profound effect, hastening the earliest birds along toward their present configuration. Sanz and his colleagues place this small bird in a "sister group" of the ancestors of today's birds—in other words, another offshoot.

Six years before the Sanz offshoot was found, another important fossil had come to light when Russian scientist E.N. Kurochkin described a true carinate—or keeled—bird from early Cretaceous deposits in Mongolia. In addition to the pronounced keel, this specimen, named *Ambiortus*, possessed many of the typically avian bones of the chest, including the wishbone. *Ambiortus* is now considered the oldest true flying bird, which is to say that it was no evolutionary side branch, like *Archaeopteryx*, but in the mainstream that led from some yet-to-be-identified reptile to today's birds.

Distinct feather impressions have been recovered from five other early Cretaceous sites in Mongolia and elsewhere in Asia, as well as in Australia—yet more evidence of the wide dispersal of birds so soon after *Archaeopteryx*. Footprints thought to be those of

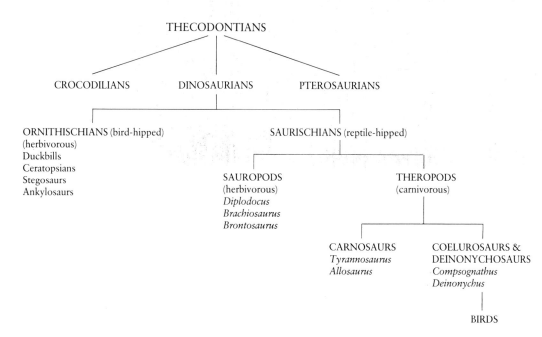

THECODONTIANS

CROCODILIANS   DINOSAURIANS   PTEROSAURIANS

ORNITHISCHIANS (bird-hipped)
(herbivorous)
Duckbills
Ceratopsians
Stegosaurs
Ankylosaurs

SAURISCHIANS (reptile-hipped)

SAUROPODS
(herbivorous)
Diplodocus
Brachiosaurus
Brontosaurus

THEROPODS
(carnivorous)

CARNOSAURS
Tyrannosaurus
Allosaurus

COELUROSAURS &
DEINONYCHOSAURS
Compsognathus
Deinonychus

BIRDS

Above, an artist puts finishing touches on a life-sized recreation of Andalgalornis, *an extinct, flightless, carnivorous bird of South America. Related to today's cranes, rails, and coots,* Andagalornis *and other phorusrhacoids flourished between 36 million and 4 million years ago. Left, although some authorities have argued that birds may have descended from crocodilians, most accept bird descent from the small dinosaurs called coelurosaurs. Note that, despite the names, birds evolved from the saurischian, or reptile-hipped, dinosaurs, rather than through the ornithischian, or bird-hipped.*

birds have been spotted from similar times in British Columbia. Even so, these early birds left tantalizingly little evidence of their existence.

The rest of our information about Cretaceous birds comes mainly from fossils of two distinct lineages associated with the sea. Representatives of both lineages were discovered within a decade of the first *Archaeopteryx*, a heady time for avian paleontology. Both finds were made in the vast chalk deposits of the Niobrara Formation in Nebraska and Kansas (the word Cretaceous is derived from the Latin word *creta*, or "chalk"). The first to turn up was a loonlike diving bird dubbed *Hesperornis*, or "western bird." It was some five feet long, with large feet, negligible wings, and a flat, unkeeled sternum. Clearly, it could not have flown.

Hesperornis's discoverer, Othniel C. Marsh, was one of the big names in the derring-do days of late-19th-century paleontology. In the winter of 1870 he had come across a few fossil bones of this bird, but, as he wrote later, the "extreme cold, and danger from hostile Indians, rendered a careful exploration at that time impossible." The next summer, with a complement of U.S. troops, he returned to brave the 120-degree heat and found an entire specimen, minus its head.

In all, some 13 different species of hesperornithiforms have been recovered since then, from five-footers to grebe-sized specimens, widely dispersed around the world. The most ancient ones found to date, of the genus *Enaliornis*, are from the early Cretaceous in England. It seems, therefore, that no sooner had birds taken to the air than one kind—which would become a highly successful animal—had given up flight to forage underwater. (Flightlessness, as we shall see, is a mode of life that birds have turned to many times in their evolution, often in a surprisingly short time.)

Foot-propelled divers, hesperornithiforms ventured hundreds of miles out to sea (although some recently described specimens were evidently freshwater birds), and may have migrated landward to breed. Fossil discoveries after the initial one showed that the hesperornithiforms, though clearly birds, had one major reptilian holdover: teeth. Successfully competing in the seas with plesiosaurs and other marine reptiles, they seem to have lived much the same kind of life as today's seals.

But the teeth were a problem for paleontologists, as was their flightlessness. Perhaps, it was surmised, birds had evolved twice—the flying kind as represented by *Archaeopteryx* and a separate, flightless lineage. Today, scholars think not. Instead, the hesperornithiform lineage began in time somewhere near the Jurassic-Cretaceous transition, arising from the main line of flying birds and then quite rapidly losing the power of flight as the hesperornithiforms adopted a diving way of life.

In addition, their bones were dense and not pneumatic, an adaptation like that of many modern birds to overcome buoyancy and make diving, and swimming with merely the head out of the water, as with anhingas, less of a problem. In many other features, such as the ability to rotate the foot sideways on the recovery stroke, hesperornithiforms were much like today's loons and grebes. But they were not ancestors: loons and most grebes can fly and have the keeled sternum necessary for it. The hesperornithiforms were keelless and flightless, and, once you have achieved that condition, there is no turning back. Like so many other creatures, the hesperornithiforms vanished around the end of the Cretaceous, hastened on their way most likely by the drying up of many of their inland seas.

The summer after Marsh's discovery of *Hesperornis* (and as it turned out he had chanced upon the largest species of this bird), his colleague Benjamin F. Mudge found the remains of a small bird with powerful wings. Though evidently headless, it resembled a tern, and Marsh named it *Ichthyornis*, "fish bird." In the same slab was the toothed jaw of what struck Marsh as a new kind of reptile, which he named after Mudge. Fame was fleeting in this case. Having removed the matrix, Marsh then found more of the jaw and the skull and concluded that he had a toothed bird on his hands, evidently a highly competent predator of Cretaceous seas, with long jaws and recurved teeth. (Mudge's reptile vanished from evolution's history.) These birds were relatively widespread throughout North America, developing several species, along with a similar

Hummingbirds evolved after the appearance of flowering plants in the Cretaceous. Many flowering plants such as these gladioli have evolved colorful blossoms and energy-rich nectar, which attract a variety of insects and birds, including hummingbirds. These assist the plants in pollination, and are in turn adapted to the gathering of nectar.

though probably unrelated bird called *Apatornis*.

These toothed, ternlike birds had also disappeared, so far as we know, by the end of the Cretaceous, when, quite suddenly in geologic terms, the land, air, and sea were rid of most kinds of reptiles. Fascinating theories abound to explain the devastating mass extinctions that took place, apparently over several million years. One proposes a huge meteoritic impact that caused a long period of year-round winter. Another proposes a similar impact into highly carboniferous rocks that released enough carbon dioxide into the atmosphere to bring about a 10,000-year-long greenhouse effect, frying many forms of life into oblivion.

In any event, some 10 million years later in an epoch called the Eocene, named for the dawn, there was already an extraordinary proliferation of life forms in a variety of environments. Abhorring vacuums, evolution already had begun to drive both birds and mammals into most of the roles that had been played by the pterosaurs and the "terrible lizards."

There were other opportunists as well, ones that also had been lurking in the Cretaceous almost since *Archaeopteryx's* time: the flowering plants, or, as they technically are called, angiosperms. Reproductively more efficient than the naked-seeded gymnosperms —cycads, palms, ginkgoes, conifers—thanks to their enclosed seeds, they could also grow faster, and, as they became adapted to being pollinated by insects and later other creatures, their distribution was assured by more than the vagaries of the wind. Opportunists themselves, they would provide innumerable opportunities for other creatures, including birds. They would become, in fact, the most various of plant types, as are birds the most various of vertebrates. It would be a time of spectacular fulfillment for those who had waited so long in the wings.

Among the mammals, the insectivores began a rapid radiation into a host of varieties, including large and small herbivores and large and small carnivores, taking over where the dinosaurs had left off. Many, of course, took the opportunity to become diurnal. Of the fossil avifauna of the late Cretaceous, most of what were not related to the hesperornithiforms were primitive shorebirds, some of the bones of which—such as those of the genus *Telmatornis*—were very similar to those of today's stone-curlews. Indeed, Alan Feduccia suggests that shorebirds may well be analogous in their evolutionary diversity to the mammals' insectivores and probably trace back to the following modern bird groups: the sandpiperlike true shorebirds; the gulls and terns; the auks, murres, and puffins; cranes, rails, and other marsh waders; flamingos and ducks; and possibly seabirds such as the petrels and pelicans—all together more

Related to the worldwide nightjar family, the nocturnal tawny frogmouth of Australia and Tasmania uses its huge bill to subdue its mainly invertebrate prey. Frogmouths bear a striking resemblance to owls in some aspects of form and habit and may point to an ancestral link between nightjars and owls.

than a thousand species living today, and certainly far more that became extinct in the intervening years.

It is worthy of note that avian paleontologists are afflicted not only by a relative dearth of fossils but also by the fact that once the main forms of many modern birds arrived on the scene they did not change much except in external features such as plumage and behavior—features unlikely to be fossilized. This greatly complicates the task of sorting out which birds are related to which in the course of evolution—one of paleontology's main functions, along with providing the all-important time dimension. Generally speaking, paleontologists have to search out often subtle features that are either "primitive" or "derived." Primitive features are those that trace back to a hypothetical common ancestor; derived features are those that

evolved in a lineage after it branched from a common ancestor. The fact that both *Ichthyornis* and *Hesperornis* had teeth doesn't mean they were very closely related, then, since this primitive characteristic was also common to reptiles. Derived features are novelties.

Beginning in the late 1970s, Feduccia collaborated with Storrs Olson of the Smithsonian's National Museum of Natural History in an exploration of the evolutionary connection between flamingos and ducks. Their work illustrates the importance of determining whether a feature is primitive or derived. One of the creatures that arose from Cretaceous shorebird stock was a highly gregarious bird called *Presbyornis*, worldwide in distribution around 50 million years ago in the Eocene. The Smithsonian's Alexander Wetmore was the first to describe this bird in 1926, from skeletal fragments, and he con-

A large predator and scavenger of arid tropical Africa, the marabou stork, above, and other storks represent one of the many genealogical riddles confronting students of avian evolution. Storks may be related to the whalebills and hammerheads, also of Africa, and may have distant links to pelicanlike birds.

The greater flamingos of Ngorongoro Crater in East Africa, right, and crab plovers, top, of the Indian Ocean coasts, may both be related to an extinct ducklike bird called Presbyornis *that left its tracks, above, and bones by the millions in Wyoming sediments. Perhaps ancestral to all ducks,* Presbyornis *was a filter-feeder that had evolved from the same ancient shorebird lineage as the plovers and the flamingos.*

sidered it to be a new kind of shorebird related to stilts and avocets. But, depending on what part of the whole skeleton one looks at, one can see a shorebird, a duck, or a flamingo. Furthermore, flamingos generally are thought to be related to storks, ibises, and herons or to ducks and geese.

In the early 1970s, scientists at the University of Wyoming found large quantities of intact fossil remains of *Presbyornis* in a vast shale deposit called the Green River Formation at the conjunction of Colorado, Utah, and Wyoming. The bird evidently had teemed on the shores of ancient Eocene lakes. It clearly had the bill and braincase of a duck, but its legs were more like those of a flamingo or an avocet.

Presbyornis was a filter-feeder, like some ducks and all flamingos. But ducks filter-feed primarily on plant material and flamingos primarily on animal matter, straining it through their beaks with a thick, mouth-filling tongue, not unlike the feeding mechanism of some baleen whales. *Presbyornis,* this mosaic of a bird, lived in huge colonies and nested in massive groups: scientists working just north of Canyon Creek Butte near the Colorado-Wyoming border came upon great numbers of *Presbyornis* bones and a plentitude of eggs. It may have been preyed on by the Eocene version of the frigate bird. Over time, the 15,000-square-mile lake in today's Wyoming and Utah fluctuated between freshwater and brackish, at some intervals becoming

Smithsonian ornithologist Storrs L. Olson, above, compares a modern albatross's wing bone, or humerus, to a fossil humerus of the largest flying seabird ever discovered. Called a pseudodontorn, or "pseudo-toothed bird," the bird's wings spanned more than 18 feet. Distantly related to the Pelicaniformes, pseudodontorns became extinct about 5 mil-lion years ago. Also related to the Pelicaniformes were the large, flightless diving birds called plotopterids, shown opposite with an outline of the largest living penguin for comparison. Plotopterids flourished in the northern Pacific about 30 million years ago.

so saline that it was full of "trona," a form of sodium carbonate that is now common only in the lakes of Africa's Rift Valley—home of enormous congregations of greater and lesser flamingos.

Olson and Feduccia subsequently found a fossil from the Eocene lakes that was very close to today's avocets and saw in it a number of characters that were, in turn, very close to corresponding features in flamingos. Thus, the ancient shorebird gave rise in one instance to an avocetlike bird that before long also produced the lineage of flamingos. It doesn't take much imagination to see the longer legs of a flamingo coming about from an avocet's—merely a change in the habitual depth in which the bird needed to wade.

On the other hand, having "opted" for the increasingly large tongue and odd-shaped bill for filter-feeding, the flamingo and its derived feeding system went down a highly special-ized path that ultimately would restrict the kinds of environments in which it could make a living. Evidently, no other avian lineage branched off from flamingos.

Meanwhile, the putative ancestral shore-bird also went on to produce the line of *Presbyornis*, with an altogether different tongue-beak configuration from flamingos' for filter-feeding. This survived happily in the freshwater periods of Eocene lakes, dredging up the algal blooms with a bill much like that of a modern duck. Assuming that the shore-lines were relatively narrow, it seems reason-able that the ducks, as they evolved, developed shorter legs capable of propelling them into deeper water to extend their foraging range. And from ducks, of course, it is also not far to geese, and swans.

If that lineage system is the case, with flamingos and ducks arising from shorebird ancestors, then where did the herons, ibises, bitterns, spoonbills, and other similar waders come from? While they are grouped to-gether, their genealogy remains beyond un-derstanding. The storks seem to bear some relationship to pelicanlike birds; the ibises stand alone—enigmas; and the herons are anatomically distinct from all the others, perhaps, as Olson suggests, a surviving early offshoot of the Gruiformes, the group that includes cranes and rails.

Nowhere is the mystery of bird evolution greater than with the birds of prey. Owls

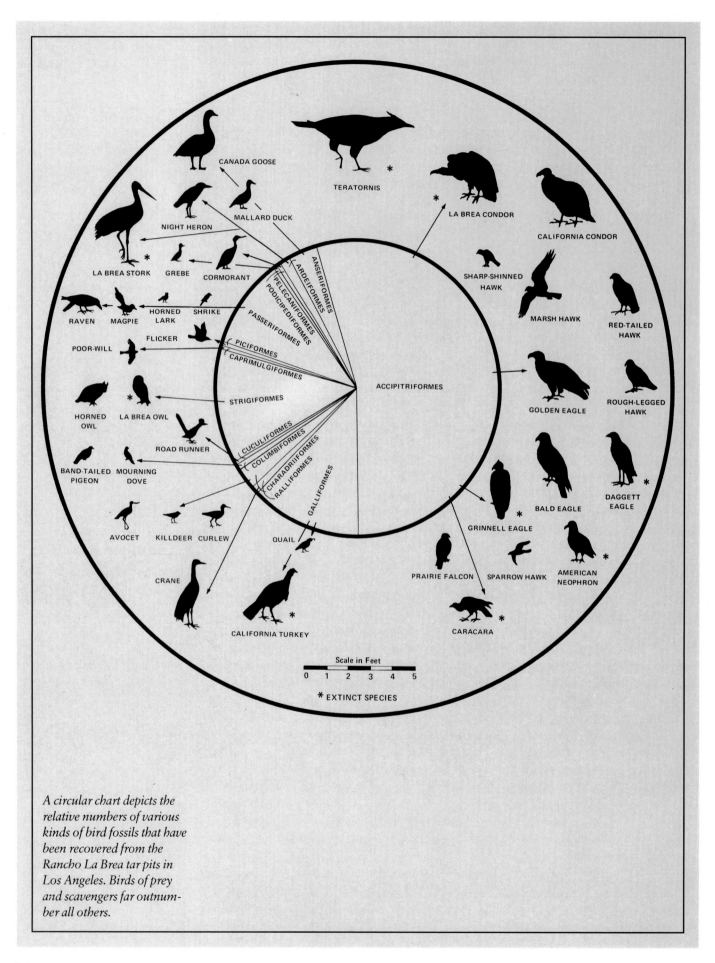

CANADA GOOSE

TERATORNIS *

LA BREA CONDOR *

CALIFORNIA CONDOR

NIGHT HERON

MALLARD DUCK

SHARP-SHINNED HAWK

LA BREA STORK *

GREBE

CORMORANT

MARSH HAWK

RED-TAILED HAWK

RAVEN

MAGPIE

HORNED LARK

SHRIKE

FLICKER

POOR-WILL

GOLDEN EAGLE

ROUGH-LEGGED HAWK

HORNED OWL

LA BREA OWL *

ROAD RUNNER

BALD EAGLE

DAGGETT EAGLE *

BAND-TAILED PIGEON

MOURNING DOVE

GRINNELL EAGLE *

AVOCET

KILLDEER

CURLEW

QUAIL

PRAIRIE FALCON

SPARROW HAWK

AMERICAN NEOPHRON *

CRANE

CALIFORNIA TURKEY *

CARACARA *

ANSERIFORMES
PELECANIFORMES
ARDEIFORMES
PODICIPEDIFORMES
PASSERIFORMES
PICIFORMES
CAPRIMULGIFORMES
STRIGIFORMES
CUCULIFORMES
COLUMBIFORMES
CHARADRIIFORMES
RALLIFORMES
GALLIFORMES
ACCIPITRIFORMES

Scale in Feet
0 1 2 3 4 5

* EXTINCT SPECIES

A circular chart depicts the relative numbers of various kinds of bird fossils that have been recovered from the Rancho La Brea tar pits in Los Angeles. Birds of prey and scavengers far outnumber all others.

Detail of an artist's recreation of the Rancho La Brea tar pits during the Pleistocene some 100,000 years ago in southern California shows saber-toothed cats and giant teratorns, vulturelike birds with wings spanning up to 12 feet, coming to feed on herbivores mired in seeping tar. The predators themselves will then fall victim to the sticky trap. South American teratorns attained wingspans of more than 24 feet; they were the largest flying birds of all time.

might possibly share an ancestor with the goatsuckers, or nightjars, which include such birds as whippoorwills and nighthawks. In the same order (the Caprimulgiformes) is an Australian bird called the frogmouth, which looks like a small, long-tailed owl, sits crossways on branches like owls, nests in hollow trees like owls, and also hatches downy young. The earliest owl fossil predates the Eocene but tells paleontologists nothing about what came before it. One thing is evident, however: the hooked beak and strong talons common to owls evolved separately from those same features as they occur in the other raptors—a case of what is called convergent evolution, where the same ecological circumstances lead to the same evolutionary conclusion on separate occasions.

The various falcons and eagles (and Eurasian vultures) may have arisen from a variety of ancestors, while the New World vultures, such as the turkey vulture and California condor, might have some ancient affinity with storks. Without the kind of missing link provided by *Presbyornis* that so clearly helps one perceive the transition from one kind of bird to another, scientists are driven to inferring from present-day birds some of the evolutionary fine-tuning that has gone on in the production of derived characteristics.

A valuable feature in this regard—especially when it comes to the pesky problem of relating land-bird lineages—is a tiny bone in the bird's middle ear. Mammals have three such bones, or ossicles, involved in transmitting vibrations to the fluids of the inner ear. Birds, on the other hand, like reptiles, have

but one, called the stapes—a kind of footplate attached to a stem that fits into the window of the inner ear. In most birds, the stapes remains quite primitive, or reptilian, and in such cases is not much help. For example, the cuckoos and their presumed allies, the touracos and hoatzins, have very similar stapes, but, since these structures are all primitive in form, they in themselves do not indicate that the three bird types are closely related. On the other hand, kingfishers and trogons and several other kinds of birds all share a large, bulbous footplate of the stapes, clearly a derived characteristic, confirming a close relationship that might not otherwise be so obvious.

Other subtle features used in analyses of relationships are the shape of the voice box (or syrinx) and the feet, especially the arrangement of toes. Any one of these features can provide a hint; a conclusion will normally be based on a fairly long list of such features. And now modern biochemical comparisons, including the analysis of DNA, the genetic material itself, are beginning to provide new clues to the mystery of bird relationships.

By the time man's hominid ancestors were groping unwittingly toward the status of being human, all of the families of birds we see today were extant. This was the beginning of the Pleistocene, some 2 million years ago. Many of the families of birds alive then—in fact 12 families comprising 125 species—have been recovered from a single place—the Rancho La Brea asphalt deposits, or tar pits, in what is now downtown Los

the DoDo & Given   by G. EDWARDS.   F.R.S. Aᵒ. 1759.

Safe on the predator-free island of Mauritius in the Indian Ocean, the dodo, above, lost the ability to fly and attained relatively large size—about 50 pounds. European sailors and their animals found the dodos easy prey; by the end of the 17th century they were extinct. The half-ton elephant birds of Madagascar, whose gigantic eggs are still found, left, had been exterminated by natives some time around the year 1000.

Angeles, opposite which sits the Page Museum, part of the Natural History Museum of Los Angeles County. Driving by, one can rubberneck at a mammoth in the clutches of the tar, shown just before it sinks into oblivion, or be awed by a saber-toothed cat on the attack. We associate this famous tourist attraction and cornucopia of information on Pleistocene faunas with the great and charismatic mammals of the age, understandably.

The great proportion of mammal types that were interred in the soggy asphalt were carnivores, probably old or diseased animals drawn no doubt by the bellows and screams of sinking mastodons, camels, and bison, only to be caught up themselves. But, where there is action, one usually finds birds in the vicinity. And from Rancho La Brea they have recovered horned larks, Canada geese, ravens, quail, cranes, killdeer, and a preponderance of birds of prey, some of which, like red-tailed hawks and bald eagles, are still with us today, while others are extinct: a raptor called a Daggett eagle and the La Brea condor, in some ways even spookier-looking than that Pleistocene holdover, now in critical condition, the California condor.

But perhaps the most amazing vulture of the Ice Ages, also represented in the tar, was *Teratornis*, possibly related to the condors and other vultures with which it shared the task of scavenging the dead, but far larger. One common teratorn species had a wingspan of 12 feet; another's approached 17. In 1980, yet another species of teratorn was found in Argentina: it stood five feet tall, and, extended, its wings reached 24 feet overall, making it the largest known flying bird ever.

Gigantism was relatively common in Pleistocene times. Mammals larger than anything today roamed the grasslands. It is no surprise, perhaps, that large carrion eaters evolved in tandem, but huge birds do seem something of a contradiction. The general scheme among birds was the creation of a structure that could largely free itself of gravitational restraints, and great size would seem counterproductive.

Yet the achievement of great size took place among noncarrion eaters as well. In 1987, Storrs Olson and Kenneth Warheit, now at the University of California at Berkeley, reported on the fossil remains of the largest sea bird known to have existed. Discovered in South Carolina, the remains were of a bony-toothed bird of the family of extinct birds called pseudodontorns, probably related to today's pelicans, with a wingspan of nearly 19 feet. The largest sea bird alive today is the wandering albatross, which weighs about 20 pounds and has a wingspan of about 11 feet. The South Carolina bird probably weighed about 90 pounds; Olson and Warheit theorize that, while the ancient pseudodontorn could raise and lower its wings, it could not have achieved a true flapping motion, which requires a rotational movement. Instead, it must have depended largely on ocean winds for gliding, and, Olson and Warheit speculate, a change in

Reaching eight to nine feet in height, moas of New Zealand were among the tallest of the birds, although outweighed by elephant birds. Reasons for the extinction of the 13 or so species of these giants are not clear, although Maori hunters may have hastened their demise.

ocean currents and wind patterns could have been what did this pelagic giant in some 5 million years ago, after 45 million years of roaming the sea in search of fish and squid.

Gigantism is found also among those birds that turned their backs on the main bird achievement—flight. As early as the Eocene, penguins were penguins, wing-propelled divers but flightless, the wings having become relatively rigid flippers. And until the Miocene era there were giant penguins roving southern seas, as well as another family of large, wing-propelled divers called Plotopteridae, which lived in the northern seas of the Pacific only. The largest species of plotopterids were almost twice the size of the largest living penguin, and they and the giant penguins vanished about 20 million years ago at the end of the early Miocene, possibly as a result of competition with seals and porpoises, which were colonizing the oceans at about that time.

But it is on land that birds have achieved their most awesome size and on land that the

use of the forelimbs, so efficiently evolved into wings, has surprisingly and so many times lapsed. Geologically speaking, it was barely an instant after the large, bipedal, carnivorous dinosaurs had abandoned the stage that a bird filled the gap. By Paleocene times, a six-footer with massive legs, tiny wings, and a head nearly the size of a horse's with a large, powerful beak roamed North America and Europe. These were the diatrymas; recently it has been suggested that they were not fierce predators but may have been on the lineage that gave rise to ducks.

South America, isolated during most of this time, produced its own flightless giants, at least 12 species in all of what are called phorusrhacids—birds that were lighter and presumably faster than diatrymas and reached five to eight feet in height. These big flesh-eaters, which also occurred in North America and Europe, apparently died out about 4 million years ago, around the time that North and South America became joined, allowing mammalian predators from the north to move

in and compete. At least one species of phorusrhacid, however, survived until the isthmian gap was closed: in the early 1960s, fossils of a bird named *Titanis walleri* were discovered in central Florida.

Elsewhere, in more isolated circumstances, earthbound giants arose and became herbivorous, a feeding mode that is extremely rare among today's birds. A few parrots and the oddball hoatzin are among the handful of truly herbivorous birds alive today. Eating plants as a steady diet calls for a special pouch, or cecum, at the beginning of the intestine to house the bacteria that digest cellulose, and flying birds as a rule cannot afford the added weight. But the moas of New Zealand and the elephant birds of Madagascar had no such problem. Almost wholly free of predators, they evolved into record size. The largest of the many species of moas was eight or nine feet tall; the largest elephant bird weighed half a ton. The elephant bird's egg, the largest bird egg ever recorded, would hold the contents of 83

chicken eggs. Both of these birds survived into historic times, probably succumbing at least in part to pressure from late-arriving human populations, as did that flightless pigeon-descendant, the dodo, on the Indian Ocean island of Mauritius.

Today's flightless giants are the ostriches, which reach eight feet in height and weigh some 300 pounds. They have survived alongside the large and speedy predators of Africa most likely because of their own fleetness—they can run at least 40 miles an hour. Paleontologists guess that the ostrich arose first in Asia about 7 million years ago, most likely—again—from the Gruiformes.

Some propose similar ancestry for the ostrich's counterparts elsewhere—South America's rheas, Australia's emus and cassowaries, the kiwi of New Zealand—which, along with the poorly flying tinamous of South America, have traditionally been lumped together under the heading of ratites. Whether all the ratites derived from a single ancestral species or from several is a question

Weak flyers, the hoatzins, above, of South American rain forests feed largely on leaves, an energy-poor diet unusual among birds. Baby hoatzins, opposite, sport claws on their "hands" that enable them to clamber about the limbs of their streamside nesting bushes. At any sign of an aerial predator, a baby hoatzin plops into the water beneath its nest. As soon as the danger has passed, it uses its claws to scramble out of the water and away from other predators lurking there.

that has haunted avian paleontologists for a century. All the ratites share a particular configuration of the bones of the palate, called the paleognathous palate, which was long thought to be a primitive characteristic. But then it was suggested that the paleognathous palate was a misnomer, and that it was in fact difficult to distinguish from the standard neognathous palate of other birds. The problem was the usual: a paucity of fossils from ancient times.

Then, in 1981, Storrs Olson and paleontologist Peter Houde reported on some fossils of flying birds from the Paleocene era. They had all the characteristics of the paleognathous palate, demonstrating that it was indeed a primitive character, which in turn meant that it could not be used as an argument for a single ancestor for all the ratites.

Three years later, Chris McGowan of the Royal Ontario Museum in Toronto studied the tarsus joint (the equivalent of the ankle) in modern flying birds and flightless ones like ostriches and emus. In both kinds, the embryos have a cartilaginous spur in the tarsus, but in flying birds it eventually ossifies and fuses into a bone called the pretibial. In all the flightless birds, however, this same spur develops into another bony process altogether: the ratites do not have pretibial bones. McGowan concluded that the ratites evolved not from any "modern" flying bird but rather from a very ancient flier. Ratites, needless to say, remain enigmatic.

There are other recent flightless birds besides the ratites. They are to be found among ducks, geese, and cormorants. There are several semiterrestrial pigeons and doves that appear to be headed toward flightlessness; and the kakapo, a parrot of New Zealand, is capable only of gliding from a tree to the ground. Parrots are derivatives of pigeons, as was the dodo. Recently extinct flightless grebes inhabited Lake Atitlan in Guatemala.

Flight is expensive. It takes a high-energy metabolism and the energy-demanding growth of a keeled sternum and big flight muscles and other associated features. Typically, the basic flight apparatus amounts to 25 percent of a bird's weight. When over time the situation changes so that flight is not needed—for finding food or avoiding death— it has a tendency to disappear. This has been especially true in the Gruiformes, and no other kind of bird today is so prone to developing flightlessness as the rails. There are no flightless rails (or any other flightless birds, for that matter, since the demise of the great auk in the mid-19th century) in North America, but flightless rails abound elsewhere. The fossil record is replete with others. More often than not, flightlessness has occurred when a rail species first establishes itself on an island or some remote place relatively free of predation, where the birds can live their secretive lives in peace.

One might well ask why, if a life without need of flight leads to flightlessness, haven't domestic chickens tended to become flightless, too? The question goes directly to the heart of the mechanism that seems to have permitted flightlessness to occur so many times from flying ancestors, and the answer comes from Olson's work on fossil and living rails. Flightlessness, it seems, is a matter of arrested development, or neoteny—the retention into adulthood of childish or embryonic features. In pigeons, rails, and grebes, the sternum with its keel does not begin to get bony until a month or more after the bird hatches. Up until that time it remains cartilaginous. At the same time, all the vital organs develop on a normal schedule: before hatching. Any arrested development of the vital organs would, of course, be fatal. But with a late-developing sternum, any environmental pressure tugging the species toward an arrested development of flight muscles and smaller wings can proceed without harm to the other features of the bird.

In the absence of predators, the tiny Laysan rail lost the power of flight but clung to existence on its Pacific island home until the great fleet movements of World War II brought rats and other pests to Laysan. Opposite, the little scarlet-chested sunbird of South Africa is representative of the passerines, or perching birds, the most successful of the bird order. Passerines universally retain the ability to fly.

A chicken's sternum, on the other hand, ossifies several days before hatching, and the bird emerges from the egg with almost full flight capacity. Any tug toward flightlessness in chickens could therefore be played out only in tandem with the arrested development of the vital organs; the chickens and their relatives have never produced a flightless species.

People long assumed that such a radical change would take tens of millions of years to come about, but there is evidence that, once the slide to flightlessness begins, it is a relatively rapid process. The common gallinule (a recently evolved bird, meaning within the Pleistocene) includes two flightless subspecies, located 250 miles apart on Tristan da Cunha and Gough islands in the South Atlantic. And there was a flightless rail on Ascension Island that must have flown there and then become flightless in much less than 1.5 million years, because that is when the volcanic island emerged as hot lava from the mid-Atlantic. Olson points out that "the span of time needed to evolve flightlessness in rails can probably be measured in generations, rather than millennia."

In this light, the emergence of huge flightless birds like diatrymas so soon after the niche was vacated by dinosaurs seems understandable. But another question arises: what was that rail doing on Ascension Island in the first place? How did the rails—thought of as poor fliers—get there? 🦅

WHEREABOUTS

Most people go through life without ever laying eyes on a rail, and even the craftiest ornithologists often need to resort to hard work and high-tech instrumentation to see them. Rails simply torment birdwatchers. They are typically skulkers, hiding in the reeds of coastal marshes and wetlands and other inaccessible places, and they tend to be crepuscular or nocturnal as well. Members of the Gruiformes, which have given rise to so many other types of birds, including some of the more notable monsters of Tertiary horizons, they seem to be lurking about, highly plastic, just waiting for the next geological/climatic transformation to take place and call for some rapid-fire biological invention.

Slogging around in rail country hoping for a glimpse, one may often go home unrequited, except for the frustrating experience of having heard them here and there in the dark, making characteristic calls that are most often compared to the clicking together of two large pebbles. And a glimpse is about all one can hope

Preceding pages: Wings raised and feathers fluffed, a king rail aggressively defends its nest. Standing more than a foot high, this denizen of inland freshwater swamps is the largest member of the elusive rail family in North America.

Ultrasecretive and elusive, a black rail peers from its marshland nest, above. What this diminutive, five-inch-high rail lacks in size, it makes up for in aggressive behavior. Often loathe to fly and thus wrongly considered to be poor flyers, rails have dispersed to and become established on some of the world's most remote oceanic islands. Opposite, a painting by J. Fenwick Lansdowne in S. Dillon Ripley's Rails of the World *depicts, from top, a bare-eyed rail from southern New Guinea and neighboring islands, the redwinged wood rail from South America, and the baldfaced rail from the Indonesian island of Celebes.*

for. Spotted in the open at a distance by an intruder, a rail tends to walk calmly toward the nearest cover—a stand of marsh grass, say—and vanish like a wraith. Their bodies are highly compressed, an adaptation for running through reeds and tall grasses that gives us the phrase "skinny as a rail." Taken by surprise at close quarters, however, they will fly up suddenly, their legs hanging clumsily below them, and hurtle off a few yards before crash-landing in the vegetation.

It was this latter habit that made hunting them feasible in times and places where people relied more heavily on wild nature for food. Alexander Wilson noted the mode of rail-hunting in his time in the eastern United States: a shallow boat was poled through the reeds at high water with a hunter poised in the bow. "The Rail generally spring singly, as the boat advances, and at a short distance ahead, are instantly shot down. . . . The sport continues till an hour or two after high water. . . . In these excursions it is not uncommon for an active and expert marksman to kill ten or twelve dozen in a tide."

In spite of what John James Audubon later lamented was ruthless overkill here—and surely elsewhere in the world—and in spite of being what appear to be relatively poor and certainly reluctant fliers, rails are found almost everywhere in the world, including (as noted previously) on small oceanic islands up to 1,500 or more miles from the nearest shore. In this they seem to be a paradox.

It has been pointed out that, once arrived, rails are likely to be adept colonizers of new territories. Birds that live on the margins, such as coastal areas and the edges of forest and savannah, are inclined to have a built-in adaptive plasticity. Having found their way to an island that is free of predators and other competition, they tend to be able to locate themselves on the coasts, become entrenched, and gradually move on back into the forests. The more omnivorous the bird (and rails have catholic tastes), the better off it is in this regard. Also, there is a tendency among rails for the young to disperse in random directions in occasional irruptive migrations that are unusual among birds. These explosions are a different matter from the predictable movements of migrant rails that travel annually from a breeding range to a winter range. Rails, it has been said, are simply weird: all of

a sudden they just take off. A tropical rail was found wandering around in Pennsylvania in 1978. While it is certain that many young rails, randomly dispersing from their traditional area, do not find salubrious habitat and perish, the practice obviously confers an advantage on the species overall. And, because the bird is given to odd irruptions of this sort, it clearly pays a rail that winds up on a distant island to develop flightlessness so that it won't one day take off and wobble perilously off to sea. But none of this explains how they travel so far.

S. Dillon Ripley, the eighth Secretary of the Smithsonian Institution and an ornithologist who has left tracks in about as many parts of the world as the rails themselves, believes that it is the very reluctance of rails to fly that has led to their widespread dispersal. Another paradox? In the tradition of Edward Lear, Ripley published a monumental monograph called *Rails of the World*, amply illustrated with paintings by J. Fenwick Lansdowne, a Canadian bird artist. In this book, Ripley pointed out that most rails, and certainly the migratory ones, have excellent flight equipment and fly "perfectly well." He went on to ask: "Could it be that these skulking birds, once airborne, are reluctant to stop? Their hesitation in flight may be balanced by an equal uncertainty in alighting." He further suggests that, being mostly sedentary in style, they have little experience from "range reconnaissance flights" and so tend to stray—in the great sweepstakes of life and geography occasionally winding up on a remote island, which is no more improbable than Pennsylvania.

Islands have played a central and romantic role in the history of zoogeography. Two of its most renowned students, Charles Darwin and Alfred Russel Wallace, found on islands confirmatory evidence for their emerging (and converging) ideas about the origin of species via natural selection. While fossil remains, in a sense, provide a means for standing in the past and looking forward to the present, the whereabouts of animals today provide a means of looking back from the present into the ancient course of evolution. In this sense, islands are very like laboratories, for on them life has experimented many times in relative seclusion.

In the case of oceanic islands—those that at

J.F.LANSDOWNE

Plant life must precede any successful colonization of a new oceanic island by birds or other animals. Ocean currents transport the seeds of many plants, such as this sprouting coconut, and birds also act as dispersal agents, carrying seeds on their bodies and in their digestive tracts.

one time or another erupted from the sea floor, such as the Hawaiian Islands—half the problem of successful colonization would appear to be simply getting there. And there must be plant life established on a new island before any animals can survive. Explaining the arrival of plants on a new island is easy: the seeds of most beach plants are well adapted to being carried by ocean currents to other places. Other seeds can float great distances through the air, as can insects and spiders. Floating piles of debris can carry all manner of seeds, plants, and even small reptiles and mammals across great distances. And, of course, birds can carry seeds on their feet in mud, stuck to their feathers, or in their digestive tracts. It is highly likely that migratory and stray birds have played a significant if incalculable role in populating islands with their flora as well as arthropod fauna. There is speculation, for example, that the ancestors of the New Zealand fruit pigeon brought to that island the very fruit—a kind of fuchsia—upon which it still regularly feeds.

Of course, when an island or island chain emerges where there was none, it may well become a convenient way station for already migratory birds. The Pacific golden plover, the western form of the American golden plover, which migrates thousands of miles from the Arctic to the east coast of South America each year, is to be found in Hawaii from August to April each year—a new migratory path and a new wintering ground. In all, members of 11 other migratory birds use Hawaii as a winter home—seabirds and shorebirds. Also, 22 wide-ranging oceanic species—albatrosses, petrels, shearwaters, tropicbirds, and terns—nest on the Hawaiian chain, a natural extension of their widespread oceanic territories.

But most of the year-rounders—especially the birds that are endemic, or peculiar, to Hawaii—must have arrived by chance as strays, perhaps blindly hastening off in a new direction like rails, or simply blown off course by storms and high winds, arriving in pairs or flocks, bewildered and lucky. It seems terribly chancy. Indeed, such long-distance dispersal is so much like a horse race of long shots that paleontologist George Gaylord Simpson christened it "sweepstakes" dispersal. But adding the factor of time, it becomes less surprising.

The main Hawaiian Islands emerged serially as volcanoes between 3.5 and 6 million years ago, the Big Island, Hawaii, being the most recent. Suppose, as botanists do, that by 5 million years ago the island forests were suitable for birds to live in. There are some 90 species of birds—contemporary and fossil—unique to the Hawaiian Islands, all derived—scientists estimate—from about 20 original immigrant species. On the average, then, it would take only one successful colonization about every 250,000 years to create the native Hawaiian avifauna.

Not by any such metronomic scheme, they blew in over the eons from various directions: coots and stilts from the New World; elepaio, a Hawaiian flycatcher, and melaphagids, or honeyeaters, from the South Pacific; millerbirds and the Laysan rail probably from Asia, island-hopping across the Pacific from the west. Once established, they adapted to their new territories and, over time, became distinctly Hawaiian. Perhaps the crown jewels of these endemic Hawaiians are the finches, or honeycreepers, which, like Darwin's finches on the Galápagos Islands, offer a stunning example of adaptive radiation.

Descending from a finch that somehow made its way 2,000 miles across the open ocean from the American mainland, the honeycreepers evolved into 45 or more species, each distinctly adapted for a slightly different way of life in the lush new habitat. Some have beaks like those of parrots or grosbeaks, for cracking and grinding seeds. The strongly decurved upper mandible of the akiapolaau is about twice as long as the straight, robust lower mandible. The bird searches for food like a woodpecker, pounding its lower beak into dead branches and tree trunks for insects and their larvae. Its upper bill is used primarily for probing. The Maui parrotbill uses its hooked beak like pliers to tear away the wood of the koa tree in search of insects. Another, the akepa, has slightly crossed mandibles evidently useful in opening leaf buds. The anianiau, endemic to Kauai, has a short, relatively straight bill with which it collects insects in loose tree bark; its cousin, the amakihi, has a slightly larger and decurved bill used for both collecting nectar from flowers and probing underneath bark for insects and grubs.

With their emergence some 5 million years ago, the Hawaiian Islands became a wintering ground for the Pacific golden plover, like the one at left in a lotus pond on the main island of Oahu, and other shorebirds and seabirds. Despite the Hawaiian archipelago's remote location in the vast Pacific, almost midway between North America and Asia, below, its islands were colonized by various birds that flew in from faraway continents and adapted to the new habitats.

The original ancestor of the Hawaiian honeycreepers was probably dependent on seeds for sustenance, but over time some of its descendants diverged from this diet and began to feed on nectar. Some of the most arresting honeycreepers have taken this nectivorous specialty to a high degree. One of the most striking and conspicuous of the honeycreepers is the iiwi, a bright crimson bird with black wings and tail reminiscent of the scarlet tanager—but there the resemblance ends. The iiwi has a long, salmon-colored decurved bill designed for sipping nectar from deep tubular flowers. Walking in the eerie mists of the cloud forest on Kauai, one will hear its rusty, discordant song and peer around to see nothing but a few shadowy branches emerging from the fog. Then suddenly, on a branch, an iiwi appears, the only point of color in the timeless grey emulsion, and all the legendary magic of Hawaii is instantaneously summed up. Iiwis are most often seen feeding on the relatively shallow blooms of the ohia tree, but are presumed to have developed their long beaks more anciently, in association with the deep flowers of lobeliads, which are thought to be a more primeval component of the Hawaiian forests. Thus, while the New Zealand fruit pigeon "made" its habitat, the habitat and particularly the flowers of Hawaii made the iiwi.

Forgetting for a moment that even 5 million years is a short time for 45 species to arise from one, and knowing that the oceanic skies are often surprisingly full of stray birds, one might ask why only about 20 immigrant species successfully colonized the Islands. While half the problem is getting there, however, the other half is finding suitable habitat in which to reproduce. Once the honeycreepers had begun to radiate into a variety of niches, those niches would be unavailable for any new immigrant (unless the newcomer were bigger and stronger). No one can say, on the other hand, why Polynesian doves and parrots found the intervening expanse of ocean too great for them. Such birds have been introduced since by man and do fine in Hawaii.

Nor are natural colonizations of islands by birds only a thing of the long-gone past. Both pied-billed grebes and fulvous whistling-ducks have established breeding populations in Hawaii within the last few years. And, in 1937, a flock of fieldfares, a European bird something like the American robin, got blown by a storm to southeastern Greenland, which they found to their liking, and where they are now well established. It is possible that one day they may become a new subspecies or species.

Madagascar, that huge island of bizarre life forms ranging from lemurs and tenrecs to the royal poinciana, also called the flamboyant tree, has evolved 46 endemic genera of birds. Once part of the African continent, Madagascar was largely in its present position by the end of the Cretaceous. Not surprisingly, it has few mammals, but, as the plethora of African birds evolved, some made it across the Mozambique Channel, and many of these set off on evolutionary journeys that were unique to the island. One such journey, which probably began with a rail-like ancestor, led to three species of birds called mesites. Flightless and completely terrestrial, mesites must climb to reach the nests they build a few feet up in a tree or bush. In two species, the female is polyandrous, mating with several males; the males incubate the eggs. Locals consider these strange birds sacred because of their legendary parental devotion. If a chick is stolen from the nest, the parent will follow the thief even into a village.

Madagascar has its own counterpart to the Hawaiian honeycreepers—albeit less exuberant, perhaps because by the time they arrived other birds had already taken up some of the available niches. These are the vanga shrikes of unknown ancestry—probably the descendants of the ancestors of Asian wood-swallows or the shrikes of Africa, Europe, Asia, and North America. In any event, when their ancestors arrived, they were arboreal and insectivorous, for that is the habit of most of the vanga shrikes today. They radiated into a number of forest habitats and evolved a variety of plumages and, as one might expect, a variety of beak shapes for different diets. One species, the sicklebill, was particularly confusing. For a while scientists placed it in several other families, until they discovered that, except for its long decurved bill, it was anatomically close to the other vangas. Another, the helmet bird, has a large and rather awkward-looking casque on its upper mandible. Yet another, the hook-billed vanga, has a bill that tends toward the shape of a true shrike's, and, with its solitary lifestyle and its diet, which consists largely of frogs, tree lizards, and chameleons, seems almost as if it were on its way to reinventing the raptor.

The island condition is especially conducive, then, to rapid speciation up to a point of equilibrium, as well as to flightlessness and gigantism, but it also calls forth other oddities. Great blue herons normally nest in trees, but on a predator-free island in Lake Michigan they can safely nest on the ground and do so. The same is true of ospreys in the Chesapeake Bay. The kea, a parrot of New Zealand, became a carnivore, its natural diet consisting of insects and worms. A Samoan pigeon nested on the ground until the arrival of whaling ships and their ever-present cats, and then quickly turned to the high trees. This same bird evolved a notched bill that acts like teeth, enabling it to tear pieces from the figlike fruits of the banyan tree, on which it chiefly feeds.

A unique habit evolved in the huia, a species of New Zealand's wattlebirds that is now extinct as a result of the loss to human

Perhaps the crown jewels of endemic Hawaiian birdlife are the finches, or honey-creepers, that evolved from a finch that flew or blew in from North America. The akiapolaau, above, lives only on the island of Hawaii. It uses the lower mandible of its unique bill to pound bark in search of insects and grubs.

purposes of its forest habitat. The huia was a large, glossy, black bird with orange wattles and white-tipped tail feathers. For a time, European scientists took the male and female huias to be two different species, since the male had an essentially straight, chisel-like beak, while the female had a longer, gracefully decurved bill. In the quest for insects in wood, the male would chisel away in the manner of a woodpecker, and what escaped him would be taken out of the now-open holes by the female. If she, in turn, failed to retrieve an insect, the male would take over, enlarging the hole.

Island life is fragile as well as conducive to inventiveness, for the next immigrant can be a new predator or a new parasite. A change in the climate can be devastating for life forms that have become perhaps a bit over-specialized and have nowhere to go. And so, of course, can such a consummate predator as man, with his penchant for altering habitats and bringing other "exotic" potential predators—dogs, pigs, cats—with him. Twenty-three of the 45 species of Hawaiian honeycreepers are extinct, most likely at least indirectly at the hand of man.

Although we know that the honeycreepers' radiation took place in Hawaii, finding

Kauai 'Akialoa
Hemignathus procerus

Grosbeak Finch
Psittirostra kona

'Akiapola'au
Hemignathus wilsoni

Palila
Psittirostra bailleui

'Ō'ū
Psittirostra psittacea

'Ākepa
Loxops coccinea

'Akikiki
Loxops maculata bairdi

Maui Parrotbill
Pseudonestor xanthophrys

'Amakihi
Loxops virens

The Hawaiian honey-creepers, such as those in the painting at left, offer a spectacular example of adaptive radiation. Some 45 species of these finches evolved and radiated into different island niches, many of which have been altered or destroyed by human activity. Today almost half of the 45 known species of honeycreepers are extinct. In early Polynesian society, cloaks, capes, and helmets fashioned from tiny, colorful honeycreeper feathers denoted rank and status. Opposite, Boki Kamauleule, governor of Oahu, and his wife, Kuini Liliha, don royal featherwork for a portrait painted by John Hayter in London in 1824.

the exact point of origin of any species can be difficult. In these days of genetic analysis at the molecular level and the ability to probe single neurons, such inquiries about the distribution of birds may seem a bit quaint—a matter, one might have thought, generally worked out by 19th-century gentlemen ornithologists.

But, though we probably know just about all of the extant species of birds (so well has humanity probed the nooks and crannies of the planet), we still don't know everything about why birds are found where they are. We don't know, for example, why some bird species are more expansive then others, or why some are almost totally cosmopolitan. Besides being nearly worldwide in distribution, what do the following bird families have in common: ducks, rails, crows, pigeons, hawks, and swallows? Nothing, as far as anyone can figure. The barn owl, a single species, is found everywhere but Antarctica and the northernmost regions of Eurasia and North America. Other cosmopolitan species include the horned lark and the osprey. Altogether, these wide-ranging species constitute, as the late ornithologist Josselyn Van Tyne wrote, "a small, curiously assorted group, and no one seems to have suggested what they have in common that puts them in this exclusive category."

To know why a bird will go only so far when another will go farther, to know that the snowy owl evidently irrupts wildly to the south on a regular cycle of four years, to wonder why the ivory-billed woodpecker could not adjust to a changing environment while its cousin, the pileated woodpecker, could—these are all matters raised by the simple question: what is that bird doing here?

One principle for guessing where a wide-ranging bird family may have originated is to locate the place where that family shows the greatest diversity. The principle doesn't work, of course, for birds such as those symbols of the north, the loons, of which there are merely four species, all circumpolar. Yet the family of murres, auklets, and dovekies is more diverse in the northern Pacific than the Atlantic and thus has been presumed to have arisen in the Pacific. Pigeons and parrots are more varied and numerous in Australia than anywhere else in the world and probably spread from there to Eurasia and Africa,

reaching the Western Hemisphere via the Asia-Alaska connection. Wood warblers can be seen as originally from North America.

This same principle, interestingly, is now being applied to the question of human origins. Geneticists using sophisticated biomedical techniques have found a far greater genetic diversity among the present-day races of Africa than among the other races of the world, and take this as confirmation that modern humans arose there and spread out to people the world, shoving aside—maybe even absorbing—the other near-humans, such as Neanderthals. Biochemical techniques are also beginning to be used on birds, and have the potential to provide valuable clues to evolutionary relationships. Analysis of the genetic material of birds, DNA, for example, is turning up some surprises. According to DNA hybridization research, the family called Corvidae—which includes crows, ravens, jays, and magpies—evidently arose first in Australia and spread from there to Eurasia and then to North America as well as into Africa and lastly, once a land bridge formed, into South America. From these corvid ancestors, today's crows and ravens apparently evolved in Eurasia and spread widely around the world, even recolonizing Australia.

Birds that were often taken to be related to crows are those of the starling family, which are, like crows, for the most part good mimics. Meanwhile, that master mimic, the mockingbird, was thought to be related to thrushes. DNA analysis has shown that the starlings and mockingbirds are both related to thrushes—and even more closely to one another—and probably shared a common ancestor, a bird that lived in the then-warmer broad-leaved forests of the Arctic, its descendants moving southward when the climate cooled.

Why some birds are so widespread and others so restricted is a matter of barriers—barriers ranging from the position of entire continental land masses to the extent of the range of a particular tree species, from the history of the Earth's climate to the presence or absence of a snail type. There are even barriers that are seemingly psychological. The brown booby, for example, will not fly the 50 miles it takes to cross the Isthmus of Panama. It is perfectly capable physically of making such a flight (which is made regularly

Heads held high and flipper-like wings extended for balance, a flock of royal penguins travels up a creek on Macquarie Island, left, in the sub-Antarctic. This South Pacific island is the only known breeding ground of this species. The snail kite, above, is limited to the tropical Americas by its specialized diet, which consists almost exclusively of the freshwater apple snail. Its range includes the Florida Everglades, where this kite prepares to feed its young. Harlequin ducks, such as the brightly patterned male at right, frequent only fast-moving water, be it along sea coasts or in inland streams.

by frigate birds and brown pelicans). It just won't do it.

In North America there are a number of nonmigratory birds, such as ruffed grouse and screech owls, that have not and evidently will not take up residence in perfectly suitable habitat on Great Lakes islands separated from the mainland by only a mile of water. And while the brown pelican will readily fly across the Isthmus of Panama, its range down the eastern edge of South America stops abruptly at the Amazon. Fine pelican country lies just south of the river, but evidently the muddy waters at the mouth are too opaque for the bird to see any fish, and so it won't venture across. The aptly named harlequin duck, a true dandy, likes to feed in a certain manner and will accept no other. Along the rugged seacoasts where it spends most of the year, and on freshwater streams during breeding season, it swims in cold, fast-flowing water, poking its bill under rocks for the larvae of aquatic insects. Much the same larvae are to be found in the lakes from which the streams originate, but the duck is not found on the lakes. Its diet can success-

Bearing the typically brilliant colors of many of the world's kingfishers, a family that numbers some 87 species, the African pygmy kingfisher measures only four inches from the tip of its beak to the end of its tail.

fully be altered in captivity, but, unless the captor provides a strong current, the duck will not eat.

Other birds are restricted by a finicky diet. The everglade kite, as well as the limpkin of the Everglades, has come to feed almost exclusively on a single kind of freshwater snail, *Pomacea paludosa*. In South America, the wetland habitat of the snail is fairly widespread and so is the kite; in the Everglades and the few other places in southern Florida where the bird nests, the habitat and the snail population, and therefore the kite population, have shrunk considerably, putting the entire system in danger. (Since there are, in fact, populations of this bird in South America, its official common name has been changed to snail kite—more precise, if less evocative.)

In the rain forests of the Amazon Basin, perhaps the most wildly diverse biological area anywhere in the universe, some highly elaborate practices have been worked out. Certain thrushlike birds, for example, are called ant followers—not because they eat ants but because they are camp followers of

army ants. As, periodically, a vast horde of army ants begins to march across the forest floor in a voracious stream, the ant followers feed on the insects that are thus stirred up. Recent research by the World Wildlife Fund has demonstrated that, if a patch of forest is isolated by forestry or the conversion to ranchland of the surrounding area, it is likely that there won't be enough territory in the isolated forest patch for the army ants' wide-ranging maneuvers. They will leave or die out, and the birds are obliged to do the same.

Of course, though most birds can fly, and most can fly farther than they do, there are large and obvious barriers. The American dipper, a bird with the fascinating habit of walking underwater in mountain streams, is found throughout the western mountains of North America. It might well be able to do fine in the streams of the Appalachians, but the vast area of the plains states has limited it to the West. Conversely, a mountain range can effectively limit a nonmigratory bird of the plains. Warm ocean currents in the northern regions of southern seas have, for some 50 million years or so, kept penguins

In a scene familiar the world over, a child chases domestic pigeons, Columba livea, *inside the Courtyard of the Moors, Cordoba, Spain, opposite above. Four young of another cosmopolitan species, the barn owl, above, stare from their Florida perch.*

totally restricted to the Southern Hemisphere. The most northerly species, the Galápagos penguin, breeds in those islands off the coast of Ecuador.

Except for those crammed together on small islands, no two of the more than 8,000 bird species have exactly the same range. They may overlap, and they always seem to be subject to change. The bird with one of the smallest ranges—albeit almost certainly because of human disturbance—is a little lark that exists exclusively and abundantly on a single island, Razo, in the Cape Verde Islands—a territory of a mere three square miles. The Kirtland's warbler breeds and nests only in the jack-pine forests of Michigan; today there are fewer than 5,000 square miles of jack-pine country.

That the ranges of birds have been in flux over long periods can readily be seen in situations where a bird has a discontinuous range. The red-shouldered hawk is widespread throughout northeastern North America but is not to be seen again until you have crossed the Rockies and the Sierras to California's coast. No one has explained this

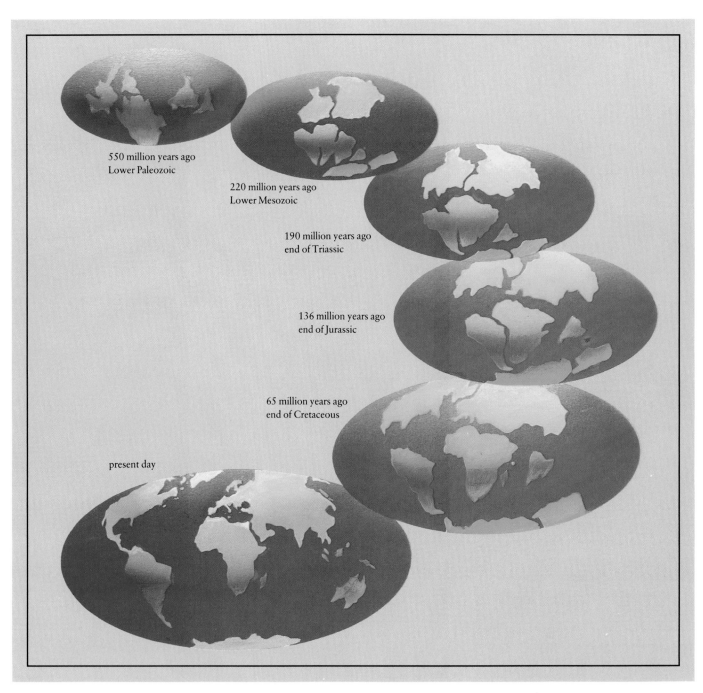

550 million years ago
Lower Paleozoic

220 million years ago
Lower Mesozoic

190 million years ago
end of Triassic

136 million years ago
end of Jurassic

65 million years ago
end of Cretaceous

present day

A series of maps illustrates the breakup of the supercontinent Pangaea, which, by some 180 million years ago, had split into Laurasia to the north and Gondwanaland to the south. Further fragmentation of these two immense land masses yielded continents as we know them today and promoted species diversity in birds and other animals.

long gap, though the finger is pointed at an increase at one time of aridity and altitude in the intervening area.

What seem to us to be imperceptibly slow changes in the configuration of the continents have obviously affected the ranges of birds. For millions of years, as now, frigid water separated North America from Asia. But at various times during the Pleistocene, which began about 2.5 million years ago and ended about 10,000 years ago, ice bound up water upon the land's surface, lowering the sea level and exposing a land bridge, thus permitting a vast exchange of life forms, including humans, between the two continents. Several species of wrens, which originated in Central America, adapted to the warmer parts of North America. But one, the winter wren, became more tolerant of colder climes and, grasping the wings of happy chance, ventured north over the now submerged Bering land bridge and established itself all across the top of Eurasia, even reaching the British Isles.

Meanwhile, to the south was a great island: South America. It had early on split away from Africa in the great migration of continents, and it remained for most of its history in remote isolation. Before the South America/Africa split in the late Cretaceous, at least 65 million years ago, a group of birds called suboscines had come into being. Today this group is represented in the New World most generally by flycatchers of the family Tyrannidae. In South America the suboscines flourished, eventually radiating into the nine families and 1,000 species living today, nearly one-eighth of all bird species. They are for the most part small birds, the most primitive of what we tend to call songbirds but what are better thought of as perching birds, or passerines.

The age of origin of the true songbirds, or oscines, remains unknown. They probably originated in Australia, although no early fossil record exists there. Scientists have discovered a fossil of a modern genus of oscine from Australia that may date to the Oligocene Epoch, which began about 38,000,000 years ago and lasted about 12,000,000 years. In any case, there is no reason to assume that the oscines originated later than other groups, although they did not spread to the Northern Hemisphere until the late Oligocene. With some 4,000 living species, the oscines are the most successful and diverse birds on the planet, and represent nearly half of all bird species.

About five and a half million years ago, faunal affairs in the Western Hemisphere changed radically with the achievement of a land connection between the two continents at Panama. The Great American Interchange soon got underway, mostly a one-sided affair. For example, carnivores of the southern continent were mostly made up of marsupial mammals, representing one solution to mammalian childbirth wherein the fetus is born early and spends time in the mother's pouch, as with the kangaroos and other mammals native to that other isolate, Australia. More effective, it seems, is the placental mammals' system; before long the placental carnivores—and herbivores—of the north had overrun the south, eventually replacing most of the marsupials. Conversely, only two southern mammals established themselves in the north—the porcupine and the opossum.

The peculiar ecological requirements of the Kirtland's warbler have limited its breeding range in historic times to fewer than 5,000 square miles of young jack-pine forest in central Michigan. Alterations of this forest ecosystem by global warming resulting from the greenhouse effect would leave the Kirtland's warbler with no habitat in which to nest.

The formation of the Panamanian land bridge some five and a half million years ago sparked an interchange of bird families between North and South America. The oscines, or true songbirds, fared far better in their colonization of new lands than did the more primitive suboscines of the south. Today the flycatchers, including the willow flycatcher, above, and the vermilion flycatcher, opposite, are the only suboscine family to be found in the United States, and most of them migrate to their ancestral south in winter.

Similarly, great waves of oscine birds flooded the south and became established, while relatively few suboscines could make it much farther north than Central America. Today the flycatchers are the only sub-oscine family to be found in the United States, and, except for the phoebe, they spend only the summer, returning to their ancestral south in winter.

As the two continents were hooking up, matters in the south were further compli-cated by the rise of the Andes as the southern continent also plowed into the huge crustal plate under the Pacific. Forging a vast barrier to the prevailing winds and a host of other climatic changes, the Andes created a variety of new habitats as well—habitats that both the oscines and the suboscines hastened to take advantage of. And not long after, in the Pleistocene, the coming and going of the Ice Ages produced alternations of dry and humid periods in the Amazon Basin, calling forth yet more speciation among the suboscines in a short period of time.

There are some scholars who say that, had it not been for the new habitats brought about by the Andean uplift and the Ice Ages, the suboscines would have fared even worse against the newcomers than they did. (Opponents of this view point out that the suboscines hold their own perfectly well in the tropics when oscine migrants from North America come to spend the winter.) Overall, however, the true songbirds—the oscines—have edged out the more primitive suboscines wherever the two groups have had to compete.

Thus is a bird's whereabouts determined in part by the motion of the continents, mountain uplift, climate change, the creation of new niches—all of what might be called the accidents of history—and in part by cer-tain features peculiar to the bird, one of these having to do with its inherent capability to vie with other species when the occasion is thrust upon it.

Extinction also has a profound effect on a bird's whereabouts, and local extinctions can determine a bird's distribution at any given time. The huge condors of the New World most likely came into being in North Amer-ica, later following large northern mammals south across the Central American land bridge. Should we lose the California condor—

in spite of heroic efforts to save it—a future observer of big condors, seeing only the Andean species, would suppose that they had arisen in the south, unless the observer had access to condor history.

In fact, the history of vultures and other birds of prey turns out to be relatively unhelpful in terms of telling us where they arose in the first place. The only place where hawks and their allies, the falcons and eagles, don't occur is Antarctica. Vultures are found in the Western Hemisphere, Asia, and Africa. No nature film of the African veldt is com-plete without a distant gyre of vultures soar-ing hungrily over a carcass, signaling its presence to others for miles and miles. Those vultures, however, with their grim, naked heads, are an altogether different family from the vultures of the New World. The Old World vultures are related to the eagles and hawks and are placed in that family. New World vultures, on the other hand, arose separately from an unknown ancestral group and developed convergently the soaring, scavenging habit and the bald head, the bet-ter not to become fouled during feeding. (We tend to shudder at this habit, though humans do eat uncooked meat and practically never any that is alive.) The two kinds of vultures differ widely, however, in such features as the feet, the nostrils, and the voice box. New World vulture babies can cheep like chicks, but the adults have no voice box at all and can break the silence only by hissing.

For a time, it seemed perfectly reasonable to assume that their current ranges explained their points of origin. But then, in 1916, scientists described two vultures from Cali-fornia's Rancho La Brea tar pits that were distinctly related to the Old World type. The scientists held up the announcement for two years, it is said, because so great a geographic leap looked fishy. Subsequently, other Old World vultures were found as fossils dating from 30 million years ago in the New World, and that is about how far back they go in the Old World as well, so now their place of origin is up for grabs. As Barry Lopez, a close observer of wildlife, has written, "It is the birds' independence from predictable human design that draws us to them."

Nevertheless, early ornithologists sought for good reason to impose various concep-tual schemes on the larger geography of

Wings and legs outstretched, a Nubian vulture, far left, prepares to land near a carcass in Kenya's Maasai Mara National Reserve. Though unrelated, Old and New World vultures, such as the lappet-faced vulture, left, and the turkey vulture, below, share the soaring, scavenging habit and such physical features as unfeathered heads, characteristics they evolved independently, or convergently.

Changes in weather patterns can have extreme effects on the ecology and distribution of birds. In the early 1980s, a severe El Niño—an invasion of unusually warm water in the eastern equatorial Pacific caused by a complex dance of ocean, wind, climate, and current—wreaked havoc on nesting seabirds throughout much of the Pacific. On Christmas Island in the central Pacific, above, a healthy one-month-old great-frigate-bird chick, opposite, stirs in a nest built over the remains of a dead chick abandoned by its parents during the severe El Niño of the previous year, 1982. Seabird populations on Christmas Island rebounded in 1983 and 1984, then suffered another setback in 1986-1987 with the onset of another El Niño.

birds. In the late 19th century, the dominant one of several schemes divided the globe into six major faunal regions: the Holarctic, comprising the Nearctic and the Palearctic; the Neotropical; the Ethiopian; the Oriental; and the Australian. Such grand abstractions provide convenient labels: loons, for example, are Holarctic, meaning that they occur around the entire northern portion of the globe. Such divisions also provide a general sense of which birds are where and, to some extent, where they might have come from. But finer-tuned geographies were needed, ones that explained more about the why of bird distribution. North America could be divided into various life zones based largely on temperature, for example, but temperature is only one of many ingredients in the distribution of any form of life, let alone something as sophisticated as a bird. Another scheme was to analyze the distribution of plants and animals by means of what are called biomes. A biome is a natural area characterized by distinctive assemblages of plants and animals, such as tundra, or grassland, or coniferous forest. All such schemes prove useful up to a point—mostly the point of providing labeled regions to monitor to see change taking place. And change they do. Birds pay little attention to the lines people draw on maps. The quaint old field of bird distribution, when stared at, turns into the fine filigree of ecology, and holds out plenty of surprises still, for it is always in flux. All it takes is a change in the weather.

On the coasts of Peru and Ecuador, there is an invasion every so often of unusually warm water. Accompanied by a rise in local sea level, it tends to happen near Christmastime and has come to be called El Niño, The Child. Its effects, however, seem anything

but redemptive. El Niños occur about once every two to seven years, with four to five years being the most frequent interval. Particularly catastrophic ones, with heavy inland flooding, are as yet unpredictable. El Niños are a result of an extremely complicated dance of ocean, wind, climate, and current that affects the entire Pacific. Accompanied by great atmospheric changes that scientists have named the "southern oscillation," they are thought to be behind the gradual but noticeable warming of the eastern equatorial Pacific. Regularly, El Niños destroy the nests of thousands of seabirds along the coast of Peru and Ecuador and also cause downswings in the supply of anchovies and other fish.

In the early 1980s, a major El Niño caught the attention of the world, and, as scientists from a host of fields fanned out to try to understand what was happening, the late Ralph Schreiber and his wife, Elizabeth, of the Natural History Museum of Los Angeles County, went to Christmas Island in the central Pacific. Since the 1940s, biologists had been making a census of the seabirds that nest there in the teeming millions—a spectacular cacophony of petrels, shearwaters, boobies, terns, and frigate birds. Most of these birds tend to lay one egg, which takes a long time incubating, followed by an extensive period of child care, a conservative strategy best used in a situation that remains stable over long periods of time. These birds depend on distant supplies of small fish and squid, taking advantage of the fact that predatory fish and sea mammals drive the smaller organisms toward the surface where the birds can get to them.

On Christmas Island in 1982-83, The Child wrought havoc. Of the 8,000 great-frigate-bird pairs that usually nest there, only some 100 turned up. In the Schreibers' study colony, where typically there should have been 90 frigate-bird nestlings, there were six that were starving and 19 already dead. Sooty terns, which nest there in the millions, are usually found flying over the island in November in preparation for nesting in December. That year, none flew. And so it went, down the list of species: rain and floods were washing away nests, drowning the burrows of petrels and shearwaters. Most birds that were present didn't bother to mate at all.

A long way from their natural range in Africa and the Old World tropics, cattle egrets, above, hover about brahma cattle in Florida. Efficient exploiters of the insects and small vertebrates kicked up by grazing cows or agricultural machinery, cattle egrets were first sighted in North America about 1941 and are now quite common on farms throughout the eastern United States. Single cattle egret at right displays special orange-buff breeding-season plumage.

The microscopic organisms called plankton that drift in the sea and provide a major food base for the chain that rises through fish to birds had suffered a population crash as well, the result of the warming of the water. The next year, the plankton population was up again off the coast of South America and less so near Christmas Island; the Schreibers pointed out that the equatorial sea is generally a poor plankton producer. Nonetheless, some of the Christmas Island birds were showing a few minimal signs of recovery. Five years later, Elizabeth Schreiber reported, the tropicbirds and crested terns seemed nearly recovered; all the others were still reeling from the calamity.

The restless Earth has much in store for birds—and some scientists now link the drought of 1988 and other natural disasters to El Niño's opposite twin, a cold phase in the eastern Pacific—but nothing so profound as the existence of that other singing species on the planet. Probably nothing since the glaciers has had so great an effect on the arrangement of birds on the planet as our activities—often deliberate and often inadvertent. Quite aside from being the chief perpetrator of species extinctions in recent times, we are also now the chief aid to bird colonization of new areas. A British observer, Colin Tudge, of the British Broadcasting Company, has called this "now one of the most significant phenomena of the natural world: second in importance, perhaps, only to extinction."

It is an ancient practice. Jason and the Argonauts probably brought the pheasant to Greece from the Orient in 1300 B.C., to spread thence to the rest of Europe. In their expansion through the islands of the Pacific, the Polynesians were mindful to bring along the chicken, as far as Hawaii and even, evidently, on pre-Columbian missions to South America. Importing food and sport birds is one thing; sentimentality is another. Songbirds have been transported here and there around the globe as nostalgic reminders of home. Poet John Keats's skylark sings in British Columbia for no other reason.

In the 1870s, some citizens of Ohio banded together to create the Cincinnati Acclimatization Society. There were many other such groups in America around that time, as well as in Australia and Great Britain, but the Cincinnatians seem to have been the group with the quintessential hurry-up attitude of American optimism. They spent some $9,000 amassing 4,000 European songbirds— blackbirds, robin redbreasts, skylarks, song thrushes, wagtails, great tits, and so forth— and on one afternoon let them all fly forth from the window of a suburban house in "a cloud of beautiful plumage," as a witness described it. The neighborhood, he went on, was "resonate with a melody of thanksgiving never heard before and probably never heard since." Indeed. Nothing came of this experiment by way of colonization. All 4,000 eventually perished without issue.

At the same time, there was afoot in certain circles in New York City the idea of bringing to American shores all of the birds mentioned in the works of Shakespeare. It would be interesting to hear a Shakespearean aside or two about this plan and its results— chiefly, the successful introduction of the European starling. In 1890, drug manufacturer Eugene Schieffelin, who had conceived the idea of importing the bard's birds, brought 80 starlings into the country and released them in March in Central Park in New York City. He let another group go the following spring, and it is said that at least one pair nested in the eaves of the American Museum of Natural History. That was all it took. Soon they were nesting in most of New York's five boroughs, and within six more years were in New Jersey and Connecticut and moving rapidly up the Hudson River. By 1917, ornithologist Edward Howe Forbush expressed the general attitude of bird people, viewing "the introduction of the starling with some apprehension." Insightfully, he pointed out that the bird had lived for millennia in Europe, during which time it had thrived in many habitats and had learned to do so near large concentrations of humans. Native American songbirds and woodpeckers, on the other hand, had had a far shorter time, only a few hundred years, to get used to large numbers of people, and thus were at a disadvantage. Already it was clear that wrens, bluebirds, flickers—any bird that nested in a hole— were being pushed aside as this aggressive and highly capable alien began populating the continent.

By 1959 starlings had reached San Diego, and their conquest of North America was

Our best-known avian immigrant, the European starling was introduced in Central Park, New York, late in the 19th century, and rapidly extended its range along the East Coast and eventually throughout the entire United States.

complete. Today it is estimated that more than 200,000,000 starlings range from Alaska to northern Mexico and from coast to coast—one of the most extraordinary human-induced faunal explosions outside of the house mouse and the Norway rat. It was the same, if not even more so, with the European house sparrow.

There is little way to predict what will take place when people attempt to transplant birds. Often, for a variety of ecologically subtle reasons, the attempt fails. Sometimes generalists will succeed; sometimes a bird that is more of a specialist will succeed. Ostriches, brought to Australia for their feathers, somehow managed to survive despite predation from local animals, ranchers, and aborigines, and despite severe bouts of rheumatism brought on by incubating their young on damp ground. The cattle egret was brought to Hawaii because of a particular and, it was thought, desirable habit. It hangs around pastures and eats the insects stirred up by cattle, even riding aboard a cow and ridding it of insect pests. In Hawaii it did just that, but also took to devouring the eggs of seabirds and competing with such birds for food.

Sometimes, accidental or intentional releases provide a fine laboratory for ornithologists to check their theories. The California house finch is naturally found in Mexico, the American Southwest, and the state of its name. There it is comfortable in a variety of habitats, including recent urban ones. At some point some were released in Hawaii (or, for all anyone knows, they got blown there by a storm). They are now one of the Islands' most common birds, and some have taken on a saffron color that replaces the crimson splash on the head and rump of the mainland bird—possibly a dietary effect. Meanwhile, bird dealers on Long Island, who were selling house finches as caged birds, let a small flock get away in 1940. Now the bird is one of the more common guests at bird feeders from eastern Canada through the Midwest and into the deep South.

A rule of thumb says that, in birds such as the house finch, color variations occur in local populations, the darker plumage appearing in those that inhabit more humid areas. The naturalized eastern house finches do seem to be darker and, in addition, to have larger bills and shorter wings, tails, legs, and toes, and also less variation in their songs than the California race. When—and if—the two populations meet along some frontier in the West, it may be that there will be two distinct species.

All it takes, sometimes, is a bit of passive collusion by people to allow a bird to explode suddenly into widespread new ranges. And the effects can be either benign or downright malignant. Sometime between World Wars I and II, the cattle egret established itself in British Guyana, probably having been blown there from its natural range in Africa (and Asia). Within a half-century, it has spread northward widely, now being a relatively common sight on farms from Texas to New York.

The cattle egret's presence seems unthreatening, but the reverse is the case with the Indian house crow. It is nearly impossible to find anyone who will pay a compliment to this bird, except, perhaps, for sadists. Native to the Indian subcontinent and ranging naturally as far east as Thailand, it has taken advantage of the shipping lanes to expand vastly up and down the African coast, throughout the islands of the Indian Ocean, and as far east as Malaysia. It frequently arrives in Australia, is found in Iran and Syria, and is universally regarded as a plague.

Intelligent and sassy, the Indian house crow forages in ports and around cargo vessels, and it often ships on board for a while. If the weather turns bad, the crows may stay with a ship for voyages of 3,000 miles and up to two weeks, picking up scraps of food from an open garbage bin or from the surface of the sea, or even getting handouts from a softhearted cook.

Once established in a new place, which is rarely a problem for these crows, they quickly become a pest. Mombasa, a busy seaport in southeastern Kenya, has lost nearly all its native species of birds to predation by the crow, which raids the nests of smaller birds and gangs up to mob and chase off birds of prey. It attacks fruit bats in their daytime roosts, takes marine life at low tide, destroys fruit, and even attacks poultry and small livestock animals such as lambs. These crows are noisy, calling raucously from before dawn on through the day, and even at night in places where there are street lights. They discourage tourists in many ways, including by entering their rooms and fouling the furniture. They have even ganged up to attack humans who strayed too near their nests. In addition, their droppings foul water supplies and carry a range of diseases, such as salmonellosis.

The crows first arrived in Mombasa in 1947, and now there are 200,000 of them spreading up and down the coast and inland, threatening wildlife, tourism, and peace of mind. By 1986, some 25 of these birds had reached the remote Seychelles Islands, a fragile ecosystem best symbolized by the white or fairy tern, which lays its single egg in the open, often balanced on the limb of a tree. The house crow, on the other hand, lays four or five eggs at a time, often twice a season, and could create utter havoc in the Seychelles in very short order. To rid the islands of this pest, the Seychelles' ministry of national development is considering various programs—poisoned bait, shooting, bounties—already in use for the rats that are imported pests there, too. But the crows, alas, are highly intelligent.

In the long run, the only answer will be for all ships' crews to receive a bonus for eliminating any entertaining Indian house crows long before their ships reach their destination. In the meantime, whenever any of these birds arrive in Australian ports, they are met by armed agents who, mindful perhaps of Alfred Hitchcock's nightmarish film *The Birds*, promptly shoot them. In the absence of a modern comment from Shakespeare on man and his dalliance with the distribution of birds, we can only quote the poet from his earlier work: "What a piece of work is man! How noble in reason!" 🦅

The pantropical white tern, also known as the fairy tern, builds no nest, but balances its single egg on a rock, a tree limb, or even a manmade structure. The graceful white tern shown above is nesting on Pearl and Hermes Reef, Hawaii.

STORRS L. OLSON AND HELEN F. JAMES

The scientific description of living species of Hawaiian birds began in 1778 when Captain James Cook and his men first explored this remote archipelago. Then, as later, the wonderful diversity of the Hawaiian finches, or honeycreepers, diverted attention from the fact that the rest of the birdlife was actually quite impoverished. Indeed, by the beginning of the 20th century, when most of the Hawaiian birds had been discovered, many species had begun to disappear at a startling rate. No one considered, however, that even more extinction might have occurred prior to the arrival of Europeans. In fact, such a possibility was dismissed out of hand by scientists, who claimed, for example, that "no serious inroads were made on the native birds by the Hawaiians."

This skein of misconceptions began to unravel in 1970 with the discovery of bones of extinct birds in sand dunes on the island of Molokai and later in dunes on Kauai. Soon archaeologists discovered other bone deposits in sinkholes in a raised limestone reef on Oahu, deposits that provided a surprisingly bountiful record of past birdlife on that island as well. Even greater riches were uncovered on the island of Maui, this time in lava tubes—caves that form during lava eruptions. Weak places in the roofs of these tubes may collapse and open up treacherous pitfalls that act as natural traps. Judging from the accumulated bones that have been found in lava tubes, such was the fate of a number of flightless birds that once lived in Hawaii.

Further excavations on four of the main islands have brought to light fossils of heavy-bodied, flightless descendants of ducks. Called moanalos, which in Hawaiian means "vanished fowl," these birds were about the size of barnyard geese, but with much more massive legs and feet and strangely shaped beaks with which they must have browsed on native vegetation. Quite probably the moanalos, like their larger counterparts, the moas of New Zealand, occupied much the same ecological role as the tortoises of the Galápagos Islands, which feed exclusively on vegetation. All of these large, island-dwelling, avian herbivores are now extinct.

Another discovery among the Hawaiian bones was flightless ibises—the first ever to be found. Unlike the long-legged ibises that are associated today with marshes, the Hawaiian ibises had rather short legs and ran around on the forest floor, probably preying on insects and snails. Their habits would have been much more like those of the kiwis of New Zealand than those of typical ibises.

Rails are the birds that are best known for reaching remote islands and becoming flightless. Only one such rail, extinct since at least the middle of the last century, was known from the main Hawaiian Islands until our fossil discoveries showed that flightless rails were once probably everywhere in the archipelago. We have found as many as 10 new species, all of which were flightless. One of these, from Molokai, is the smallest known rail and was surely among the smallest of all flightless birds.

The most widespread predatory bird in the Hawaiian Islands today is the pueo, or short-eared owl, which is the same species

An extinct flightless Hawaiian ibis, seen in the painting opposite, shares the forest understory with two extinct flightless rails. The first flightless species of this bird family to be discovered, the flightless Hawaiian ibis came to light in 1976. Like those of other flightless Hawaiian birds, the remains of the Hawaiian ibis, such as those below on Maui, have been found in lava tubes. Recent fossil discoveries have doubled the number of endemic Hawaiian bird species known to have existed before the arrival of the Polynesians some 1,600 years ago.

Fossil collectors sift sand at Kauai's Makawehi dunes, which perch over sea cliffs on the island's southeast coast. This site yielded hundreds of honeycreeper bones as well as those of other bird families.

found on the mainland. It probably colonized the Islands after the Hawaiians cleared land and thus created habitat suitable for the owl, and also introduced food in the form of the Pacific rat. Before the arrival of people, however, a different owl lived in the Islands, of which four species have been discovered so far. These were descendants of such owls as the barred owl of North America, but they had longer, more slender legs and shorter wings, thus resembling in their proportions such bird-catchers as Cooper's and sharp-shinned hawks. And we know that the owls *were* bird-catchers: the

fossilized remains of their pellets contain the bones of small birds.

Rare among our fossils are bones of a small hawk quite unlike the living Hawaiian hawk. This extinct hawk was descended from harriers, such as that of North America, but, unlike those long-winged hawks, this species had short wings and must also have been specialized for feeding on birds. Chief among the raptors was an eagle, very similar to the bald eagle, that was probably the only significant predator on the moanalos and adult ibises.

Among the Hawaiian honeycreepers,

we have found bones of at least 15 new species, including at least three new genera. One of the most interesting of these is a gigantic finch-billed species, rivaling the largest known finches in massiveness of beak.

Everywhere we have worked in Hawaii we have found bones of living or recently extinct birds on islands where they had not been known before. The palila, for example, an endangered finch that today is found only above 5,000-feet elevation on Hawaii's Mauna Kea volcano, once occurred at sea level on Oahu. What today is called the Maui parrotbill was once also on Molokai. The Hawaiian crow, known only from the Big Island, where it is now all but extinct, may have lived also on Maui and had at least two much larger cousins on Molokai and Oahu. Bones of the Hawaiian goose, or nene, also thought to have been confined originally to the island of Hawaii, are found throughout the archipelago. Even the Laysan finch and Nihoa finch, which survive only on tiny, remote islands in the northwestern Hawaiian chain, left bones behind on Oahu and Molokai to show that today's populations are but remnants of once more widespread species.

Of the archipelago's 92 unique species of birds now known, with the fossil record taken into account, only 48, or 52 percent, were discovered before the fossil excavations began. And we know that the fossil record is incomplete.

What happened to cause such massive extinctions, and when? With few exceptions, all dated deposits are only a few thousand years old or less, much younger than the last ice age that might have triggered climatically caused extinctions. From radiocarbon dates and from the association of bones of extinct birds with those of rats and lizards and with shells of snails that were introduced by Polynesians, we know that these now-vanished birds were still present and thriving in the Islands when the first people arrived some

A complete skull of the extinct Hawaiian long-legged owl, top, was uncovered in the highly fossiliferous Moomomi dunes on the island of Molokai. Scientists have even found fossilized pellets regurgitated by these owls. The particularly well-preserved fossil owl pellet above, found in Kauai's Makawehi dunes, contained the bones of three species of honeycreepers.

Many of Hawaii's endemic birds have become extinct or endangered since the Islands were colonized first by Polynesians and later by Europeans. The akialoas, such as the Oahu akialoa, above, are now extinct, as are the five Hawaiian species of Old World honeyeaters, including the Hawaii oo, above right. Hawaii's state bird, the nene, opposite, is endemic to the island of Hawaii; specialized features, such as reduced webbing between the toes, enable it to live on thinly vegetated lava flows. Captive-breeding programs have attempted to restore the nene population, which suffered great reductions after 1850 due primarily to hunting, ranching, and other development.

1,600 years ago. The influence of these human settlers is strongly implicated in the severe depletion of the avifauna.

Direct hunting for food would have presented an immediate threat to birds, especially to the large, flightless birds, and was certainly a factor in the reduction or extinction of seabird populations nesting in the Islands. Pigs, dogs, and especially the Pacific rat introduced by the Hawaiians may have played a role in extinction, as might diseases brought in by introduced chickens. But probably the greatest damage was wrought through habitat destruction as lowland forests were cleared for the extensive crops that were later to sustain large Polynesian populations on most of the main islands. Almost all dry-forest vegetation was lost through cutting and burning, so that the only native vegetation remaining was the cold, wet rain forests on mountainsides unsuited for agriculture. With the lowland vegetation gone, the majority of Hawaii's animal species also disappeared forever.

Are the Hawaiian Islands an exception in the amount of prehistoric extinction they suffered? The answer is an emphatic no. On every island where bones have been preserved and collected the story is the same.

Between roughly a quarter and a third of all historically known species of birds are endemic to islands. If we consider that these may represent half or fewer of the species that were present on islands before the arrival of people, then human-caused extinctions on islands, most of which have taken place within the past 2,000 years, may have effected one of the swiftest and most pervasive catastrophes in the entire history of avian evolution. Unfortunately, this process continues, and island species are still being lost at an alarming rate.

Curator Storrs L. Olson and his wife, Helen F. James, both of whom work in the Division of Birds in the Smithsonian's National Museum of Natural History, began their investigation of Hawaiian fossil birds in 1976.

F.W.Frohawk del.et lith.

West, Newman imp

BERNICLA SANDVICENSIS

*P*oets have always sung about birds, but poets are, for the most part, egoists who empathize with birds as fellow singers. Except for Percy Bysshe Shelley, the romantic English poet who grew ecstatic about the skylark that "singing still dost soar, and soaring ever singest," poets have mostly overlooked as incidental to their purposes the fact that birds fly. For a true paean to bird flight, it is necessary to turn to prose—that of the enigmatic Henry David Thoreau, who, one April during his sojourn at Walden Pond, looked up from fishing on a riverbank when he heard a strange rattling sound:

> *I observed a very slight and graceful hawk, like a night-hawk, alternately soaring like a ripple and tumbling a rod or two over and over, showing the underside of its wings, which gleamed like a satin ribbon in the sun, or like the pearly inside of a shell. This sight reminded me of falconry and what noblesse and poetry are associated with that sport. The Merlin it seemed to me it might be called: but I care not for its name. It was the*

most ethereal flight I had ever witnessed. It did not simply flutter like a butterfly, nor soar like the larger hawks, but it sported with proud reliance in the fields of air; mounting again and again with its strange chuckle, it repeated its free and beautiful fall, turning over and over like a kite, and then recovering from its lofty tumbling, as if it had never set its foot on terra firma. *It appeared to have no companion in the universe,—sporting there alone,—and to need none but the morning and the ether with which it played. It was not lonely, but made all the earth lonely beneath it. Where was the parent which hatched it, its kindred, and its father in the heavens? The tenant of the air, it seemed related to the earth but by an egg hatched some time in the crevice of a crag;—or was its native nest made in the angle of a cloud, woven of the rainbow's trimmings and the sunset sky, and lined with some sort of midsummer haze caught up from earth? Its eyre now some cliffy cloud.*

While literary critics have pointed to Thoreau's description of the pigeon hawk, or, as it is now indeed called, the merlin, as the most lyrical hymn to bird flight in English prose, they have yet to explain why flight has stymied most literary artists despite its obvious tug on the human soul. Even in the 90 years or so during which man has attached wings and engines to himself and has actually flown, aviation has produced not a single novel of particular literary stature (as the whaling industry did in *Moby Dick*). Perhaps

the flying creature truly has no companion in the universe and the artist is destined to remain anchored to the ground. Where poets fear to tread, however, scientists walk in, determined to get to the bottom of things.

Getting to the bottom of things in this case means understanding the evolution and aerodynamics of flight in birds. And, whatever fossil contender winds up being acknowledged as the first bird, its true name is serendipity, which is defined as the faculty for making desirable discoveries by accident. How many times, for example, did the scales of reptiles almost begin a series of changes that might, under the right circumstances, have become something like feathers? How many times did such changes take place in the absence of certain other mutations or in the absence of the right selective pressures from the environment to encourage them on their way?

No one will ever know the answer to such questions, but the first true bird had to have undergone a series of *related* alterations from the reptilian model more or less simultaneously. Feathers by themselves would have done little if anything to get a small, long-armed tyrannosaurus into the air. No single factor enables a bird to fly, but all the factors enabling a bird to fly are virtually the same in all birds. Thus, despite their astonishing variety, in terms of their basic body architecture birds are very much alike.

Mammals, by comparison, exhibit vast differences in body shape and size. They can be exceedingly sleek and slender, like a weasel, or almost preposterously fat, like a male sea lion. They are built to run on four legs, hop on two, swim, fly, burrow, crawl, climb, even to swing by the tail. The largest mammal, the blue whale, may weigh 150 tons—59 million times as much as the smallest shrew. The ostrich, however, the largest living bird, weighs only 64 *thousand* times the smallest hummingbird.

The reason for the greater uniformity in size among birds is that they are virtually all designed around one overriding principle: aerodynamics. Even flightlessness in birds is clearly derivative of their original adaptation to the air. As zoologist Carl Welty wrote, "Birds simply dare not deviate widely from sound aerodynamic design. Nature liquidates deviationists much more consistently and

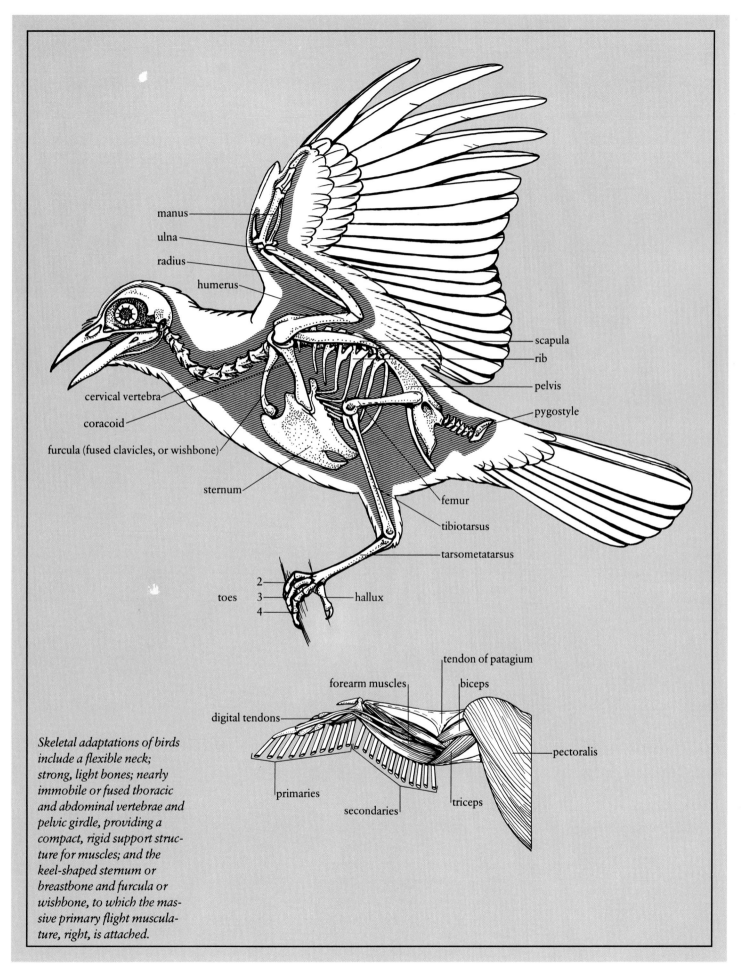

manus

ulna

radius

humerus

cervical vertebra

coracoid

furcula (fused clavicles, or wishbone)

sternum

scapula

rib

pelvis

pygostyle

femur

tibiotarsus

tarsometatarsus

toes

2

3

4

hallux

Skeletal adaptations of birds include a flexible neck; strong, light bones; nearly immobile or fused thoracic and abdominal vertebrae and pelvic girdle, providing a compact, rigid support structure for muscles; and the keel-shaped sternum or breastbone and furcula or wishbone, to which the massive primary flight musculature, right, is attached.

tendon of patagium

biceps

forearm muscles

digital tendons

pectoralis

primaries

secondaries

triceps

drastically than does any totalitarian dictator."

Besides wings and feathers, the obvious features for flight, birds evolved a strong, keeled breastbone to serve as an anchor for large flight muscles and thin, hollow bones that in many cases are fused together. Birds needed warmbloodedness, which they may have inherited from reptilian ancestors or evolved independently, as did the mammals. They needed a large, efficient heart, a greatly refined respiratory system, and a high-energy metabolism, which in turn called for a high-energy diet. But for a few exceptions that tend to prove the rule, browsing leaves and grazing grass like antelope were out.

Some of the price birds paid for flight is less obvious. Sweat glands would add weight and dampen feathers, so birds have other ways to get rid of excess heat. One is by panting; a pigeon at rest breathes at a rate of about 30 breaths per minute, but a small increase in body temperature will raise this rate to 200. Reproductive organs are added weight, so in some male birds one of the testes may become vestigial, and in most female birds only one ovary develops, although, if the active one is removed, in some birds the other will develop in its stead. For most of the year, a bird's reproductive organs are reduced in size, with such factors as hormones and length of day triggering them to swell to operational size only when they are needed. A starling's reproductive organs weigh 1,500 times more in breeding season than at other times.

Virtually everything about birds, in other words, is modified to meet the two basic requirements of all flying machines: low weight and high power. And, as in all engineering designs, most solutions are compromises. A hollow tube is far lighter but not as strong as a solid rod. Add a few well-designed internal struts to a hollow tube, and the result is a great gain in strength for a small addition in weight. Inside the wing bone of a vulture, one finds diagonal struts up and down the length like an endlessly repeated WW. In some airplane wings and steel structural members, engineers use a nearly identical configuration called the Warren truss, named for the engineer who invented it for the second time.

Similarly, the bird's skull is relatively light

in proportion to its body. Its bones are hollow, filled with a network of tiny trusses and struts. Heavy teeth and jaw muscles are sacrificed, their work taken over by a lightweight gizzard located in the abdomen near the bird's center of gravity, just as the luggage compartment of an airplane is not up forward but amidships. The skull of a pigeon weighs, proportionately, about one-sixth that of a rat. Perhaps the most astonishing example of lightness is the frigate bird. While it has a wingspan of seven feet, its entire skeleton, including the skull, weighs a mere four ounces—less than its feathers and the same weight as two Grade A large chicken eggs.

The fusion of various bones, such as vertebrae, wing bones, and skull, is a means to provide less weight but also greater rigidity of the skeleton to withstand the rigors of flying—although not in every case. The bones must also be flexible. The fusion in birds of what we call collarbones (or clavicles) into the familiar wishbone (or furcula) used to be seen as part of the general strengthening of the chest area. But recently, using high-speed X-ray movies, scientists peered at the skeleton of a European starling thrashing away in a wind tunnel and noted what generations of children making wishes with the Thanksgiving turkey's wishbone knew. It is highly flexible: you have to hang it up somewhere for several days before it is brittle enough to be used for wishing. Watching the starling's wishbone in action, the scientists saw it open and close with each wing beat and realized that it serves as a spring. It stores energy on the downbeat and releases it to the wings on the upbeat. The wishbone may also assist the bird in breathing, pumping air throughout its respiratory system as it alternately bends and recoils.

While some birds move slowly, on the ground or in the air, life for most birds generally seems quicker than ours. Flight confers speed, maneuverability—great gifts in the business of avoiding predators and catching insects and getting from a breeding ground to a winter home. The split-second maneuvers of birds can seem almost impossible: the way, for example, woodland birds can dart through branches and leaves at such a high rate or fly directly into the smallest hole without evidently slowing down. Imagine driving right up to your garage door at 35 miles per hour. The nervous system of birds had to be able to accommodate this speeding up of life. Compared with the brains of terrestrial vertebrates other than mammals, the bird's brain is far more developed in those centers that integrate motor activities, such as the cerebral hemispheres and the cerebellum. In the inner ear, well-developed canals and other structures provide the means for extremely rapid assessment of flight equilibrium.

Except for birds of prey, birds' visual acuity is about the same as ours, and in some songbirds it is less. But birds excel us in the speed with which they can assimilate detail within the visual field. At a glance, they can register a complete scene that would take us several seconds or more of scanning to perceive as a whole. By analogy, a bird's "cockpit instrumentation" is suited for the high-speed coordination of a jet fighter rather than the plodding of a pickup truck.

Speed calls for high energy, and the chemical factory of a bird works faster than that of other vertebrates. Chemical reactions go faster if they take place at a higher temperature. The normal body temperature of a bird is 10 degrees Fahrenheit higher than a human's, and, as a result, the high-calorie diets of birds—fruits, seeds, insects, worms, fish, rodents, and so forth—are more rapidly converted to energy. A young stork, for example, may convert up to 33 percent of its food into actual growth, compared with perhaps a 10-percent utilization of food for a typical growing mammal. Digestion is efficient and fast: a young blue jay completes the digestive cycle in less than an hour and a half (also tactically a weight-reduction scheme).

In the activity we call aerobics, birds leave people in the dust. A bird's heart (which is four-chambered like ours, although different in certain details) is proportionately larger. A canary's heart is four times larger than ours in proportion to body weight, a hummingbird's almost six times larger. While the human heart averages some 70 beats per minute, the canary's pumps at a rate of 514, the hummingbird's at 615. Blood pressure is proportionately higher as well: a chicken's blood pressure exceeds that of an average person by 50 percent. The concentration of blood sugar is twice as high in birds as in mammals.

But it is the bird's respiratory system that

would put even a decathlon champion to shame. We breathe with our lungs, and so does a bird. But a bird can also breathe with its legs, in a sense. A great English surgeon, John Hunter, showed in 1758 that a bird with its windpipe completely blocked could continue to breathe if a hole was made from the outside into a wing bone or leg bone. This is a result of a unique avian development—air sacs that take up some of the volume of the chest and abdomen. Discovered first in 1653 by the English anatomist William Harvey (who elucidated the circulation of blood in mammals), and counted by an Italian physicist in 1679 among the features that lighten a bird for flight, the air sacs originate in the lungs and penetrate various parts of the body, including some of the bones.

The lungs exchange gases, removing carbon dioxide from the blood and bringing oxygen to it. The oxygenated blood takes this crucial gas to the cells of the body where it "burns" food in a chemical reaction that provides the body with the energy it needs. Depleted of oxygen and full of carbon dioxide, the blood returns to the lungs and loses this freight, acquiring more oxygen. In mammalian lungs there is always some oxygen present but always some carbon dioxide as well: fresh air and stale air. This system

The damselfly, opposite, retains the four-winged, primitive flight mechanism of many early insects. First to fly, insects took to the air at least 300 million years ago; their flight structures are completely different from those of vertebrates. Unlike birds, bats spread their fingers to fly. This nocturnal Mexican fishing bat, above, skims still water on leathery wings, scanning for fish with sonarlike echolocation.

Fast, agile long-billed dowitchers and other shorebirds make prodigious flights during migration, refueling at critical way stations along their routes.

works perfectly well for flight, even for bats, those flying mammals. In fact, flight, for birds as well as bats, requires only a 10- to 15-fold increase in oxygen consumption—an increase no greater than that needed by a human track runner (though no marathoner can run as long as many birds can fly). If the standard mammalian lung is sufficient to sustain flight, then why is the bird's respiratory system so elaborately different? Several years ago, Knut Schmidt-Nielsen of Duke University proposed that the avian air-sac/lung system permitted flight at high altitudes. It had been shown that at an altitude of about 20,000 feet a mouse was rendered comatose, while a sparrow at the same altitude could fly perfectly well.

Schmidt-Nielsen tracked gas through the avian system. Most of the air taken in when the bird inhales, he found, does not go to the lungs but bypasses them and winds up in the rearward air sacs. Unlike ours, the bird's lungs contract on inhalation. During exhalation the lungs open up and air from the rear air sacs passes through them, on to the forward air sacs and from there outdoors. The net effect of this is to set up a continuous flow of fresh air across the lungs from the rear forward. Meanwhile, there is a continuous flow of blood across the lungs in the opposite direction, and the two continuous flows maximize the uptake of oxygen at every point along the way. In other words, this system makes it possible for a bird to extract considerably more oxygen from each breath than can any mammal. (A secondary function of the air sacs evidently is to provide a large area of damp surface that evaporates away excess heat.)

How efficient is it to fly? According to Vance Tucker, also of Duke University, flying has it all over the locomotion of ground animals in terms of speed and endurance. Ducks cruise at speeds between 40 and 50 miles per hour. A cheetah, the fastest land animal, can achieve 70 miles per hour, but only for a short distance, after which it is so exhausted it needs a half-hour to recover. Neal Smith of the Smithsonian Tropical Research Institute in Panama has shown that broad-winged and Swainson's hawks, by carefully using thermal updrafts and other air conditions, can soar from southern Texas and other southwestern regions of the United States all the way to Central and South America in their annual migration, traveling thousands of miles without ever needing to eat. In terms of energy cost (how many calories are burned over a given distance), flying also wins. "A walking or running mammal," Tucker has written, "expends 10 to 15 times more energy to cover a given distance than a bird of the same size does . . . a pigeon flies more economically than a light plane. Moreover, a Canada goose may be able to perform better than a jet transport."

As we all know to our dismay, however, airplanes wear out and so do bodies. While flight allows birds to get from here to there more efficiently than those of us with feet of clay, birds presumably pay a high cost for it, the flip side of aerobics. Oxygen gives us the fire of life, but it is the oxidization of the body's cells over time that is the aging process.

With their wondrous ability to extract oxygen, their white-hot metabolism, and their quickened existence, birds in general live short lives—a toll that has something to do with flying. A major aspect of longevity, of course, is size: small birds tend to be short-lived, large birds tend to be quite long-lived. The smaller the animal (for birds and mammals, that is), the higher its surface-to-volume ratio and thus the faster it radiates body heat. So the small must eat more frequently to keep their temperature high, and, quick little furnaces that they are, they tend to burn out before long.

The high metabolic rate of birds is costly. Thus it is to the bird's advantage to conserve energy by flying as little as possible, and this

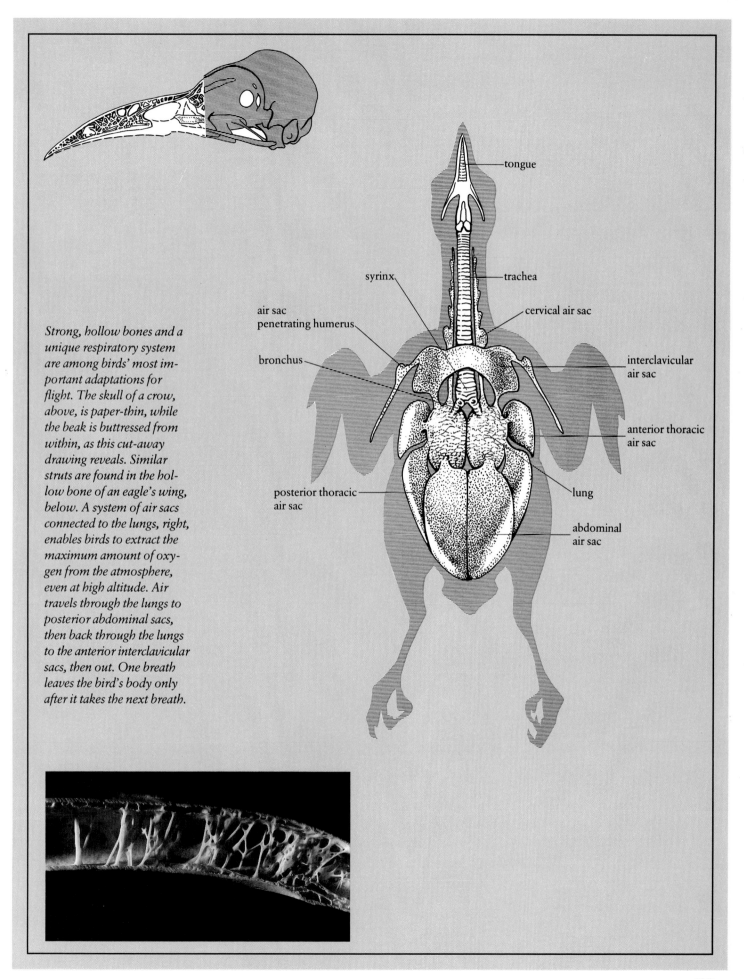

Strong, hollow bones and a unique respiratory system are among birds' most important adaptations for flight. The skull of a crow, above, is paper-thin, while the beak is buttressed from within, as this cut-away drawing reveals. Similar struts are found in the hollow bone of an eagle's wing, below. A system of air sacs connected to the lungs, right, enables birds to extract the maximum amount of oxygen from the atmosphere, even at high altitude. Air travels through the lungs to posterior abdominal sacs, then back through the lungs to the anterior interclavicular sacs, then out. One breath leaves the bird's body only after it takes the next breath.

tongue

syrinx

trachea

air sac penetrating humerus

cervical air sac

bronchus

interclavicular air sac

anterior thoracic air sac

posterior thoracic air sac

lung

abdominal air sac

is what they tend to do. Except in the rarest circumstance, birds never fly for what we might call the fun of it. As seen in many cases of flightlessness in birds, it is mainly predators that keep birds in the air. In their absence, birds tend to give up the entire expensive business of flight and act more like mammals.

Certain modes of flight are more efficient than others. The amount of energy it takes to soar in circles, making only fine adjustments to use thermal updrafts, clearly is next to nothing compared with the blinding buzz of the hummingbird. But both modes require wings, and all bird wings function on the same basic principle: the airfoil. Hold a sheet of paper horizontally in front of you from the two near corners and blow over the upper surface. The free end of the paper will rise.

That is an airfoil. The air going over the upper surface is faster than that below, reducing the pressure above the paper and allowing the pressure below to lift the paper up.

On a bird's (and an airplane's) wing, there is a greater curvature of the upper surface so the air has to go faster above than below, resulting in that same pressure drop, or lift. Lift can be increased by raising the forward

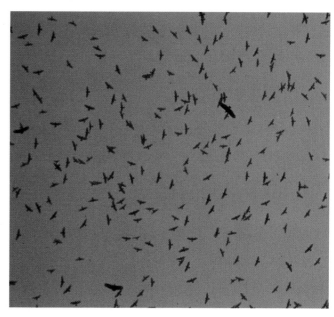

or leading edge of the wing, further lowering the pressure on the upper side: typical bird flight takes place with the angle of attack about 13 degrees off the horizontal. It is the "arm" section of the wing that provides lift; the outer part or "hand" is the propeller.

As we saw in chapter 2, however, the bird's hand hardly resembles yours. The first digit is greatly reduced and functions separately from the other two, which have been partly fused into one digit. In flapping flight, this hand moves forward and down, then backward and up, over and over, the tip describing a figure eight with each stroke. The major flight muscles are located amidships, their contraction and relaxation working long, light tendons. Smaller muscles in the "wrist" add power to the propeller section.

It is the wing feathers and, to a degree, the tail feathers that provide the aerodynamic surface that makes flight possible for birds. The secondary feathers of the arm furnish most of the lift, while the primaries of the hand supply the surfaces needed for propulsion. The leading feathers of the hand, coming off the first digit, are short and stiff.

To hover, the ruby-throated hummingbird, left, beats its wings hundreds of times per minute; it must sip energy-rich nectar constantly to fuel its efforts. Migrating raptors such as these broad-winged and Swainson's hawks, above, may fast for much of their journey, but efficient soaring on rising air currents reduces their energy requirements. As many as 300,000 to 400,000 migrants per day may funnel south over the Isthmus of Panama.

Jointly called the alula, they can function separately from the other primaries: they can be moved away from the others, creating a slot. Like a stream going through a narrows, air speeds up when it goes through a slot and thus increases lift. In addition, the primaries, though they work in unison, will separate into slots simply from the force of the air, creating more narrows, all with the same effect.

With those flight feathers now in place, it is possible to return to the business of lift and other aerodynamic matters with which the bird must contend. Lift can be increased by raising the angle of attack, but, at about 15 to 20 degrees, the stream of air no longer can follow the smooth upper surface of the wing and instead breaks off into turbulence, which causes loss of lift. This is the stalling angle. To postpone a stall, the bird can raise the alula, which normally rides tight against the leading edge of the hand, thus creating an additional slot and giving the bird increased lift.

As with airplanes, the most critical times in flight seem to be taking off and landing. Some birds have great difficulty getting into the air, although once there they do fine. Loons and large waterfowl, including geese and swans, have to run across the water all the while flapping their wings in order to produce enough speed to achieve the needed lift to become airborne. (Much of this is, from an engineering standpoint, a matter of the ratio of body weight to wing-surface area, and much of it is related to wing shape.)

One of the more comical sights in nature is an albatross coming in to some oceanic island for a landing: as often as not these ultimate gliders, capable of spending even months aloft gliding over the seas by manipulating the wind and the air currents off the waves, will swoop in to land and crash in a cumbersome, unathletic jumble. Once righted, the bird goes on about its business unperturbed. It may be because of this slap-

Takeoffs and landings impose special problems for large birds. Tundra swans, opposite, must run on the water to achieve takeoff speed. Laysan albatrosses, right, may stay at sea so long they "forget" how to land and crash—most often harmlessly—when they return to breed and nest.

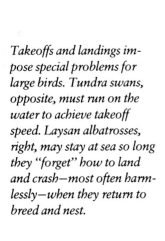

So beautifully adapted to
flight that their skeletons,
above, weigh less than their
feathers, frigate birds are
both effortless soarers and
agile pirates. Right, great frigate birds ride the trades over
Whale Skate Island, Hawaii;
below, a great frigate bird
harasses a red-footed booby
to make it disgorge fish.

Frigate birds live, mate, and nest on tropical coasts and islands around the world. Left, an overshooting frigate bird misses a morsel on a Galápagos Islands beach; below, a Galápagos male inflates his throat sac in courtship display; far left, on the nest, Christmas Island, central Pacific Ocean.

stick association with the land that sailors came to call them gooneybirds.

Birds with well-developed tails tend to be good at landing, and for obvious reasons. A quick spreading and lowering of the tail at the appropriate moment, tied to a high angle of attack by the wings, causes an immediate and controllable stall. Some birds also use the tail as a kind of rudder, twisting it to one side or another to change direction, which can also be accomplished by changing the angle of attack—or the shape—of one wing compared with the other.

The difficulty of getting airborne depends partly, of course, on where the bird is. Without a good breeze, an albatross is likely to remain grounded. A cliff-dwelling bird, or one in a tree, merely has to head off into the air; the force of gravity supplies the necessary speed to achieve lift. The large wood stork uses a technique approaching that of the helicopter, its wings sweeping back and forth nearly horizontally. The great egret leaps off the ground with its legs and beats its great wings rapidly and fully. The entire wing becomes the propeller section, leaving practically no area to provide lift. Instead, the bird spreads its tail out wide, creating a lift-giving slot behind the wings.

Always opposing lift (and speed) is drag, the force of the air against the wing's forward motion. The greater the angle of attack, the

albatross

falcon

buteo or soaring hawk

partridge

The shapes of birds' wings are supremely adapted to their life-styles, and fall into four basic designs: (from top) the very long, slim wings that enable such seabirds as albatrosses and shearwaters to soar at high speeds in strong winds; the shorter high-speed wings of falcons, terns, and swifts; the long, wide, slotted wings of birds that soar over land; and the short, wide, many-slotted elliptical wings of forest, ground, and perching birds.

greater also is the drag. One constant form of drag is caused by the air that has passed along the bottom surface of the wing, curling back up over the top of the trailing edge. This is particularly strong at the wingtip and is called wingtip vortex. One way of minimizing its overall effects is to have longer wings, thus making a larger, longer lift surface. Another way is to have broader wings. And, of course, on this basic plan of airfoil and propeller, birds have developed as many variations on a theme as Vivaldi, each suited to a particular need or set of needs in the business of flying.

In general, however, there seem to be four basic wing shapes in birds. The most common is the elliptical wing typically found on birds that have to make their way through restricted openings, such as the leafy branches of a tree. This type of wing has a low aspect ratio, meaning that it is comparatively broad in relation to its length. It has, as a result, a relatively low wingtip vortex and confers on the bird a high amount of lift. Chickens, pheasants, and quail have such wings, accompanied as well by a high degree of slotting—a necessity in getting these relatively heavy birds off the ground for their short flights. Woodpeckers and doves are elliptically winged, as are most of the perching birds, including crows and ravens. The more active the bird, the more likely it is to take

advantage of the role of slots. More than half the length of a gray catbird's wing is given over to slots, giving the appearance of a wing modeled on venetian blinds.

The opposite is the high-aspect-ratio wing, in which the length is far greater than the width, like the wing of a glider plane, the analogue in aviation for the great gliders of the ocean—albatrosses, tropicbirds, and the like. Particularly common to the roughest and windiest southern seas, where the prevailing winds blow east to west and rarely let up, albatrosses are the unchallenged champion gliders. The largest, the wandering albatross, has a wingspan of 11 feet (the wings being less than a foot wide at their widest point), and, as it takes advantage of even the smallest updrafts that result from the eternal dance of wind and wave, it can fly almost effortlessly, with seldom a wing beat. Slotting is rare among such gliders' wings: the vortexes at the wingtips are too far apart to make much difference. Sailors in southern latitudes often will find themselves accompanied all day by an albatross making gentle S-curves behind, beside, and ahead of their vessel, utter masters of the breeze. A banded albatross was found to have circumnavigated the globe in fewer than 80 days. An albatrossian cousin, the much smaller Manx shearwater, is known to have covered 3,400 miles in a bit more than 12 days, which is to say

Landing, a golden eagle, opposite above, displays the slotted, broad wing typical of many large, terrestrial soaring birds. Above, the ring-necked pheasant's rounded, stubby wings lift the ground-living bird on brief flights from danger.

about 270 miles a day, using the same technique of wheeling above the wave tops, catching each helpful updraft.

While albatrosses are the champion windjammers, and shearwaters (some of which annually circle the entire Pacific) may be the most traveled of birds, the frigate birds have been called the most aerial. Hopeless on land, they nest in bushes or trees on oceanic shores, using the slight addition in elevation to gain the needed speed to get airborne. Once in the air—and they rarely land in the water, where they quickly become waterlogged—they "soar motionless, by the hour hanging steadily, quietly in the sky," as Oliver Austin, Jr., describes their flight in his book *Birds of the World*. As noted, their skeletons weigh but four ounces, the rest of their bodily equipment bringing them to a maximum of four pounds. Given a seven-foot wingspan, they have the greatest ratio of lifting-surface area to body weight of any bird, and they flaunt it, chasing boobies, gulls, pelicans, cormorants, and other seabirds—usually within sight of land—until these harassed birds give up their own prey, which the frigate bird swoops down to pluck from midair. This habit has given these spectacular fliers the reputation of piracy, as has their habit of preying on the young of other seabirds, but most of their diet, such as flying fish and jellyfish, they take on the wing fastidiously and without a splash from the ocean's surface or just above.

A third basic wing type is the high-speed wing, long and relatively slim, often with swept-back hands without slotting. More suited for fast, level flying than maneuverability and quick takeoffs, this is the wing of the falcon, of terns and sandpipers, swifts and swallows, and hummingbirds. It is among birds with such wings that many of the spectacular records in speed and aerial prowess are to be found. A peregrine falcon will fly normally between 40 and 60 miles per hour, but when it dives after prey, it may achieve speeds approaching 200. The fastest normal wing-flapping flight ever clocked was of the white-throated needle-tailed swift in India: a reported 219 miles per hour.

Swifts compete (in our minds) with frigate birds as the most aerial and with shearwaters as the greatest airborne travelers. Swifts live exclusively on flying insects and floating

A gray jay or "whiskey jack," opposite, fluffs up contour feathers against winter cold. Gray jays inhabit North America's far north and mountain west where bitter winters are the rule and downy insulation essential. Above, barbs have separated in these brown pelican flight feathers found on a beach. Gentle stroking will interlock their tiny, hooklike barbules again.

spiders (a kind of aerial plankton, so plentiful are they) and will spend virtually all day as airborne insect traps. In breeding season, a European swift was estimated to fly 560 miles a day; a banded American chimney swift that lived for nine years is estimated to have flown well over a million miles in its lifetime, including its annual migration to the Amazon Basin and back. The endurance of swifts is astonishing. They have been seen heading out to sea from Great Britain in the evening, returning in the morning, suggesting that under the right circumstances they can forage throughout the day *and* the night without landing.

Unique in flight and flight characteristics are the hummingbirds, evidently descended from some swiftlike ancestor. In all, there are today some 319 species of hummingbirds, all restricted to the Western Hemisphere, all adapted to sipping high-energy nectar from flowers, and—more than any other birds—playing an active role in the pollination of flowering plants, from which they also take trapped insects for protein. Master hoverers, they have evolved a system that is most akin to that of helicopters, enabling them to fly directly up, sideways, even backward at will. Their flight musculature is about 30 percent of their weight, proportionately greater than that of any other bird, and some of this added weight is given over to muscles that provide extra power on the upstroke. The wing is mostly hand (propeller) and is attached to the shoulder in such a manner that it can swivel uniquely, permitting the hummingbird to adjust the wing's angle of attack on the powered upstroke as well as on the downstroke. Add to this the fact that for some small hummers, the wing beat is some 70 per second, a rate higher than any other bird's, and you have much of the secret of these astonishing little packets of energy darting here and there at speeds of more than 30 miles per hour—what some would say are the most highly evolved of birds.

The fourth basic wing type is the slotted high-lift wing, which brings to mind eagles and most birds of prey (but not falcons, which rely more on speed and thus are equipped with high-speed, scimitar-shaped wings). This wing has a relatively low aspect ratio with a strong camber and a typically high degree of slotting. The result is a great

deal of lift, needed not just to get the bird aloft and keep it there—these birds are the great soarers—but also because the bird will (if it is good at its job) find itself hauling fair-sized prey in its talons.

The shape of the wing is one thing, but there is also an important mathematical consideration involved in bird flight—the ratio of wing-surface area to body weight. If you double the surface area of a solid—such as a cube or, for that matter, a bird—you triple (not double) its volume. This geometrical fact predicts that, if you were somehow to double a particular bird's wing-surface area, you would also triple the bird's overall weight. A chimney swift, for example has a wing-surface area of about 120 square centimeters and weighs about 20 grams. If you doubled its wing-surface area to 240, you would expect a bird of some 60 grams. Nature has almost done this for us: the red-winged blackbird's wing-surface area is about 250 and it weighs about 70 grams—close enough.

Mathematically this can be stated as follows: wing-surface area is equivalent to weight to the two-thirds power, or weight$^{2/3}$. In other words, if you square the weight and then take the cube root of that number, you should have the wing-surface area. It turns out that this magical bit of natural math holds roughly true for most birds—the swift, the blackbird, doves, swans, and chickadees, and many others. On the other hand, some birds, such as hummingbirds, loons, and geese, have wing-surface areas that are *less* than weight$^{2/3}$, and they make very poor soarers. Similarly, the good soarers, such as eagles, herons, gulls, and purple martins, have wing-surface areas larger than weight$^{2/3}$.

All birds that fly are especially sensitive to the air. Anything from a small gust to a gale affects their progress through the sky, and they all make constant adjustments. But soaring birds seem especially gifted in sensing the invisible motions of the air. Wind blowing across an obstruction—a wave, a sand dune, a shoreline, a hill—causes an updraft. An albatross takes advantage of these evanescent updrafts in series, ascending and descending, gliding for hours near the surface of the sea. A gull soaring along the beach is vectoring easily along the continuous updraft, at right angles to the offshore breeze hitting the

Feathers require constant care. Opposite, a Louisiana heron preens flight feathers with its bill. A specialized claw on the middle toe of the great blue heron, above, and certain other birds provides a "feather comb" for preening. An anhinga or "snakebird" of Florida and the American tropics dries its non-water-repellent wings after swimming for fish.

slight rise of shoreline. The same is true of hawks as they soar southward along north-south-running mountain ridges on their autumnal migration. On land, an open area of field will warm up faster than surrounding woodland, and the air over it rises in a great column. Vultures will soar in circles on these thermals, defining their edges. Meanwhile, over the sea, warming water sends air up in groups of thermal columns, and gulls may be seen soaring in circles around them. If there is a fresh wind—at least 24 miles per hour—it will tend to blow these columns of air over sideways. Each column of warm air rotates, even when prone, and this causes another updraft between the columns. Gulls and other seabirds will soar along these invisible updrafts, straight into the wind, gaining altitude as they go.

Even as a bird gains altitude while soaring, it is in fact in a descending mode. It rises because the current of air is rising faster than the bird is dropping. This sounds like a very efficient means of travel, and it is, but the actual efficiencies of ascending and descending flight are not always what seem obvious. Wind-tunnel flights of parakeets have shown that efficiency—in terms of energy expenditure—is a combination of many factors, espe-

cially speed. Flight for a parakeet at 12 miles per hour is not as efficient as it is at its normal cruising speed of 22. On the other hand, ascending at an angle of about five degrees while flying at 12 miles per hour turns out not to take much more energy than merely flying at that speed. And as the speed of ascending flight increases toward cruising speed, the overall cost of ascent keeps going down (as flight itself becomes more efficient). In this equation, one can see that for some birds it might be possible to save energy over an entire journey by spending a good deal of the time descending (with minimum cost) and ascending at not much greater cost than straight flying. Such is the flight pattern of goldfinches and woodpeckers—an undulating path through the air. It also turns out to be the pattern of certain migratory birds that may ascend and descend repeatedly through 20,000 feet during their vast sojourns aloft. Aeronautical engineers have yet to devise as fuel-efficient a system for airplanes. They also envy birds their feathers.

It is the manipulation of feathers—by the bird and by the air—that allows for many of the subtle maneuvers of birds in flight and on takeoff and landing. It is feathers that permit birds to fly relatively soundlessly: imagine the human misery if birds made proportionately as much noise in flight as airplanes. It is also feathers that turn what are chunky and awkwardly shaped bodies into streamlined, aerodynamically sound fuselages. Feathers keep birds warm, dry, and aloft, and they also provide the canvas upon which natural selection has done some of its most extraordinary artwork. That birds spend a good deal of time preening, dusting, oiling, and otherwise caring for their feathers is no surprise:

The spectacular courtship plumage of the great egret, left, nearly brought about its extinction by hunters for the millinery trade in the 19th and early 20th centuries. Right, prized by nobility of the ancient civilizations of Central America, the plumage of the resplendent quetzal has earned it top place on today's list of the world's most beautiful birds.

feathers are probably the most important pieces of avian apparatus.

Each flight feather itself is an aerodynamic marvel. The forward vane is narrower than the rear vane, and air pressure acts differentially on the feather, pressing more heavily on the wider vane and twisting the feather to the proper angle. In this the quill colludes, being rigid toward the base but flexible and flatter toward the tip.

Most birds have 10 primary feathers on each wing—these being the propeller feathers, which emerge from the three-fingered hand—though more primitive birds such as grebes and flamingos have 12, and herons, ducks, and gulls have 11. What are thought to be more specialized birds, such as swallows, Hawaiian honeycreepers, the New World wood warblers, and finches, have nine. Flightless birds tend to have even fewer (although the ostrich has 19). Secondary feathers—the lift feathers on the arm—vary widely in number depending on the length of that part of the wing. An albatross has a whopping 32 secondary feathers on each wing, a turkey vulture 18, a northern bobwhite 10. The fewest on any bird is the hummingbird's six or seven. Over all these feathers are tiers of coverts, cleverly arranged in overlapping series on both the top and bottom of the wing, lending strength, among other things, to the entire flight array.

Tail feathers are counted in pairs. While most birds have six pairs of tail feathers, this, too, varies widely: hummingbirds, swifts, cuckoos, and others have five pairs; some cuckoos have a mere four. Other birds have far more. The white pelican has 12 pairs, and the champion appears to be the white-tailed wattled pheasant with 16 pairs. It used to be thought that the ostrich had 30 tail-feather pairs— plumes that were much in demand by the millinery trade and were one reason Australians imported the birds— but ornithologists now say that the ostrich has but seven pairs, while the other plumes are another kind of feather altogether. This technical distinction by itself has not diminished the demand for these adornments. Like flight feathers, tail feathers are overlaid by coverts, swimming birds having more coverts than tail feathers. In peacocks and in breeding males of the resplendent quetzal, a peren-

nial candidate for the title of the world's most beautiful bird, it is the tail coverts that have developed into the birds' fantastic plumage.

All told, the flight feathers and their associated coverts account for a small proportion of the feathers that cover a bird. The ruby-throated hummingbird has fewer than a thousand feathers overall, while the whistling swan has more than 25,000. Most of these feathers are contour feathers, all of which typically grow from specific tracts on the skin (waterfowl are "tractless"), and down, which can grow almost anywhere and which provides insulation. There are also vaneless and nearly vaneless bristles that on some birds, such as ostriches and cuckoos, appear as mammalianlike eyelashes, and that many insect-chasing birds have around the mouth, increasing the area of the trap and also perhaps playing some sensory role, like whiskers on a dog.

Contour feathers usually have well-formed vanes but are downy at the base. They cover the body and give it its aerodynamic shape, though in many instances they have evolved into highly elaborate structures for display, as in such bizarre and beautiful creatures as the birds of paradise. Contour feathers grade into other types called semiplumes that are less well-vaned and more loosely webbed. These provide insulation, flexibility around joints, and, in waterbirds, buoyancy.

In association with contour feathers are odd hairlike feathers called filoplumes with vestigial vanes at the ends. These feathers, which generally lie under the contour feathers, baffled ornithologists for some time. They were suspected of having some sensory role, and recently West German scientists studying pigeons found that the filoplumes are directly connected to sensory receptors in the skin that detect mechanical stimuli— that is, motion. If the filoplume, or the nearby contour feather, is waggled, the signal is transmitted directly by the filoplume to the bird's central nervous system. A contour feather that is out of place can cause a loss of heat. Perhaps more important, a contour feather that is ruffled cuts down on the streamlining of the bird's body. And it may also be that a change in pressure on a contour feather during flight, once signaled via the filoplume to the central nervous system, plays a role in the constant fine-tuning called

for in the conduct of flight. So the filoplume would seem to provide a direct and very specific bit of information to the bird—what we might think of as an itch, saying that something is out of place, or at least changing.

There apparently is nothing—no feature—of these superb athletes that does not owe its original design and function to the overriding task of flight, the amazingly complex talent birds possess that is so unimaginably liberating and, at the same time, so elegant a straitjacket. 🦅

Broad, slotted wings give the large, heavy sandhill crane grace as it flies thousands of miles between its breeding and wintering grounds. Masters of migration, cranes, herons, storks, hawks, eagles, and vultures often soar majestically from thermal to thermal, using relatively little energy in flapping flight.

SUBSISTENCE

*T*en thousand years ago in North America, the ice began to ease its hold on the land. Northern areas of what is now the United States were emerging from the glaciers' frigid grip, and trees such as oaks, beeches, and chestnuts, long relegated to southern refuges, began to colonize the north, at first along river systems where warm gulf air and rich soil created salubrious habitats. Scientists have discovered that the oaks in particular migrated north very fast, far faster than many trees with light seeds capable of being dispersed by the wind. How could this be? Squirrels are famous for burying acorns, but they rarely transport them far from the parent tree.

The answer, most likely, is that felonious dandy, the blue jay. An omnivore, the blue jay gets its brigandish reputation from the fact that it occasionally feeds on the eggs or young of smaller birds, though its main animal food is composed of a variety of insects and small mammals and amphibians. But three-quarters of a blue jay's diet is vegetable, and a

Preceding pages: The bright red berries of a mountain ash in autumn attract a flock of Bohemian waxwings. By voiding the seeds away from the tree, the birds help it to propagate.

great proportion of that is acorns and beechnuts. This bird has a specially strengthened lower mandible with which, mouth open, it pounds such nuts to crack them open, and a reinforced skull to withstand the jarring blows. More to the point, blue jays are among the few species of birds that might be thought of as capitalists, creating assets for future use. In addition to the strong lower mandible, the blue jay has an expandable throat and esophagus in which it can hold three large acorns or up to 14 beechnuts. And in the autumn, the jays busy themselves foraging for such nuts, carrying them from the forest to their home territories—often located in less forested, bushier areas that may be as distant as five miles away from the foraging grounds. The jay doesn't take just any nut; instead, it will take a nut in the beak and rattle it, sensing somehow if it is viable. If it isn't, the bird simply drops it on the ground. Once loaded up with what appear to be good nuts, it may take one more and hold it in the beak and head home, flying low along potential cover lest a hawk attack while it is slowed by the excess baggage.

Once in its home territory, the jay disgorges the nuts and, one by one, caches them under the grass or in the soft soil. It then covers the caches with plant debris, in a

behavior that may keep nosy mammals from getting them but that adventitiously keeps the nuts from drying out, thus enhancing the likelihood of germination. In studies in Wisconsin, W. Carter Johnson and Curtis S. Adkisson found that 88 percent of the nuts cached by blue jays were viable, while a random sample of nuts from the same trees produced only 10 percent viable ones.

The caches provide sustenance for the jays in winter and their nestlings in the spring, and those that are left go on to produce more nut-bearing trees to the benefit of future generations of blue jays. In one study, it was found that 50 jays transported 150,000 acorns in a period of a month—almost 60 percent of the entire production of 11 pin oaks. Such industriousness, it is estimated, could easily account for the fact that oak forests chased the receding glaciers at a rate of nearly 400 yards per year, far faster than even the spruce trees, whose light, windborne seeds permitted them to advance northward only some 280 yards per year. And today, in areas where farmland and human habitation reduce the oak forests to isolated remnants, the jays play an important role in regenerating them and maintaining their genetic diversity. Most other jays around the world exhibit similar behavior: the scrub

jay of California will even cache marbles.

Another planter of forests is a jay relative, Clark's nutcracker, a gray, black, and white bird found at high elevations in the juniper and pine forests of the Rocky Mountains and the Sierras. This bird, along with its European counterpart, is also an omnivore but specializes in the seeds of coniferous trees, which it caches by the hundreds, often marking the caches with pebbles or twigs. Studies have shown that a nutcracker will recover up to 80 percent of its stores—but rarely does it recover the stores of another nutcracker. Mammals such as squirrels as often as not recover nuts stored by others, suggesting that they find them chiefly by the sense of smell, rather than any specific memory of their own previous caching activities. The nutcrackers, on the other hand, appear to use a visual memory to guide them. The pebble and twig markers suggest this, but that there is something even more remarkable afoot by way of memory is suggested by nutcrackers that have been spotted digging through snow as deep as half a foot to recover previously cached seeds.

To add experimental evidence to anecdote, Russell Balda of Northern Arizona University put a Eurasian nutcracker named Hans into a laboratory room the floor of which was covered with sand. Given a large quantity of seeds, Hans ate his fill and buried the rest. Then he was removed from the room. After 18 days, he was let back in and recovered his seeds with an accuracy of 92 percent. Even when the seeds were removed and the sand raked over, Hans would dig around only where seeds once had been, suggesting that the bird's poorly developed sense of smell was not at work but rather something people rarely ascribe to the bird brain: a well-developed memory.

In mammal brains, it is believed that learning and memory take place in the six-layered cerebral cortex. The brain of birds has but three such layers. However, recent research has shown that the embryonic cells that develop into the neocortex (the extra three layers) in mammals are present in birds, too, and give rise to a portion of the brain called the hyperstriatum, which appears to have a similar chemistry to the neocortex and to transmit similar impulses. So there is reason to believe that a bird can have the equivalent

One of the handsomest birds of the eastern United States, a blue jay can hold acorns in its throat and beak, opposite. Loaded up, opposite above, it flies as far as five miles to cache the nuts in the ground for future consumption. Stores not recovered may sprout and aid in reforesting the area, and may have been responsible for the rapid northward spread of oak forests after the Ice Age. Above, working its way head-first down a tree trunk, a white-breasted nuthatch may find food missed by trunk ascenders. A hoarder, it hides seeds in crevices in the bark.

brain power of at least some mammals, and it is therefore not too surprising that the nutcracker's memory is brought to bear on that most crucial aspect of existence: food. Such memory of where they have hidden something is commonly noted among crows and ravens as well as their corvid cousins, the jays and nutcrackers. Similarly, Alan Kamil of the University of Massachusetts has pointed out that the amakihi, one of the Hawaiian honeycreepers, will not revisit a flower that it has already searched for nectar, even though the search seems to leave no telltale mark on the flower.

In any event, even the relatively brilliant Hans was not perfect. Some of a nutcracker's cache goes unretrieved and thus promotes the growth of the forest trees that the bird so heavily relies on.

Various other birds also are hoarders, but their form of storing food apparently does not alter the environment in any significant way. Nuthatches will store food at all times of the year, typically sticking seeds into crevices in the bark of trees (where they often are found and eaten by titmice and chickadees). The acorn woodpecker of the western United States may be the champion hoarder. It chisels out tight-fitting holes in the trunks of trees and presses acorns into them: one single ponderosa pine was found to contain 30,000 acorns. Oddly, the acorn woodpeckers in northern Colombia do not store nuts.

A modified form of food storage is practiced by a few predatory birds. The American kestrel will set aside the uneaten remains of prey for later use, as will the peregrine falcon and some owls, while shrikes have made this a specialty, impaling small animals like mice and birds on thorns or even the barbs of barbed-wire fences, creating a larder for use as much as a week later. But, except for those few birds that have evolved such practices (the sort of capitalist "virtue" that attracted Aesop to ants), subsistence for birds—the obtaining of fuel to keep their hot little metabolisms going—is a day-to-day, in some cases moment-to-moment affair, an ever-present necessity from which there is little respite.

Energy-intensive to an extreme, most birds spend many of their waking hours feeding, looking for food, or going to places where food might be. This quest is what we observ-

Perhaps the champion hoarders of the bird world are acorn woodpeckers of the western United States, whose winter granaries, such as the one in the fencepost below, may hold 30,000 nuts.

ers most frequently see going on. To stoke their furnaces, birds eat a great deal more compared with their weight than, say, we do. A four-pound goose will consume the equivalent of 4.4 percent of its body weight each day; a one-pound pigeon eats 6.5 percent of its weight, which is roughly equivalent to a 150-pound human consuming 10 pounds of food a day. The smaller the bird, the greater its requirement proportionately: while a mourning dove (smaller than a pigeon) eats 11 percent of its weight daily, a titmouse that weighs less than half an ounce requires 30 percent of its body weight daily to sustain itself. Hummingbirds eat up to twice their weight in nectar each day.

Such specifics can, however, be misleading. Food value, as computed in calories or usable energy, is equally important. Animal food is easier to digest than plant food. A carnivorous bird, like many raptors, may assimilate 90 percent of the food value of its prey. Vultures and other scavengers may do even better, since meat that has begun to decay is assimilated even more efficiently. Insects are animals, of course, but they normally are covered as adults with a tough outer skeleton of chitin that is barely digestible: insectivorous birds reach digestive efficiencies of 70 to 80 percent. On the other hand, adult insects do not provide those that dine upon them with much by way of calcium. Birds such as swallows that feed almost exclusively on flying insects get their calcium by taking bits of mollusk shells. And anyone with a nest of barn swallows on the property will find that it takes only a day or two before the swallows will eagerly accept the property owner's crushed chicken eggshells thrown out in the yard.

The superior value of animal food is shown in birds by the fact that many birds that depend on fruit for food nonetheless will catch animal food, usually insects, to get their young broods off to a good start. This is part of what is called the altricial strategy, altricial referring to young that hatch in a helpless state, as among songbirds. The opposite is precocial—young that hatch with their eyes open, with down feathers covering their bodies, and usually with the ability to walk and leave the nest in a few days or even hours, as with quail, chickens, ducks, and others. The precocial condition is advanta-

Lacking talons, a loggerhead shrike, or "butcher bird," left, impales its prey—here, a sparrow—on thorns, barbed wire, or sharp pieces of wood to secure it for eating. It may return up to a week later to feed from its "larder." The American kestrel, right, eats mostly insects, but may cache birds and small mammals when food is plentiful.

geous for birds that nest on the ground or in other easily preyed upon places. A well-constructed nest off the ground, however, can, in a sense, be built anywhere, and, being relatively free of predators, allows the parents a grace period to raise utterly dependent young to the point at which they can fend for themselves. Nevertheless, there is always danger, and the shorter this period of dependency the better. So the parents, even if they themselves eat nothing but fruit, will give only the highly nutrient-rich and digestible insect fare to their young. The great insect blooms common in the North Temperate Zone and farther north have fostered the altricial strategy of migratory songbirds, and this strategy itself may be behind the remarkable success of the songbirds in terms of sheer numbers of species and widespread distribution.

Of the food that plants afford, seeds are perhaps the richest and most assimilable—they can provide an 80 percent efficiency rating. (The lowest rating is for decaying wood: millipedes relegated to such a diet convert only about 15 percent of their food to usable energy.) Cattle and elephants and other browsers and grazers that eat leaves and grass come in at a low 30 to 40 percent. Such herbivores had to invent a new digestive system along the way to handle such indigestible stuff, and it is little wonder that it is almost entirely flightless birds that have the stomach for the life of the browser. Indeed, it is fair to say that the less digestible the food a bird eats, the more sedentary the bird.

A case in point is the hoatzin, that weird anachronism of cuckoo ancestry that lives in South America. The hoatzin has a highly specialized crop that comes in two parts and

takes up nearly a third of the forward part of its body, even shoving aside the sternum and reducing the keel and flight muscles to the degree that the hoatzin flies only short distances. The function of the extended crop? The hoatzin eats leaves; it is one of the relatively few birds with such a diet. Others include certain grouse and ptarmigans: more than half a blue grouse's diet is pine needles.

Leaves, as well as grass, are slow to release their energy content and thus must remain in the bird for a long time, adding weight that is counterproductive to flight or any other form of escape. The owl parrot of New Zealand feeds chiefly on leaves and grass; it is flightless, capable only of gliding down from a tree it has climbed, and mammalian predators introduced to its island home are rendering this parrot rare. Another New Zealand bird, the takahe, a large, flightless gallinule, also feeds largely on grass. It has no particular internal modifications for this work, as do the hoatzin and the owl parrot. Instead of storing food, it simply eats prodigious amounts, voiding up to eight yards of fecal matter each day.

There is virtually no class of organism that does not provide food for one bird species or another, and this fact helps explain avian diversity and near ubiquity on the planet. The lesser flamingo, pumping nutrient-rich water through its "baleen"-lined beak, is gorging almost exclusively on blue-green algae and diatoms, some of the most primitive and simple of life forms. At the opposite end of the scale, the Philippine eagle eats primates, among other foods. A beached whale is carrion for gulls, and the kelp gulls of South America annoy live whales by pecking at their fat. There are picky eaters among birds as well, specialists such as the snail kite, but even most specialists enjoy a bit of dietary variety. Hummingbirds eat mostly nectar but also feed on insects that have drowned in the flowers or gotten caught in spider webs, and some of the larger hummingbirds actively hunt insects on the wing. The yellow-bellied sapsucker is a practiced borer of trees, drilling different kinds of holes in different seasons or trees, the better to get the sap to flow. Yet it also will eat insects, especially hornets attracted to the running sap, along with fruit and some of the inner bark of the tree.

The most obvious adaptation of birds to their food is the beak, and birds have gone to remarkable extremes in this department. The cardinal's beak, for example, like that of other finches, has evolved as a highly efficient seed-cracker. It is short and heavy, backed by strong muscles. A seed will be held in one of the grooves along the sides of the upper mandible, while the lower mandible, which is sharp-edged, moves forward, breaking the seed's hard outer shell. One of the most beloved of American birds, providing a splash of tropical red in the gray days of winter, the cardinal was naturally a bird of the South, but its range is extending northward as far as New England, where it takes advantage of seed proffered in winter at suburban feeding stations.

The birds with beaks adapted to a seed diet, which include sparrows, finches, buntings, and towhees, represent a relatively recent development in evolution. The kinds of plants that yield such seeds—grasses and sedge, for example—became widespread only in the Miocene era, some 25 million years ago. Other birds, such as the larks and pigeons, adopted a seed diet in part, but finchlike birds—descended from some sparrow ancestor—took to the new food source with a vengeance and radiated into more than 400 species, almost all with beaks specifically adapted to the diet.

The powerful effect of an available food source on evolution can hardly be seen better than in a comparison of the beak of a swift with those of likely swiftian relatives, the hummingbirds. A swift's beak is short and tiny and slightly decurved, while the mouth (when open) is a great gaping trap. (The beaks of swallows evolved convergently to

this form.) The sword-billed hummingbird's beak, to take an extreme case, is longer than the rest of its body and can reach into the deepest of flowers.

One of the oddest beak adaptations is that of the skimmers, coastal birds often seen in late afternoon and early evening flying gracefully along the water's edge in search of small fish and shrimp. Uniquely, the lower mandible is longer than the upper, and it cuts the surface of the water as the bird flies just over it. When the lower mandible strikes a minnow or shrimp, the upper mandible clamps down, its sharp edge fitting between the two sharp edges of the lower mandible, thus securing the slippery prey. Strong neck muscles and extra bone in the neck and head allow the bird to withstand the shock of these impacts. Unusual musculature associated with the beak has also helped the starling become an especially successful forager. Most birds can close their beaks with considerable force, but the starling can also open its beak with power. Thus, looking for insects just below the surface of the ground, it will thrust its beak into the ground and open it, tearing a two-inch gash in the soil. This action is far more likely to expose an insect than mere probing.

When it comes to bills, nothing seems so ridiculous (in a beautiful sort of way) or so inexplicable as the bills of toucans. Huge, often larger than the body of the bird, and brightly colored, they would seem as much a hindrance as a help in eating fruit (their main diet) or insects . . . or anything, for that matter. They are very light, being honeycombed with fibers, but appear cumbersome nonetheless. Ornithologists are at a loss to explain these bills. They could have evolved to eat some especially large, soft fruit that has since vanished from the scene, or just to reach farther from a perch, or perhaps as an apparatus to convey a threat, or possibly a device to aid in recognition or courtship. No one knows.

While particular bills evolved along with particular food preferences, many birds that remain much alike in such outward characteristics have developed different forms of dietary specialization, and a moment's thought leads to the reason. Specialization tends to separate a bird from competition for resources. As bird ecologists look at the

A male cardinal enjoys a seasonal meal of berries, above. Its short, heavy, conical beak, typical of finches, has evolved for eating seeds, the richest and most assimilable of all plant foods. The grooved upper mandible holds the seed as the sharp-edged lower mandible comes forward to crush and husk the hull, left.

A newly hatched ruffed grouse, above, sports thick down and bright eyes. It soon will be able to leave the nest and flee predators—part of the precocial strategy of ground-nesting birds. A black-winged stilt, left, finds its own food from the start, but trumpeter swan cygnets, top, are ushered on early trips.

Much more care is needed to raise altricial birds. Blind, naked, and helpless at birth, robins, above, are dependent on their parents for protection and food. Like the yellow warbler chicks at right, they will be fed protein-rich insects to speed development. Even after fledging, baby azure-winged magpies, top, and other tree-nesting chicks are fed by their parents.

habits of birds, they find that small differences between what two species eat or how they eat can make all the difference in their ability to coexist. For example, warblers have a preference for seeking out insects in particular parts of a tree. Thus a single spruce tree may host a bay-breasted warbler in the lower half, foraging near the trunk; a black-throated green warbler in the middle out near the tips of the branches; and a Cape May warbler in the upper branches—all of them minding their own business. There can even be gender differences in feeding behavior, the extreme case being the extinct huias of New Zealand, which evolved different bill shapes altogether for the two sexes. However, one also sees male indigo buntings foraging high in the tops of trees while the females typically forage closer to the ground.

For many birds there is also a great seasonal variation in diet. In December, for example, a black-billed magpie may depend almost entirely on carrion, grain, and some wild fruit. In February, it switches from grain and fruit to small mammals, along with carrion. In September, more than half its food is grasshoppers. Many birds, especially those in the temperate zones, must be opportunists when it comes to diet. Birds that eat fruit exclusively, or nearly exclusively, such as toucans, parrots, and some pigeons, are found in the tropics, where warmth and a vastly greater variety of trees make fruit available year-round. Fruit, of course, "wants" to be eaten, while animals, including insects,

The diets of birds include most classes of organisms, from tiny insects found in the flower nectar favored by the green-crowned brilliant, right, and other hummingbirds, to the monkeys sometimes preyed upon by the fierce but endangered Philippine eagle, left.

don't. Many fruiting trees and bushes, particularly in the tropics, need birds to eat their fruit and distribute the seeds by voiding them elsewhere: it is no wonder that most fruits and berries are brightly colored and readily seen by the color vision of birds. While fruit (and other plant food) yields somewhat less food value to the bird than animal food, it is far easier to find and "capture."

It turns out that for most small birds—think of the swift plying the airy ocean's insect plankton or the chickadee at a bird feeder—their food is common and easily obtained once found, so they can afford to be specialists in food preference. On the other hand, a hawk making lazy circles in the sky is in fact busily looking for prey and may have to keep looking for hours. Spotting a small animal down below, it swoops down on it in an instant and takes it, whatever it may be. With such a long time needed for the search, the hawk can't afford to be picky. Long searching times tend to produce dietary generalists. A cormorant has a different problem. Like loons, grebes, and mergansers, the cormorant dives underwater and then looks around for fish. Fish tend to be fairly common so it doesn't take much time to spot prey. But pursuit takes a good deal of time and effort. In such a situation, a bird tends to specialize in prey that provides the greatest payoff measured against the length of pursuit: that is, the largest fish it can handle.

Birds that eat fruits and berries, then, tend to promote the continuation of plants. Even

With its strong, overlapping mandibles, the red crossbill, above, pries apart the scales of pine cones to extract the seed. A long, slightly upturned bill helps the saddle-billed stork, right, scoop up fish from shallow waters, but the purpose of its "saddle" is an enigma. When a brown pelican bags a fish, opposite, it may trap three gallons of water in its huge pouched bill. Saline secretions from ingested sea water run down a groove in the top. The only bird with a lower mandible longer than its upper, the black skimmer, opposite top, fishes on the wing. As the submerged lower mandible hits a minnow, the upper mandible snaps shut, trapping the prey. The only thing certain about the toucan's colorful bill, opposite bottom, is that if it weren't so fibrous and light, the bird would fall over.

seed-eaters often drop seeds with the same effect. Furthermore, even if birds were to eat all of the seeds off a particular conifer one winter, this would not affect the production of seeds the following year, whereas a local mammal population is quite obviously affected by the number of adults that fall prey before breeding season. It is generally believed that a cycle exists, at least on the local level, between predators and their prey. If voles increase greatly, then the owls that prey on them may later increase to a point where voles are so heavily preyed upon that their population decreases, leading to a phased decrease in the owls.

A dramatic variation on this theme is the periodic irruption of snowy owls into the south beyond their normal range. These birds depend primarily on lemmings as prey, and, while the popular lore that lemmings charge off periodically in mass suicide is not true, they and some other rodents do have large, cyclic population buildups and sudden crashes. During the lemming buildup, the population of snowy owls tends to grow. When the lemmings drop off, the owls either must seek a different prey, which some do, or leave. Thus, every three to five years, in autumn, large numbers of snowy owls head south and reach the United States, where some, but not most, find food to tide them over the winter.

Even nonpredatory birds can find themselves caught up with such cycles. In Siberia, brant (once known as barnacle geese) breed in the same area as lemmings. When the lemmings are on the rise, the geese have been found to breed well, too. But when the

lemming population plummets, the geese do poorly. While it is possible the geese are subject to some internal cycle of their own, it is more likely that in poor lemming years the resident foxes and skuas turn to goose eggs and young goslings.

In the 1940s, ethologist Lukas Tinbergen set out to analyze the effect on the population of house sparrows of kestrel predation in Holland. The hawks, he found, removed about 8 percent of the existing house sparrows during one month, May, accounting for 80 percent of all house sparrow mortality. That seems like a significant control mechanism on house sparrows, but the facts appear

contrary. If the hawks were not present, would the sparrow population grow? In the late 19th and early 20th centuries, British gamekeepers, with their typical interventionist instincts, eliminated most kestrels from most of England, but no one in that nation of avid birdwatchers reported a dramatic increase in house sparrows during that period, nor a dramatic reduction after 1939, when kestrels were reprieved and began to become numerous again. If predators take those weakened by age or illness, it can be argued that their controlling effects on populations are limited: the old and ailing die soon anyway. One thing, however, is sure. No raptor is so numerous or voracious as to eliminate its prey population, any more than insectivorous birds clear an area of insects. A bustling houseful of purple martins may make a dent in mosquito populations, but they cannot, as advertised, rid one's backyard of mosquitoes.

The quest for food is almost constant for birds. A red-tailed hawk was found to have gone for five days without eating anything, but it was foraging, looking from morning till night each day. There are times, however, when certain birds willingly starve themselves. A male penguin will stand on the Antarctic ice for two months with its egg resting on its feet by way of incubation. By the time the chick hatches, the male will have lost half his weight. Most birds that experience the cold of winter, or the rigors of migration, have the capacity to store up subcutaneous fat reserves that will tide them over. And in lieu of a meal, a bird can take a bath in the sun.

Many birds sun themselves during the period of molt, often to the point of thermal stress, signaled by heavy panting. It has been suggested that additional heat, however uncomfortable, somehow relieves the irritation of skin and follicle during the loss of feathers. Perhaps the heat causes mites and lice that parasitize both feathers and skin to increase their own movements and thus become easier to remove. Sunbathing also promotes the synthesis of vitamin D, which tends to be lacking in birds with a largely plant-derived diet. The preen glands of some birds produce an oily chemical that is transformed into vitamin D by sunlight: when the bird smears the oil over its feathers, it ingests some as well, along with the recently synthesized

With its long, sensitive bill, a dunlin, opposite, probes the shoreline for insects and tiny crustaceans while a merganser, right, may dive for many seconds for its fish fare. Powerful talons bear down on a rodent as a snowy owl silently pounces, below.

Breeding season draws a colony of king penguins to the rocky coast of Antarctica, opposite. In the harsh climate, a pair lays only one egg. By turns, one parent cradles the egg on its feet, incubating it beneath a fold of belly skin, above left, while its mate returns to sea to feed. A hatchling also gets swaddled against the cold, above, until it grows a thick down coat, top left, and, after a year, the colorful, watertight plumage of an adult.

vitamin. It is interesting to note that the two bird families with the least development of preen glands are the exclusively insectivorous swifts and the nightjars. Some birds, though, and possibly most birds, take advantage of the sun's warmth on days when air temperatures are low to save themselves some energy-expensive foraging.

Like most birds, the white-crowned sparrow has a distinct daily pattern of feeding activity, with peaks an hour or two after dawn and an hour or two before sunset. But years ago it was found that these sparrows do less foraging at midday on sunny days than on cloudy days. Laboratory experiments with sun lamps mimicking the sun showed that even when it was very cold the birds would markedly decrease their rate of feeding. Calculations indicated that the radiation from the lamps provided a substitute for more than 15 percent of the birds' total caloric needs. In warming the outer feathers, the sun bath evidently deters heat loss significantly. The sun (a sun lamp) radiates heat across a wide spectrum of wavelengths, some of which are visible as light and some of which—the far-red—are invisible. Dark plumage absorbs virtually all the wavelengths of visible light, while white feathers reflect most of them. Meanwhile, the invisible far-red wavelengths are absorbed equally by any color

feathers. And this difference may serve to explain a strange phenomenon in nature called Gloger's rule.

Gloger's rule states that, as you move from drier habitats to wetter ones, the animals—from insects to birds—tend to become darker. The usual explanation for this is that a darker color makes an animal less conspicuous against darker, moister soil. But that would not explain why a purple martin, which spends the better part of its day in the sky, would be darker in a more humid environment. The answer seems to lie in the fact that humidity sharply reduces the amount of far-red radiation that reaches the Earth's surface. If one can assume that there is some energetic cost in producing pigmentation in feathers, then it follows that birds do not "want" to be dark, all other things being equal. But the cost would be worth it if a damp environment is removing the far-red radiation, making it necessary to rely on visible light, which is best absorbed by dark plumage. In a dry environment, on the other hand, light plumage, which is less costly, will absorb the available far-red perfectly well, and in such a place a bird is free to be light-colored.

Whether the environment is damp or moist, birds—especially small ones—are always at some risk of starvation. So intense is the metabolism of the hummingbird that it

Poised to strike, a green heron waits for a fish. Green herons have been known to drop leaves on the water as bait and, in Japan at least, to break off twigs at an optimal length for luring fish.

would starve to death during the night if it did not enter a state of torpidity. At night the hummingbird's heart rate drops and its body temperature falls to about 70 degrees Fahrenheit. In this manner, it uses less fuel from the previous day's gleanings, and it returns to normal as the air temperature rises the next morning. Some insectivorous birds, such as swifts and nighthawks, have been found to be dormant (actually appearing quite dead) during extreme cold spells when their insect prey vanishes, but fly off normally once they are warmed up. Of course, prolonged cold—that is, winter—and the loss of food supplies for many kinds of birds is what lies at the heart of their annual migrations. But one insect-eater manages to stay behind all winter without ever seeing an insect. As Oliver Austin, Jr., wrote: "When Arizona Indians a century or more ago told of birds that slept away the winter in crevices in rocky cliffs, this was duly recorded by cultural anthropologists, but dismissed by ornithologists as a charming Indian folk tale. It wasn't until the early 1950s that the skeptical white man learned that this tall Indian tale is quite true." Common poor-wills, it turns out, creep into crevices in canyon walls when cold weather begins to thin insect populations, and the birds experience a 20 percent drop in body weight. Their body temperature drops to about 65 degrees Fahrenheit, their digestion shuts down, and breathing almost ceases. In this state they pass the winter, as close as a bird comes to hibernation, "coming to" when the weather is warm enough to produce nighttime insects.

Such stratagems aside, hunger remains a driving force in birddom, and avian evolution has produced about as many ways of finding food as there are bird types—some methods being characterized by cooperation, tool-use, learning, and what might well be called intelligence. On one of the Galápagos Islands, the sharp-billed ground finch (also called the vampire finch) has developed a taste for blood. It hops onto the backs of nesting boobies and bites them on the back of the wing, then drinks the blood. The same species of finch does not do this on the other islands where it occurs, suggesting that this is something that one island race has learned to do, rather than inheriting it in its genetic program.

Many birds, especially in the tropics, for-age in large flocks of mixed species. Aside from sheer sociability, such flocks may be advantageous to the birds by providing more eyes on the lookout for predators, or confusion when a predator does arrive. Certain South American shrike-tanagers forage in flocks, and there are (controversial) claims that, when their foraging takes them out of the trees onto open ground, one member of the flock is somehow appointed to be a guard, watching out for predators while the others feed. In some cases, it has been reported, the guard shrike-tanager will see a flock member nearby with a particularly attractive morsel and sound the alarm call. The birds drop everything and the guard gets the morsel. A sea gull, spotting a piece of food, also may sound the alarm, causing other gulls to hesitate while the alarmist gets the jump on them.

Such attempts at deceit are not always successful. The bald eagle, as Ben Franklin dourly pointed out, is something of a pirate, attacking ospreys or other eagles that have caught a fish and taking it away. Very rarely, fights break out between two eagles, but more often an eagle that has caught a fish and is attacked by another gives up and drops the fish. Looking into these felonious matters, Andrew J. Hansen of Oak Ridge National Laboratory in Tennessee found that it is a question of "asymmetry." The chief asymmetry is size. A smaller eagle assesses the pirate's size and, if it is bigger, gives up the fish in order to avoid a costly struggle. Not surprisingly, then, small eagles tend to fish while larger ones tend to pirate. Another asymmetry is hunger. The hungrier eagle is more likely to be fierce; hunger is shown by means of displays of head, neck, and wing feathers. Thus a large eagle approaches the owner of a fish and raises its feathers, signaling that it is mean and hungry. The owner, which may well have already eaten some of the fish and not be truly as hungry as the pirate, might fake it by raising its own feathers in a mock display, but when its neck feathers are raised, its distended crop is visible and the game is up. The bigger and hungrier eagle invariably wins.

On encountering a school of fish, double-crested cormorants often will gather in a long, curved line, swimming toward the fish and diving after them, evidently acting to

In the Galápagos Islands, the woodpecker finch uses a cactus spine to probe for grubs and insects in tree bark, top, then quickly drops its specially tailored instrument to grab the quarry, above.

hem the fish in. White pelicans take this even further, forming an arc on the water, and, wings flapping, drive fish into the shallows where they can more easily be caught. Cooperation is perhaps the last thing one might expect from raptorial birds, which normally are seen alone, although there have been reports of mated pairs hunting together. In 1988, James Bednarz of the University of New Mexico found that Harris's hawks often form hunting parties of up to six individuals. The team consists of a family group—an adult pair, young adults they have raised, and juveniles from the previous breeding season. Their tactics include surprise attacks from many directions, the flushing of prey by one while the others stand ready to attack, and relay attacks. By such methods the hawks can bring down prey that is larger than the birds themselves—a jack rabbit, for example, which weighs more than three times as much as an adult male hawk. The larger the hunting party, the more successful it is at finding and killing prey.

A few birds use objects as extensions of their bodies—that is to say, tools—and why tool use has arisen among these birds (all unrelated) and not others remains in question. The Galápagos woodpecker finch will pick up a cactus spine and use it to poke into crevices for insects, dropping the spine when the prey emerges. The Egyptian vulture is

Flock-feeding white pelicans, below, swim in a semicircle to herd fish and maximize their catch. Such cooperation is rare among birds, but most at least avoid fights. Even amid winter hardship, grey herons, opposite, will soon settle their squabble over a fish rather than risk injury.

known to drop stones on ostrich eggs to break them open; there are unconfirmed reports that the black-breasted buzzard kite of Australia will chase an emu from its nest, pick up a stone, fly up, and drop the stone on the emu's egg to break it open. Brown-headed nuthatches have been found to pry a piece of bark off a tree, fly to another tree, and use the bark to pry off yet other bits of bark to get at insects underneath. Green herons have long been known to toss an object like a leaf or twig into the water, crouching down to wait and grab whatever fish is curious or bold enough to be attracted to the bait. But green herons in a park in Japan have been found to use a wider variety of bait, even biscuits. On a few occasions, the herons took what evidently were oversize twigs, held them in their feet, and broke them off with their beaks before using them as bait.

Tool use is difficult to analyze. It is evidently something that has to be learned, rather than behavior that arises from a built-in genetic program. Some tool use would appear to be mere trial-and-error learning. A captive blue jay, for example, was observed tearing off a piece of paper and using it to reach into an adjoining cage to sweep birdseed within the range of its beak. Rather than having thought through the problem and realized its solution, it is more likely that the

jay was merely fooling around with the paper and accidentally swept up some seeds. Before long the behavior was learned, just as a dog learns to come when it is called. Such behavior, even though involving the use of a tool, is what scientists call cognitively simple.

Sea gulls perform a task akin to tool use that appears to be cognitively complex. Like ravens, they will pick up objects, in this case shells, fly up, and drop them on hard surfaces in order to break them open to get at the food inside.

Looking for something common among the avian tool users (and mammalian ones), scientists have pointed out that in general it is the need to extract foods that are secreted or embedded in an opaque material that has tugged these creatures along the path to the use of tools. So, once again, as with the nutcrackers and their memory, it is food that seems to have called forth some of the birds' outstanding cognitive feats. Others who have looked into the matter of tool use among birds are loath to attribute to these creatures mental abilities with such loaded names as cognitive mapping and intelligence. It is possible, for example, that the tool-using gulls (which are usually older ones, four or five years of age) have simply been conditioned in the same way mice can be conditioned to perform certain feats by the providing of a penalty or an award. The topic of animal psychology is an intellectual minefield.

It has been said that it is impossible to separate food and foraging behavior from microhabitat and habitat. In other words, the ultimate key to the whereabouts of a bird is the availability of food, which is generally perceived, as well, as the chief limiting factor for the size of a given bird population. In the 1950s, the British ecologist David Lack adduced four pieces of circumstantial evidence for food as the limiting factor. Actual fights among birds are very uncommon, he noted, but fighting for food in winter is a "regular feature" of the behavior of some birds, such as crows. "Presumably such behavior would not have been evolved unless the birds were short of food," Lack wrote. Also, if food were not a limiting factor, then the differentiation of feeding habits, such as that of the several warblers in one tree, would not have come about. Such differentiation is essential if food is a limiting factor, however, "since if

two species compete for food, the chance of both being equally well adapted is negligible, so that one will eliminate the other." Further, populations of birds are always greater where their food supply is abundant. Perhaps most important, however, is the apparent fact that few adult birds die from either predation or disease.

Virtually every wild bird is parasitized by a variety of mites, lice, and ticks. At least 70 different kinds of parasites could be found on a single pigeon. But in general, and for obvious reasons, it is to a parasite's evolutionary interest not to kill its host. Birds and their parasites have evolved a *modus vivendi*— in fact, many. For example, a screech owl's nest is a relatively unclean place: insect larvae roam in the litter of feces and uneaten prey. But screech owls are known to import live-in help. Some of them carry to the nest blind snakes that typically spend their lives underground. The snakes settle into their new residence and tend to stay till the nest is abandoned. Scientists at Baylor University found that nearly one out of five screech owl nests will have a live-in snake, which reduces insect parasitism on the young owls. The young birds in snake-patrolled nests grow faster and have a better rate of survival.

Parasitism takes its greatest toll on nestlings (for which predation is a major factor as well), but there are many strategies for reducing its effect. Starlings, for example, often return to a nest used the year before

A party of cliff swallows, above, gathers mud with which to mold their jug-shaped nests, opposite. Colonies are havens for parasites that often prove fatal to nestlings, but communal life has its benefits. The birds feed on swarms of insects, so when one returns to its nest, its beak full of bugs, others notice, follow it on its next foray, and share the find.

and restore it to usable shape. But a re-used nest is more likely to harbor parasites than a new one. One of the last chores of a nest-restoring starling, however, is to search out green shoots of any of nine particular plants, each of which is toxic to one or another parasite, and weave them into the nest before eggs are laid.

Birds that nest in large groups, or colonies, also run a high risk of parasitism of the young, as well as the rapid spread of disease. Cliff swallows build nests of mud on the walls of canyons and cliffs, sometimes with thousands of nests in a single colony. The nests are usually infested with a bug that sucks blood at night from both nestlings and adults, and the larger the colony the worse the infestation. Mortality may be twice as severe in a large colony than in a small one. On the other hand, the adult birds do inspect a previous year's nest, and, if it is infested, they build a new one, giving themselves a few weeks' head start on the parasites. They may abandon a whole colony if the infestation is especially severe, alternating nesting sites from year to year.

Nevertheless, they still pay a high price in nestling mortality for their social habit. Why? It turns out, not surprisingly perhaps, to be a matter of food and foraging. According to Charles and Mary Brown of Yale University, cliff swallows feed on local concentrations of airborne insects—clouds of bugs that are formed here and there by convection currents, or great mating swarms. Such patches of insects may come together for 20 or 30 minutes before dissipating, during which time they can support as many as 500 swallows. An adult swallow returning to its nest with a mouthful of insects for its young is highly noticeable. And as it feeds its young, the swallow habitually rocks back and forth. A swallow that has been unsuccessful in finding food, on the other hand, simply clings to the entrance of its nest and watches. When the successful swallow leaves, the unsuccessful one follows. The colony is thus an information center, letting all its members in on the whereabouts of food. At any given time, about 20 percent of the birds forage by themselves, and it may well be that these momentary soloists are the ones that come across a new patch of insects. There are evidently no members of the colony that are solely leaders, or solely followers, or solely solitary feeders.

Mortality among eggs and nestlings varies enormously from species to species. In some hole-nesting species, survival from egg to fledgling may be over 60 percent, but in many species the survival rate hovers around 45 percent. Most of this is the result of predation and parasitism and disease. But in many species, the youngest simply don't get enough to eat and starve. Goldfinch nests are so tightly constructed that they can hold water for days: some goldfinch young drown. Red-winged blackbirds sometimes mistakenly attach their nests to dead stalks and live stalks: as the latter grow the nest eventually tips over.

Prodigious numbers of birds die as a result of accidents, especially during migrations and, in particular, night migrations, when they can crash into any number of objects, both natural and manmade. Epidemics of one disease or another periodically break out—especially among species that are

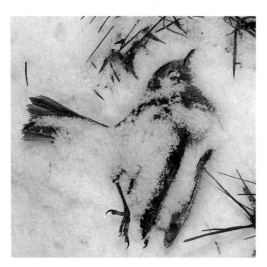

crowded, as ducks often are. Poisons of one sort or another kill birds. A newly introduced plant can be toxic to a curious forager. Upon seeing one of their kind in a paroxysm as a result of ingesting poison, many birds, such as ravens and starlings, will not only avoid the place thereafter but also shun the individual bird if it recovers; this suggests that natural poisons have long been a problem birds have had to learn to avoid.

Nevertheless, scientists believe that most birds die as a result of lack of food. Weakened by illness or age, they become cut off from the food supply and starve. That few starving birds are observed, as David Lack pointed out, is probably due to the fact that birds starve very quickly, a matter of only a few days or less. Left to their own devices and to those of the world they evolved in, bird populations appear to be limited by the availability of food, and the other factors play ancillary roles . . . until recently. Now the chief limiting factor for many bird populations is increasingly the role of humanity. By introducing splendid new obstacles such as skyscrapers for migrating birds to crash into, by introducing lead shot into wildlife refuges, by introducing insecticides such as DDT and strychnine bait to kill animals that prey on livestock, by introducing rats and goats and other new predators to islands—all around the globe people are raising the odds against birds. And nowhere is this limiting factor more potent a threat to the subsistence of these lives than in the destruction of habitat— which is to say, where the food is. 🐦

Winter claims a European robin, opposite, most likely through freezing hastened by starvation. Just when birds need even more food than usual to keep warm, it becomes scarce and harder to find. Small birds, such as the black-capped chickadee, above, are especially vulnerable and may become quite tame when food is scarce.

By late April and early May, the northern part of the globe has leaned well into the sun. Measurable, plottable lines of temperature gradients called isotherms move farther and farther north on the weather maps, and all of life pays them heed. In Cape Cod, "dark, matted marshes lie open, prostrate and torn, with their coarse grasses expressing raw strength under the ripping winds and the enveloping tides. The season gradually delivers them and they start to grow again. In out of the ocean waters and the long shores winding down to the southern continent, in out of wild snow squalls, sun spearing through mountainous clouds, water spouts and rain, low-lying mists, thick fog, and that brilliant light free again to ripen the waters, they drift in crying."

It is the arrival of what Cape Cod naturalist John Hay thinks of as arrow birds, fisherfolk—the terns, buoyantly pressing north in a journey that began thousands of miles south, far beyond the equator, only a few weeks earlier, when that part of the planet reciprocally leaned

MIGRATION

Preceding pages: In a misty winter dawn, snow geese rise at Bosque del Apache National Wildlife Refuge, New Mexico. Each year, 1.5 to 2 million snow geese migrate between breeding grounds in Canada's far north and the southern United States and Mexico.

too far from the sun. This is but a minor adjustment in geophysical terms, a matter of degrees, but withal a withdrawal of warmth sufficient to set the terns and millions and millions of other birds off to stream up the planet over oceans, along coasts, over land, by day, by night, alongside mountain chains, over passes, across deserts, barely over the treetops, past humanity's great urban creations, to arrive depleted, hungry, often near exhaustion and in desperate need to undertake yet another exhausting and dangerous task: to breed.

These arrivals—the magical day, for example, when the dawn sky suddenly is filled with swallows—have long been noted, as have their counterparts, the vanishings of autumn. And they have long held mystery. In one of his typically humiliating conversations with God, Job was asked, "Is it by your wisdom that the hawk soars, and spreads his wings to the south?"

Aristotle knew about migration, too (it is hard to miss, after all), and astutely noticed that "creatures are fatter in migrating." But his observations were limited, and he also thought that swallows hibernated locally in the mud. It is easy to snort at such concepts, but it wasn't until global explorers began bringing back bird skins from remote places to the museums of Europe that people began to get a true sense of the extent and reality of bird migration. It was not until the early part of this century that we found out that some Arctic terns migrate virtually from one pole to the other and back each year—an annual tour of some 25,000 miles—and understood that bird migration is limited less by the endurance of birds than by the size of the planet.

Such spectacular feats by some birds tend to draw attention away from the fact that life is motion and that there are many forms of migration. The sea is full of migrants. Plankton drift with the currents but also migrate daily up and down. Sea turtles and whales are capable of long-distance feats of navigation and travel comparable to those of the birds. The vast tide of wildebeest that crosses the African plains each year in search of the new grass has left many observers speechless. Even butterflies migrate, as do some people still. Bird migration, however, is the most conspicuous, given birds' ubiquity and their exceptional mobility derived from flight.

Technically, migration is like the tern's—an annual round trip from breeding grounds to wintering grounds—but there are forms of quasi-migration as well. The wandering albatross migrates eastward perpetually, circling the southern part of the globe over and over, pausing every two years on various islands to breed; albatross young take so long to raise that adults can breed only in alternative years. Another form of migration is nomadism, no-

Champion migrant is the Arctic tern, which may fly for eight months of the year and cover 22,000 miles in its annual peregrination between the Arctic and Antarctic. Opposite above, an Arctic tern hovers over the sea near Anchorage, Alaska; opposite, an Arctic tern on the tundra of Canada's Ellesmere Island, far north of the Arctic Circle; above, Arctic terns on Machias Seal Island, Bay of Fundy, near the southern limit of their nesting range.

where so evident as in Australia, the vast portion of which gets very little rainfall. What rain does fall comes unpredictably here and there, and, like all desert dwellers, including the Aborigines, the birds have learned to take advantage of momentary bounty. With a rain, plants quickly grow, flower, and put forth seed and fruit. Many birds, including parakeets and lorikeets, roam widely, gathering what they can where they can, breeding in no special place but wherever it is convenient. And, just as the biological processes of plants in such regions have evolved to take place quickly, so have those of the birds. For one species of Australian wood-swallow, courtship and mating are complete within two hours after a rain begins; there is no time for long and drawn-out affairs in the desert. Within weeks the birds, including their new young, will have to move on.

Such migratory patterns aside, it is the regular, metronomic arrivals of the north-south migrants that catch the human imagination the most. The Arctic tern may well be the champion migrant in terms of actual distance. It nests in the far northern parts of the world, as its name suggests, with a few breeding along the Atlantic coast as far south as Massachusetts. In the northern extremes of its range it depends for food on tiny crustaceans called krill, which inhabit frigid water. They drop in abundance as the Arctic summer wanes, and so the terns head off on routes that avoid warmer seas, like the western Atlantic. Some of the terns that nest in North America as far west as Alaska head across the Arctic Ocean and the north Atlantic to the coast of France, then south to Africa and either around the Cape of Good Hope to the colder regions of the Indian Ocean or westward across the south Atlantic to the South American coast. Some may cross the Atlantic from the bulge of Africa and then proceed south. Meanwhile, Arctic terns from Alaska stream south along the west coasts of North and South America, meeting up with the others on the coasts of Antarctica. Along the way, they will have taken small fish, but they return to krill in their wintering grounds, leaving fish to other, larger terns. While geographically the greatest, this long journey can be relatively leisurely, the terns stopping to feed and rest along the way. As a result of their bipolar existence, Arctic terns spend more hours in daylight than any other bird—with most of their year spent in days of 24-hour light.

The return of the swallows is a sure sign that spring has sprung throughout the temperate parts of the globe. Indeed, although the hibernation myth has been dispelled, swallows have engendered other persistent mythology, such as the precision of their annual arrival at such places as San Juan Capistrano and less famous claimants to swallow chronicity. It is believed that they always return on a certain day, and, while they usually do arrive at about the same time each year, that has far less to do with the birds than with the weather. Barn swallows, for example, follow the northward advance of the 48-degree isotherm with fine accuracy, for it is at that temperature that insects begin to take to the air. A cold snap at Capistrano in mid-March will send its swallows south again, regardless of when they arrived, which is usually slightly ahead of the claimed moment.

Some of the true subtleties in migratory "strategy" and timing are put into relief by the swallows and swifts of Europe and western Asia. All of the barn swallows that breed in this region spend their winter in Africa south of the Sahara. Twice each year, they all must cross this vast expanse of land too arid to support much by way of flying insects. Therefore they make the crossing without any sustenance, often arriving at the other side so exhausted they can be picked off the branches on which they pause to rest. The Mediterranean presents far less of a problem since most birds skirt it, crossing the water at Gibraltar and the Bosphorus.

One can glimpse ancient swallow history in their migratory patterns. Those that breed in central Europe winter just south of the Sahara in central Africa. But swallows that breed farther north add some 3,000 miles to their annual journey, wintering in the far south of Africa. Presumably, when the glaciers began receding north, swallows explored northward for new breeding sites, extending their range and probably their numbers. But the wintering grounds of central Africa would already have been taken by the central European swallows, so those that pioneered the north were thus also fated to explore the far south.

Familiar for their effortless
aerobatics over summer
meadows and lawns, little
barn swallows also perform
prodigious feats during migration. Some may travel as
far as 7,000 miles to winter
in Argentina.

In early March, the barn swallows begin to show up in Europe, swooping and glimmering over ponds and lakes where the season's first insects hatch. Along with bank swallows, they are the first of the aerial feeders to show up. Next come the house martins, birds that typically fly higher than the swallows in their quest for insect food. By the time they arrive some two weeks after the swallows, the air is yet warmer and the insects can rise higher. Even later come the most aerial of all "land" birds—the high-flying swifts, birds that in fact never deliberately alight on the ground and typically forage even higher than the martins. As with the several kinds of warblers foraging on a single tree, the separation of foraging styles of these aerial feeders plays a role in the metronomic business of migration.

Along with many other birds, such as terns and shorebirds, these aerial feeders are what can be called archetypal migrants. Their breeding grounds and wintering grounds are completely separate. Such a bird is the American golden plover, and so is its smaller western counterpart, the lesser or Pacific golden plover. The American golden plover breeds across the northernmost fringe of North America westward into Alaska, where the Pacific subspecies takes over, breeding westward from there halfway across Asia. Throughout the summer, the plover feeds on insects along the grassy coasts, on the tundra, and on ponds, but such a life is impossible once the season heads into the days of darkness and ice, and the only other similar

habitat for the American plovers is on the pampas of eastern Argentina. So, with the onset of fall, they stream southeastward, assembling in Newfoundland and Nova Scotia. From there they fly straight south across 2,300 miles of Atlantic Ocean, then make their way through Brazil and Uruguay to the pampas. All in all, it is a trip of some 7,000 miles. More extraordinary, perhaps, the return trip is mostly overland, east of the Andes into Central America, then across the Gulf of Mexico and up the Mississippi, onward to the Canadian Arctic. And even more extraordinary than this looped course—which requires knowledge of two routes—is that the newly fledged plovers do not take the risky route across the Atlantic but instead, leaving later than the adults, make their first southerly migration along the route adults use to go north—the overland route. The young plovers thus inherit the tendency to follow one route south as juveniles and later switch routes as adults.

At the same time, the Pacific golden plover simply heads south over the land mass of Asia or over the Pacific Ocean, as the case may be, wintering in the Australasian region and on oceanic islands from Hawaii to New Zealand. The Pacific migration raises another question: the chances of fetching up on a pinpoint island must be very low unless the birds have some extraordinary powers of navigation. The answer lies in part with Aristotle's observation about migrating animals being fat. Golden plovers trapped on Wake Island in the northwest Pacific in autumn were found to have still enough extra fat reserves to keep flying another 4,000 miles south. Similarly, plovers found headed northward on Wake Island in the spring had ample reserves to make it to the Aleutians.

There is evidence that the change in length of day triggers a hormonal reaction in some birds that, among other things, alters their metabolism in such a way that they begin to store fat. This may occur in particular in those birds that will spend the winter in the cold, or those that will make prodigious migratory flights. Much of this fat is deposited next to the flight muscles, which draw on it as a marathoner will swig a high-energy drink. The bobolink, which breeds in damp pastures from Nebraska to the East Coast, switches its diet in the fall from insects to seeds and then

A downy day-old American golden plover chick glows in an Alaskan tundra morning. If it survives, the chick will spend the winter thousands of miles away in South America.

The American golden plover flies an elliptical route during migration, heading out over the Atlantic Ocean in late summer from breeding grounds in the Alaskan and Canadian Arctic, arriving eventually at wintering areas as far south as Argentina and Uruguay. Returning in spring to nest, the birds fly up the center of North America.

erupts in great migratory flocks that cross the Caribbean, stopping off at Cuba and Jamaica before the 500-mile nonstop flight to South America. The bobolink accumulates so much fat for this trans-Caribbean journey that in Jamaica it is known as the butterbird.

The smaller the bird, the more remarkable seem its migratory exploits. The tiny ruby-throated hummingbird breeds as far north as Canada, and on its way back to Central America can make the seemingly impossible 500-mile flight across the Gulf of Mexico. Only a few of the tiny wood warblers of the New World remain in North America for the winter; the rest must make their way to Central and South America. Of these, the black-poll has the longest journey to make, some individuals breeding as far north as the timberline of Canada and Alaska. Though they are called the Arctic terns of the warblers, their migratory route is more like that of the American golden plover. Before fall, all the blackpolls head southeast, gathering inland in Massachusetts for about three weeks. Arriving there at less than a half-ounce in weight, they nearly double their weight, mostly in the form of fat. Then, of a cold evening, they leave with enough fat in reserve to fly nonstop for some 100 hours. Flying south at an altitude between 2,000 and 4,000 feet and at an average speed of 23 miles per hour, they can thus reach the coast of South America directly, or stop over in the Antilles to wait out bad weather.

Some migration is less spectacular. Many birds are partial migrants, performing what Robin Baker of the University of Manchester calls a seasonal shift in the center of gravity of the population. For example, in the summer, the European starling's range extends northward well into Canada as far as Hudson Bay and southward to approximately the U.S.-Mexico border. In the winter, starling country extends only into southern Canada but south far into Mexico. In the great region where the two ranges overlap, starlings are free to be relatively sedentary; at the extremes, they become migrants.

In certain situations, some members of a population may choose to migrate, others not. A string of harsh winters would tend to favor the migrants, while a warming trend would tend to favor the sedentary. In any event, true archetypal migration, as with

Bobolinks such as the singing male above and red-winged and yellow-headed blackbirds, right, sometimes flock in enormous numbers, hence their grouping as "troupial" birds (from the verb, to troupe, or to travel in groups). Bobolinks winter in South America; most red-wings and yellow-headed blackbirds retreat to the southern United States and Mexico.

swifts, can be seen as one end of a continuum of arrangements, at the other end of which is the truly sedentary species, such as the house sparrow, whose breeding and wintering grounds are identical and encompass only a few square miles. In partial migration it may be that, in balancing the risks of migration with the risks of staying put, nature, as Baker says, "is undecided."

For surely migration is a great risk. Most birds that stray into utterly unsuitable habitats—the wrong continent, for example—are migrants, blown off course and more often than not doomed. Many simply must fail to complete the long journey and fall by the wayside. And flying a long way puts one at risk of being preyed on. It is said that migration is such an urgent, single-minded activity that a predator (or a hunter) can pick off a bird from the flock without the others paying much if any attention. Errors in navigation, especially over large expanses of water, can be lethal.

But, with all the risks involved, if migration were not worth it, natural selection would have weeded out any bird with such a tendency. And the manner in which a species migrates can minimize its risks. Blackbirds and finches migrate along their relatively short routes by flying just above the trees, near cover. Most small land birds that migrate to and from the tropics over long distances do their traveling at night. This makes them invisible to most predators and also gives them daylight hours in which to settle down and forage along the way. During migration time, the night sky will be filled with birds calling to one another, probably a means of letting each other know where they are, to aid in staying together and also perhaps to avoid midair collisions. So much of bird migration takes place at night, in fact, that for most of human history we missed it altogether. (Scientists have been able to track night migrants only since the invention of radar: early radar operators kept seeing inexplicable "angels" on their screens. It gradually dawned on them that these angels conformed to the probable speed and direction of migrating birds. Since then, radar has become a valuable instrument in migration studies— though not a perfect one. It is difficult to tell one species from another when they appear as blips on a radar screen.)

175

Strong fliers among the smaller birds can risk flying by day—notably the aerial feeders, which are fast enough to be relatively immune to predation and, unlike others, can feed while on the move. The great soaring birds, making use of columns of rising warm air to migrate almost effortlessly, must migrate over land and by day since such thermals don't occur over the water or at night. In much of Europe the white stork is a beloved migrant, considered to be good luck, and many Europeans encourage these birds to breed on their roofs. After the breeding season, the storks head for Africa by two different routes. There is an invisible dividing line that, for the white stork, lies north-south through the very center of the continent. The storks to the west of it head for Gibraltar; those east of it head for the Bosphorus—many of them thus adding considerable distance to their routes but minimizing the distance they must fly over thermal-free water. Other birds that don't depend on gliding and soaring will fly the shorter route straight across the Mediterranean. Some birds—seabirds, shorebirds, geese, and ducks—fly both day and night. All strong fliers, they usually have a long way to go, often with nonstop legs that take more than 24 hours.

Most of the small night migrants accomplish their journeys between 2,000 and 3,000 feet in altitude; shorebirds often climb to 20,000. Geese and some large raptors will

Radar tracking of migration below, reveals that millions of songbirds and others ride strong northwest winds far out into the Atlantic beyond Bermuda before picking up northeast trade winds that blow them into the Caribbean Islands. The average nonstop time of flight for such tiny migrants as warblers is between 80 and 90 hours. Such flights probably represent the greatest feats of sustained effort known. Believing that white storks bring good luck, townspeople in villages such as this one in France's Alsace maintain nests for storks returning from wintering grounds in Africa.

approach 30,000 feet, the altitude reached by the bar-headed goose, which migrates regularly across the high peaks of the Himalayas. (The absolute altitude record for birds is that of an African vulture called Rüppell's griffon. It died in a collision with an airplane at 37,000 feet, and its feathers later were identified at the Smithsonian.)

Speed of migration varies enormously, as one would expect, but much of bird migration is accomplished at rates that are astonishing. The blackpoll warbler may make about 30 miles a day northward through the United States, but, in a final rush to reach its northernmost region, it moves at an average of 200 miles a day. American golden plovers make the 2,300-mile trip from Nova Scotia to South America in two days, averaging 50 miles an hour.

As astonishing as such distances and speeds are, what is more remarkable is that migration can occur at all. How do birds know when it is time to leave? They often do so before there is any sign that the seasonal party is over. How do they know where to go? Many migrants are extremely loyal, returning to the same locale each year, sometimes even the same nest. A purple martin may return to the same nesting box for its entire life. How much of this is instinct, how much learned in life? Such questions have puzzled people for centuries, and ornithologists recently have begun to find a variety of answers.

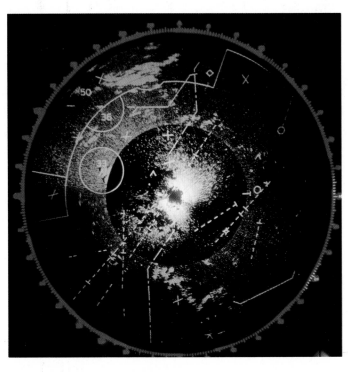

The thistleseed-loving American goldfinch, above, will travel in small flocks to winter grounds across the southern United States and northern Mexico. The insect-eating northern parula, right, of our eastern summer forests, may winter farther down in Central America and the Caribbean.

Most birds have a home range, an area where as adults they carry out most if not all their activities, but they tend to be familiar with a far larger area. As noted, many birds are partial migrants and have essentially two home ranges—breeding and wintering—within their larger familiar area. The two home ranges may overlap or be separate or—in the case of long-distance migrants—very far apart. But the two far-off ranges of the migrant are connected by familiar territory: the migration route. How does this familiarity come about?

Young birds, between the time they fledge and the time they settle down to breed, tend to be restless (like other young vertebrates, including human ones) and roam about, as in the dispersal of young rails—in essence, exploring. By means of experiments with caged birds and those otherwise cut off from their natural surroundings, it has been learned that these birds are restless at the same seasons as their counterparts in the wild, the young more so than adults, the migrants more so in spring and autumn; and, the longer their typical migration in nature, the more restless they are. This restlessness—and its degree and timing—is inherited, along with a preferred direction. Generally, a migrant bird prefers the direction of the equator in autumn and

the nearest pole in spring. That much at least is inherited, or instinctive. A bird that instinctively preferred the wrong direction for the time of year would more than likely perish; those that go in the right direction are more apt to survive to reproduce. It is likely that the rest is learned.

So a restless young bird, impelled by the onset of autumn to head off in its preferred direction, pausing along the way, being blown a bit off course by crosswinds, doubling back, but generally headed the right way, is extending its familiar area. Along the way, it may and probably does internalize a great deal of information that makes the journey far more straightforward the second time. In many instances, the young bird migrates in the company of adults, making the necessary learning all the more simple. But there are many instances where the young birds leave before or after the adults and still make the trip. At one extreme is the shining bronze-cuckoo, which is reared in southern Australia and Tasmania, migrating in late March (its autumn) northward to New Guinea and the other islands along that latitude. Like many Old World cuckoos, this one is parasitic: it lays its eggs in the nests of other species. A young one has no parent to teach it where to go when the time comes to leave, only an

Ancestor of most domestic ducks, adaptable to human presence, the mallard is the most common wild duck of many temperate regions of the world. It nests in much of North America and may winter as far north as the warmer areas of Alaska and Canada, all the way down to the West Indies and Mexico.

HAWKS ALONG THE GOSHUTES

Raptor migrations are among the most stirring spectacles in nature. Few fail to thrill at the sight of thousands of hawks drifting south on a strong northwest breeze over Hawk Mountain, Pennsylvania, or Cape May, New Jersey. Such raptor-watching vantage points are rare in the West. One is 7,600 feet high in the Goshute Mountains of northeastern Nevada. Here, along one of the largest western raptor flyways, the Western Foundation for Raptor Conservation conducts annual trapping, banding, and observation programs to monitor movements of the 20 or so species of eagles, vultures, hawks, and falcons that use the flyway.

Opposite left, staff members Jim Daly and Fred Tilly identify and count passing raptors. Opposite top, biologist Jim Zook removes a Cooper's hawk from a net, and, opposite above, records data in a processing blind. Above, biologist Jennifer DeLeon holds an immature golden eagle before releasing it to continue its southbound journey. Right, project founder and leader Steve Hoffman with a marsh hawk, or northern harrier. As a late-summer rain pelts the distant desert, Fred Tilly enters much-needed data on raptor movements in a field notebook.

inherited preference for a compass direction.

On the other hand, many geese spend their entire first year with their parents, going with them on the annual migration to and from the wintering grounds. It is only after that that they begin their own restless exploratory behavior and, as a result, may in their second year find another route to a different wintering ground, which they tend to follow thereafter.

Experimental proof was added to field observation when a Dutch ornithologist, A.C. Perdeck, put himself in the place of an adventitious gale and "blew" some starlings off course during their southwestward migration from the Baltic area to wintering grounds in northern France and the British Isles. Collecting the birds midroute in The Hague, he took them some 400 miles off course and released them in Switzerland. Playing yet another trick on them, he let the adults in his flock go separately from the young ones. The young ones continued southwest into Spain, their inherited directional preference. The adults quickly corrected their course and proceeded *north*westward to their normal wintering areas.

Clearly the adults had learned something earlier about their destination: where it was with regard to other clues, other signposts of some sort, beyond their new experience, for presumably they had never before visited Switzerland. Beyond that, some of the young starlings not only returned that autumn to the place of their birth but also returned the following year in spring to the wintering grounds where they had fetched up accidentally the year before.

A host of experimentation began to shed light on the nature of bird migration and on what sets off migratory behavior in a bird. It turned out that the onset of such behavior is related to the annual growth and shrinkage of the sex organs. Barely present at all in the winter (a weight-saving tactic), these organs are swollen and ready when breeding season begins. It was found that while they were changing—either growing or shrinking—the birds were most restless. It was discovered that birds have an annual hormonal cycle that, even in the absence of environmental cues, triggers itself. This can be "tuned" by the environment—by such factors, for example, as the change in the amount of daylight—but

In a critical congruence of annual cycles, shorebirds and horseshoe crabs come together each May in Delaware Bay. When tides are high, more than a million horseshoe crabs lay their eggs on New Jersey and Delaware beaches. At the same time, shorebirds wing in from Central and South America to gorge on the eggs, a feast that refuels them for the remainder of their journey to Arctic breeding grounds. Above, semipalmated plovers; sanderlings; and western, least, and semipalmated sandpipers mingle on a beach in Peru before taking wing for the north. Left, red knots, dunlins, and ruddy turnstones join local laughing gulls and herring gulls to feed on horseshoe crab eggs at New Jersey's Reed's Beach. A ruddy turnstone, opposite above, digs for egg clusters at Port Mahon, Delaware.

Their familiar V-formations and haunting calls heard from aloft make Canada geese the very symbol of fall migration for many who live near the great waterfowl flyways of North America. These "honkers" cruise high above the ranges of south-central Alaska.

it is basically self-regulating. As tyrannical and fine-tuned as this biological clock may be, it is not all-powerful. Few birds will undertake migration if the conditions are not right: they wait out bad weather and take the next appropriate weather front.

What of navigation? Experiments, again with starlings, have suggested that the sun plays a role. Starlings were put in enclosures from which they could see nothing but the sky. At the proper season, when they should have been migrating southwestward, they tended to move restlessly about at the southwestern side of their enclosures. They could see no landmarks. When mirrors were used to change the angle at which the birds perceived the passage of the sun, the birds made equivalent changes in their directionality. Somehow they were making judgments from the sun and therefore also had to have been affected by the changing angle of the sun throughout the daylight hours.

But what then of birds that migrate at night, even on inky-black nights with no moon? Similar experiments were undertaken with birds that could see nothing but the stars as represented by planetariums. It became evident that the patterns of the stars were as effective as the sun as navigational guideposts. For humans, the difficult business of navigating by the stars is made simpler by the fact that the North Star remains in a fixed position while the others wheel around it. But planetarium experiments with indigo buntings by Stephen Emlen of Cornell University eliminated the North Star as well as the associated Big Dipper and even the entire Milky Way, and the birds still knew their proper position in relation to the remaining firmament. And what of birds that migrate during days when overcast conditions obscure the position of the sun? No problem, evidently: they are able to read the polarized patterns of light caused by diffraction. Indeed, it has been found that a night migrant may be able to read the polarized light just before sunset on a cloudy day and use that to orient itself for the nighttime journey, although clouds continue to obscure the stars.

Just how so diminutive an organ as the much-maligned bird brain is capable of programming into itself such changing environmental information as is garnered on its maiden voyages is beyond our present under-

The eastern phoebe is one of a few North American flycatchers that do not return in winter to their ancestral homelands in the tropics of Central and South America. The phoebes and other flycatchers evolved and flourished in South America; only when the Isthmus of Panama rose did they emigrate north.

standing, but it surely deserves the respect of a species that requires a printed map to find its way around a shopping mall. And there is more to it than astronomy. Of course, landmarks are important. A mountain range that one kept to one's left on the way south is relatively easy to recall, even to keep to the right on the way north. Often even the smallest oceanic island will have a large cloud over it like a great pennant, visible from huge distances when one is flying at 5,000 feet or more. One need only be within an arc of several hundred miles to find it. There is also evidence that pigeons, at least, can use even their poor sense of smell as a navigational aid, and it has been shown that a number of animals, including birds and whales, can sense the patterns of the Earth's magnetic field. Several birds have been found to contain in the forward part of their heads a tiny string of magnetite molecules; as a change in the magnetic field puts torque on this tiny chain, the birds may somehow sense it. How much more delicate a sensation would a molecular tickle be than the subcutaneous itch brought about by a small wiggle of a single filoplume. (There is some evidence that even humans can respond, however unconsciously, to the Earth's magnetic fields, but no one yet has found any operative magnetic gauge in us.)

Beyond all that, it has been shown that certain features of the globe, such as mountain chains, emit sounds at extremely low frequencies called infrasound, with slightly different sound signatures for each feature. It is known that pigeons can sense these sounds, perhaps yet another potential source of data for the mental map a bird builds up as reference for the repetition of its annual treks across the planet.

Migration evolved independently among different species or groups of birds, so it is reasonable to assume that different groups of birds use different bits of environmental data, different senses, different techniques—or, more to the point, different arrays of all these—as the means to memorize their routes, or, in a sense, to canalize and refine a successful route out of the exploration that results from an instinctive urge to head off in a particular direction. While scientists still can only imagine what array of cues and senses a given species relies upon for its successful

migration, the ultimate question of success in the migratory life boils down to the talents of the individual bird. For now, while we can glimpse the outlines of bird migration (as John Hay, bound to Cape Cod, could glimpse only a portion of the terns' annual trek and had to imagine their actual journey through the weather), it continues, in its details, to confound us and will do so until, and perhaps even after, we have figured out how to climb inside the head of an individual bird and accompany it on its incredible journey.

We are hampered by our own natural anthropocentrism. Ultimately we can understand only what our particularly configured senses and brains and technology will permit. A bird's universe may finally be beyond our grasp. Another (avoidable) barrier is that we tend toward nationalism, or at least regionalism. We think of arriving migrants as somehow "ours." Our warblers. After all, they breed here—their most important function—so they are ours.

Migratory birds don't make such distinctions, of course, and they can confound even the rule about breeding grounds. The wheatear, a dapper little thrush that has taken to open country, is one of the planet's great migrants, wintering—all of them—in the arid lands of sub-Saharan Africa. But over the millennia they have extended their breeding range northward through Europe, across Siberia to northern Alaska and western Canada. At the same time they have extended across the stormiest of seas from the British Isles to Iceland, on to Greenland and again to Canada. Now their two breeding ranges in Canada are separated by a mere 500 miles. All things being equal, they probably one day will breed all the way around the northern tier of the globe—anybody's birds in breeding season, but they all return by traditional routes to winter in Africa. Who is to claim the wheatear, then, some of which are estimated to spend two-thirds of each year in transit, traveling their routes back and forth, touching the lives of people in dozens of countries?

The answer is twofold: no one and everyone along its path. The great streamings of birds up and down the planet are some of the most precise choreography in nature, and to participate in them, even as a momentary observer, is to rise for a moment at least beyond the confines of one's own imagination, to imagine senses beyond ours . . . and to wonder about our conventional responsibilities.

A year is not an arbitrary construct, though our calendar year is and thus needs occasional fine adjustment. A natural year is defined as the revolution of the Earth around the sun, and any marked annual cycle on Earth must originate from this fundamental phenomenon. The annual cycle of hormones in a migrant bird derives of necessity from the sun and its ancient workings with the Earth, no matter how independently the bird may appear to function.

But there are other cycles, the next most evident being that of the moon. Offshore near the edge of the continental shelf in the Atlantic, creatures whose direct ancestry is far older than that of any bird emerge from the muck in spring, tipped off by the moon, and begin to crawl across the ocean floor toward land. These are horseshoe crabs—in fact, arthropods, unchanged in form for millions and millions of years. Feeding on hapless marine worms on the bottom, the horseshoe crabs crawl shoreward, the males and then the larger females arriving with uncanny precision at the time of the spring high tide in late May. As the females begin to leave the surf, the males vie to attach themselves to a female and thus be able to fertilize her eggs. Once attached, the pair inches up the beach, there to bury thousands of olive-green-to-brown, jelly-like eggs in the sand. Many crabs get stranded, giving the beach the next day the appearance of an abandoned World War I battlefield, helmets lying here and there, casualties in the urgent business of reproduction, as directed by the capricious moon and its cycles that drive the tides. For historic biological reasons unknown, the chief concentration of horseshoe crab reproduction along the Atlantic beach is in Delaware Bay. A lesser concentration is in the area of Cape Cod. But the crabs have been striving toward these beaches each year for millions of years, even before so great an ocean separated the Old World from the New. Long after these ancestral patterns had become fixed in this most conservative of creatures, birds evolved, among them shorebirds.

Each year, long before the horseshoe crabs hit the beach, thousands of birds called red knots and millions of other shorebirds

Normally aggressive, an eastern kingbird, above, lies passively in a bird bander's gentle but firm grip. Top, also known as tyrant flycatchers for their fearless defense of nesting territory, eastern kingbirds nest over much of North America, winter in South America.

Uxorious male rose-breasted grosbeaks carol sweetly from their nests in northern deciduous forests, but return to Central and South America in winter. Opposite, a northern parula delivers a fat cankerworm to its nest. The tiny warblers often build their nests in Spanish moss or old-man's-beard.

wintering in South America—ruddy turnstones, sanderlings, semipalmated sandpipers, dunlins—experience their big hormonal changes. And just about the time the female horseshoe crabs have performed their duty on the beach, the knots and their cohorts arrive on a tight schedule on the way north to the tundra, where before long the insects will bloom in great clouds.

It takes about two weeks for the horseshoe crab eggs to develop through several stages into what look like small trilobites and, with the help of the neap tide, swim on down the beach to the sea and a perilous journey to adulthood. Vast numbers of them never make it to the sea at all: the knots and the other shorebirds probe the high-tide line with their bills and devour, each one, more than 100,000 eggs in the two weeks they remain in the area, nearly doubling their own weight in preparation for the long leg to the tundra.

Timing is everything. If the knots arrive at their high Arctic breeding grounds too late, their young hatchlings (which feed themselves) will miss the flushes of insects in early July, and the species' population will be jeopardized. And so the knots' arrival in Delaware is timed to the horseshoe crabs' arrival, and the breeding grounds of horseshoe crabs recently have been perceived as a necessary oasis along the route of these shorebirds. Among shorebirds, only two that spend time in North America—the piping plover and the Eskimo curlew—are considered endangered. Red knots are not on the list, there being uncounted thousands of them. But, as coastal land development increases and larger numbers of people migrate to the beaches, ancient breeding grounds are endangered, and so then is the life cycle of knots, sanderlings, ruddy turnstones, and others.

Migrants are not just passers-through, like so many tourists. Nor are they vacationers in the warm wintering grounds. They are what might be called bicultural—organized members of two homes as well as the routes in between. Indeed, more often than not, the migratory birds we in the Northern Hemisphere are accustomed to as "ours" spend more of the year in their wintering grounds and might more properly be called "theirs" if such distinctions are to be made. The implications of this became crystal clear when the Smithsonian Institution hosted a conference at the National Zoo's research center in Front Royal, Virginia, in 1977.

There, some 60 tropical biologists shared their recent findings about the finely tuned adaptations of migrant species to tropical niches, some of which are quite different from those the birds inhabit in their breeding grounds. John W. Fitzpatrick, now of the Field Museum of Natural History in Chicago, reported on the tyrant flycatchers, that highly successful group of suboscines (almost songbirds) that in the New World tropics have proliferated into some 375 species, of which 30 migrate into the United States and Canada to breed. Of these 30, all but the phoebes return to the tropics south of the United States to winter.

The tyrant flycatchers that breed in the north are mostly somber-colored birds that perch alone on the branches of trees, waiting for an insect to fly nearby. Then the bird makes a short sally out to catch it and returns to the perch to eat. One genus, the *Empidonax* flycatchers, consists of small, olive birds that look so much alike they defy field identification at the species level except by those expert in the fine differences of their songs. All flycatchers are aggressive when it comes to defending territories, but none is so pugnacious as the genus of kingbirds, of which the black-and-white eastern kingbird is perhaps the best known. Aptly named, kingbirds will brook no interference in their affairs; they will rush forth to attack a (far larger) crow that has come too close, or even larger birds, mobbing them to distraction, even landing on their backs in midflight to peck their heads.

What happens to these migrants when they return south? Do they find a paradise there, or a place overrun by year-round residents where competition is severe? Do they establish winter territories and defend them, or do they take up a nomadic way of life on the fringes of things, taking what they can get? What do the more than 300 resident flycatcher species make of them? The traditional view was that they (and most other migrants) spend the winter filling in the ecological cracks left unfilled by residents. But in fact the situation is more complex.

The flycatchers that breed in the western part of North America generally inhabit relatively dry pine/oak forests. In autumn, they

stream southward through similar if more arid habitat along the mountains of Mexico, fetching up in Mexico and Guatemala. Meanwhile, most of the flycatchers that breed in the eastern part of North America do so in more humid broad-leaved woods, and such habitat is not to be found in abundance until one reaches Costa Rica, Panama, and places farther south in South America. Most of the eastern species get to these wintering grounds by flying across the Gulf of Mexico, some of them going as far south as Amazonia. The two groups, eastern and western, overlap slightly in southern Mexico. In studies there made of 15 *Empidonax* flycatchers—eight migrant species and seven resident species—it was found that the western migrants tended to winter in higher, drier areas, the eastern ones in lower, moister ones. And there, for eight months of the year, the migrants established definite territories, while the less populous year-round residents lived in marginal areas. A similar study of warblers in Central America and the Caribbean revealed the same phenomenon: the migrants form stable communities there as well.

The situation is different for the flycatchers that winter in South America. The eastern kingbird is one of these, feisty to a fault in breeding season when it lives in isolated pairs. In migration and on its wintering grounds in the Amazon, it changes both its diet and its personality. Even before it leaves the north it switches from insects to fruit (sassafras, a northern representative of a tropical plant group known for its highly nutritious fruit) and becomes gregarious and subordinate. The birds travel in large flocks, descending on fruiting trees to be harassed by local flycatchers. Instead of fighting back, they take refuge in numbers: a bird under attack simply melts into the middle of the flock.

In a sense, the kingbirds' nonbreeding foraging strategy is convergent on that of the cedar waxwings: like them, the kingbirds become experts each year at exploiting superabundant but widely dispersed fruit. The white tip of the tail, like the yellow tip of the cedar waxwing's tail, is believed to be a mechanism to keep the wintering kingbirds in tight flocks. Most resident species, on the other hand, have territories to defend and simply cannot stay in flocks. The eastern kingbirds, in fact, don't winter in any one place but

instead follow the ripening fruit with the tropical dry season—in particular the fruit of one tree known as *Didymopanax morototoni*. Its fruit ripens earliest in South America, and the kingbirds track it northward into Central America before returning to North America. One gets the uncanny sense that the eastern kingbirds have somehow played into the hands of the *Didymopanax* trees, which need some bird or another to disperse their seeds. Fruiting ever northward in their range, the trees give the kingbirds a kind of send-off to the Northern Temperate Zone, a place freer of predators such as snakes and a place that offers the kingbirds bounteous blooms of insects (and the chance to be flycatchers for a while) by which to sustain themselves and rear their young.

Another voracious insect-eater when in the north is the orchard oriole, related as are all orioles to blackbirds, grackles, and cowbirds, but somehow, to our minds, a more elegant and sweeter bird, not evidently given to such unseemly, edgy swarms as their fellow troupials. But, in the tropics during the winter, the orchard oriole swarms indeed and becomes a bit nasty, especially the older males. A chief focus of the attention of orchard oriole flocks in the south is a flowering tree, *Erythrina fusca*, the flowers of which typically are folded up on themselves and hard to open. Some 13 bird species will feed on the rich nectar of these flowers, all but the orchard oriole piercing the petal with their beaks. The oriole, on the other hand—in this case the rusty-colored adult male, which chases away any orchard oriole females or youthful males—has the trick of springing the *Erythrina* flowers open. Then the flowers' stamens and styles hit the bird's throat and upper chest, sprinkling him with pollen.

Thus, the male orchard oriole is a primary pollinator for this tree, but it goes even further than that. A male orchard oriole will tolerate the presence of another only up to a certain distance; any closer, a squabble may occur. It turns out that the flower of the *Erythrina* tree, once opened *and drained* of nectar by an orchard oriole, displays the same rusty color as the male, probably providing an aversive signal to another male and sending him off to another flower if not another tree. It seems evident that the tree and the oriole co-evolved, the color and complexity of the flower in a sense bringing about the behavior of the bird. In any event, migratory birds such as the orchard oriole are clearly tropical as well as northern birds, superbly adapted to life in both regions.

In an entirely different geographical situation—the high mountain passes of the Himalayas in the remote country of Bhutan— S. Dillon Ripley, then Secretary of the Smithsonian, noted in the early '70s yet another phenomenon in migratory birds—one he called "competitive exclusion." In these high regions, 16,000 feet and up, the great soarers and fliers such as hawks and cranes fly south, taking advantage of the warmer air currents rising off ridges to soar almost effortlessly on the updrafts. On the ground, autumnal blooms of insects bring forth moths, butterflies, bees, beetles, and ants, and scrubby bushes are loaded with berries. Great flocks of hungry migrant finches, thrushes, and chats move low to the ground; so many thrushes will land on a berry bush that its branches may break. "Migration was all around us," Ripley wrote, but "where were the resident species?" In due course, he found them, a few representatives of some 30 resident species, "but they [were] few in number, nothing like the vast flocks of migrant rosefinches or mountain finches." The residents also tend to produce small broods. The reason, he theorized, is that there are so many voracious migrants each spring and fall— driven, single-minded hordes—that they consume most of the available food all at once, and "the locals cannot compete."

If we sit back for a while from our studies and our great compilations of statistical data on migrant birds, we realize how small, how free of artificial boundaries the world is to them. We in North America may make, and have made, efforts to preserve the breeding habitats of "our" birds, although there has been increasing fragmentation of their breeding grounds here, even elimination locally. But they also "belong" to Central and South America, and the migrants, along with the resident birds, play out a fully integrated ecological existence that differs radically or subtly from their northern existence. Without knowing the intimate details of their bicultural existence, how they use and sustain habitats here and there, we can at best be poor stewards. 🐦

The American robin's cheery voice often brightens northern woods before winter has retreated. Its scientific name, Turdus migratorius—the migratory thrush—reflects the robin's prominence as an early, and noticeable, arrival.

COMMUNICATION

Arguably, the most pleasant sound in the world is made by a thrush singing from the woods at the end of the day. A Connecticut naturalist, Hamilton Gibson, once took note of the fact that the thrush's liquid song is often compared to the music of a flute, and he elaborated the simile. The wood thrush is like a wooden flute, he said, but the hermit thrush, with its higher pitch and rapid trill of rising and falling notes, is like a *silver* flute. A romantic hearing any thrush's vespers might well imagine it is the woodland god Pan playing his pipes, a kind of sigh for a love lost, a nymph who turned him down—and indeed the panpipes were named for a nymph who escaped Pan's ardor by turning into a patch of musical reeds. She was called Syrinx, and that is the name ornithologists, with a fine poetic propriety, have given to the voice box of the birds.

Birds spend a good deal of time communicating among themselves, and they have many ways of doing so, many of them nonvocal. What we call body language is universal

Preceding pages: Paddling furiously in a rushing display, three western grebes rise out of the water in Medicine Lake National Wildlife Refuge in northeastern Montana. The spectacular courtship displays of these grebes help them identify members of the opposite sex.

Of the song of the wood thrush, above, Thoreau wrote: "Whenever a man hears it he is young, and Nature is in her spring; whenever he hears it, it is a new world and a free country, and the gates of heaven are not shut against him."

among birds and has long been under scientific scrutiny. An example is the eagle communicating his hunger and piratical intentions by fluffing his neck and head feathers. Male mockingbirds, meeting at the common edge of their territories, will engage in a dance, hopping sideways back and forth like two boxers sparring. Courtship displays (which apparently serve to alter aggressive feelings into a psychological state suited to forming at least a temporary bond and mating) are probably more numerous than species of birds. Many of them involve elaborate and stylized choreography, such as that of the whooping crane, in which the male bows to the female, leaps up with wings flapping, and then jumps up and down. A pair of western grebes will race across the water side by side, necks bent downward, wings out, propelled entirely and at great speed by their feet. Avocets by the dozen dance in circles, in near perfect synchrony, keeping the beat, as it were, by means of particular head movements—a kind of sign language.

For some birds, the ritual is accomplished in the air. Nighthawks dive downward, pulling up just above the ground and creating a loud boom from the air acting on their feathers. The male peregrine falcon executes a series of dives often up to a mile long, during which it somersaults and performs barrel rolls at great speed. Many woodpeckers signal their nuptial intentions by drumming on a tree. During the breeding season, the esophagus of the sage grouse becomes capable of distending up to 25 times its normal size. The bird fills this enlarged passageway with air, contracts its neck muscles, and emits what has been described as a soft, hollow "plopping" sound.

Most communication among birds, however, is vocal, and the organ that makes this possible is the syrinx, unique to birds. In humans and other mammals, the voice derives from the larynx, which is located in the upper part of the windpipe: exhaled air moves the vocal chords, which produce the various sounds. Birds have a larynx, but it has no vocal chords and serves chiefly to regulate the amount of air coming into the windpipe, or trachea.

The avian syrinx is located at the other end of the trachea, where it separates into two pipes called bronchi that lead into the lungs—

closer amidships, conferring aerodynamic advantage. In some Central and South American songbirds, the syrinx is confined to the lower end of the trachea; cuckoos and a few other birds, including some owls, have two syringes located in the bronchi. But for most birds the vocal organ is to be found at the juncture of the trachea and the bronchi. The actual position doesn't seem to make much difference in vocal ability: what is important in this regard is the muscles that surround the syringeal membranes, which act as sound producers.

While, for example, the turkey vulture has no syrinx at all, ostriches and some storks have a syrinx but no syringeal muscles, and they too are limited to hisses and grunts. A pigeon has but one pair of syringeal muscles, while mockingbirds, crows, and other virtuosos, including starlings, have between seven and nine pairs. As air passes from the bronchi to the trachea, it sets the syringeal membranes to vibrating. And, much as the strings of a musical instrument vibrate at varying pitches according to their length, the variety of bird sounds is produced by control of the tension of the membranes by the associated muscles. There is evidence that the rest of the vocal tract plays a role as a resonator, and the typical movements of the head and neck of a singing bird probably are associated with these fine adjustments.

In any event, outfitted with their unique voice box, birds have developed the art of vocal communication to a level exceeded only by humankind. One need go no farther than a semirural backyard to be astonished by the number and variety of songs and calls, often rising to near cacophony, all presumably conveying information of one sort or another. What is all the noise about? As British ornithologist Edward Armstrong wrote a quarter of a century ago, "Difficulties throng the path of anyone who seeks to tabulate the various kinds of information conveyed by bird utterances."

One of the difficulties for a long time was the fact that humans simply cannot hear bird sounds the same way a bird does. But with the invention in midcentury of electronic devices that can convert sounds into two-dimensional renderings on paper, called spectrograms, the sounds of birds (and any other sound, for that matter) now can be "seen" in exhaustive detail and analyzed. One of the first findings from such recordings was that most bird utterances contain many more notes and much greater variation in pitch than the human ear can detect: birds hear a greater range of sounds and with faster discrimination than we can, just as they can appreciate a large visual field faster than we.

Another difficulty has been that people tend to think about communication in human terms, chiefly as data or ideas transmitted by abstractions called words (or numbers) put together in an inherently logical matrix called grammar. In human communication, the sound of a word, once learned, is utterly irrelevant. "Oiseau" in French and "tsiro" in the language of the Hopi Indians are quite different in sound structure, and both differ from the English "bird." It is the abstract nature of human language and thought that puts human destiny partly outside normal biological evolution, in the sense that for us there are many other powerful factors involved besides natural selection.

But birds and other creatures are imprisoned (as are we, ultimately) by natural selective pressures, so understanding bird communication means that we must understand it as sheer biology. And one of the tenets of biology is that the physical structure of an organ or a behavior is related to its function. In the 1970s, scientists used the spectrograph and the resulting spectrograms to study the similarity of sounds in birds and mammals. Before long they had arrived at a theory of animal communication called the motivation-structural rules model.

When a dog is glad to see you, or when it is fearful, it emits high-pitched sounds we call whines, which on a spectrogram show up as a thin line. The more fearful or happy the dog, the more the line tends to rise, that is, the higher-pitched the sound. On the opposite end, an aggressive, angry dog makes a low, harsh, atonal sound we call a growl, which at its angriest shows up as a broad horizontal band. In between is the bark, a sign of interest—neither fear nor aggression—which shows up as a chevron, a line that goes up and then down.

On paper, birds have the same system. The attentive chipping of a wren, for example, looks like the bark of a dog (and if you slow down a recording of a wren's chip, it sounds

PLATE I.

A plate from A History of North American Birds *(1874), by Spencer Baird, Thomas Brewer, and Robert Ridgway, features the similar-looking, sweet-voiced thrushes of North America, including the wood thrush, veery, hermit thrush, and Swainson's thrush.*

like a dog's bark as well). A nesting catbird will growl at a starling that approaches too near. A sea gull under attack or the threat of attack by a larger gull will emit a high-pitched alarm call (which, as we have seen, some gulls will use to confound their associates). Through such sound symbols, an animal can express its state of mind on a number of important matters. A low, growling sound may have the effect of making the (unseen) growler seem larger, more threatening. A higher-pitched sound suggests a nonthreatening smallness. By such messages, actual combat often can be avoided, saving everyone a lot of energy.

There are situations in which an animal is afflicted by more than one motivational state at a time—both hostility and fear, for example. Both feelings may be expressed, perhaps, in a kind of shriek that shows up on a spectrogram as a broad, harsh sound rising in frequency. The hissing of a goose is thus explained, though tangentially. A nesting goose confronted by a fox tends to want to flee for its life but at the same time defend its young. A vocal sound probably would involuntarily include both states of mind, signaling the fox that though the goose was hostile it was also scared half to death, and thus giving the fox a psychological advantage. Over eons of goose evolution, natural selection has favored those geese that, in such a situation, withheld the

The dances and duets of cranes serve to strengthen the male-female pair bond, which in these birds lasts for life. With wings raised and graceful necks extended, a pair of red-crowned cranes, opposite, trumpets a loud, resonant unison call. Above, a male crowned crane in Kenya bows and turns in display for mate. Both birds may then leap into the air.

197

expression of emotion through the voice and emitted a nonvocal sound—a hiss—to accompany their threatening body language.

The motivation-structural rules model, once announced in 1977, seemed to have universal application—even to the elaborate languages of humans. Angry parents tend to lower the pitch of their voices when scolding a misbehaving child; high praise, on the other hand, and affection are generally delivered at a higher pitch. Researchers at the University of Rhode Island found that in 50 kinds of animals, ranging from shrews to elephants, this symbolic sound system was nearly universal. An exception was that, among some mammals, the sound for fear and the sound for appeasement differed more than the model predicted.

Stimulated by these findings, Edwin Gould of the Smithsonian's National Zoo conducted research on nocturnal animals and those that do not rely on sight as a primary means of communication. He found that with these animals the rate of repetition of a vocalization, in addition to pitch, is important in expressing motivational state. According to

A high-stepping blue-footed booby, above, shows off his bright blue feet during an elaborate courtship display on the Galápagos Islands. Royal albatross pair, right, engages in mutual preening or allopreening on Enderby Island in the South Pacific. The interloper displaying behind them may be a young male.

Gould, a baby mouse emits a constant pulsing noise. If it is touched, it increases the rate of pulsing, showing that it is more excited. Anyone who has had the experience of hand-rearing baby birds knows the increasing rate of screeches young birds produce, reaching a frantic locustlike crescendo that subsides only as the morsel of food reaches the gullet.

Thus, in a varying mixture of sound structure and rate of repetition, bird calls express important states of mind among members of one species and across species lines—even, evidently, between such distant groups as mammals and birds. The model explains differences in alarm calls that have long been perceived. A chipping sparrow on a high perch, for example, will emit "chip" notes if it sees a cat below (meaning "Attention!") but a high-pitched "zeeee" when a more dangerous hawk is seen overhead. There is physics involved here, as in everything. Sound travels as waves, and the longer the wavelength, the lower the sound. A bird determines the location of a sound source by virtue of the difference in time at which each ear picks up the wavelengths of sound. But,

once the wavelength is less than two times the distance between the hearer's ears (that is, once it is high-pitched enough), the information about location is blurred. A more fearful, high-pitched "zeeee" can be heard from farther off but obscures the position of the alarmist; a lower-pitched "chip" brings nearby neighbors to attention regarding a minor threat—a threat sufficiently less dangerous that it makes little difference if the threat knows where the alarmist is at the moment. Similarly, the call-to-arms of a kingbird intent on mobbing a predator is low-pitched, letting others know more accurately where the action is.

Researchers at the University of Missouri have suggested that in some cases the high-pitched alarm call may have the effect of ventriloquism on large predatory birds. Several years ago, Charles Brown and colleagues played a red-winged blackbird's alarm call over a loudspeaker to caged red-tailed hawks and horned owls. The predators would turn with considerable accuracy to face the direction of the call. But, in response to the robin's "seeet" of alarm, the predators would be off

The hollow, thumping sounds of a ruffed grouse, left, drumming atop a log, resound through a Virginia wood in early springtime. The drumming sound serves to attract potential mates and warn off rival males. A crow-sized pileated woodpecker, above, hammers its beak against a tree to send out a similar message.

Birds use threat displays to keep members of their own species from invading their territories and to drive off or discourage potential predators. A sun bittern in Central America, opposite top, spreads its wings and tail to startle an intruder away from its nest. Similarly, an alert rufous-fronted fantail, above, of Guam, acts to defend its nest and young. The fantail's displays proved useless against the inadvertently introduced brown tree snake, however, and today the species is extinct. Opposite bottom, a killdeer engages in its "broken-wing act" to divert the attention of a predator.

by as much as 84 degrees at first, and the more they turned their heads to zero in on the sound, the farther off the mark they got— up to 125 degrees off.

The high-pitched alarm evidently plays tricks with a design "flaw" in the avian ear. An air passage connects the two inner ears of birds: sound can go in one ear and out the other, thus hitting both sides of each eardrum. The higher-pitched call causes a change in phase on one side of the eardrum that cancels out the sound in that ear, creating an acoustical illusion whereby the predator thinks it is hearing the alarm from the side of its head opposite the source of the alarm. This is especially troublesome to an owl, whose head is twice as wide as the wavelength of the "seeet" call.

Any call, then, provides some information about location, either true or fallacious. Many paired birds constantly emit calls that keep each other in touch as they forage. Such a call says "here I am," but it also carries an implied question: "where are you?" The information may serve in the bonding process, but it is also probably a distance-adjusting device, keeping the two out of each other's immediate foraging area.

Birds sometimes utter calls when there is no listener, no "intent" to communicate anything. A prime example is the high shriek a bird emits when caught in the talons of a hawk. Ornithologists say that the bird doesn't intend to call for help. It is simply that, over the eons, crying out in such a situation has turned out to be the best behavior: the call may confuse the predator sometimes, or it may even alert a bigger predator. For example, there is an account of a backyard robin being attacked by a merlin. The cry of the robin evidently alerted a nearby red-tailed hawk, which swooped down on the merlin. In the ensuing confusion, the robin escaped minus a few feathers. Natural selection simply has favored such behavior on the part of the attacked, and it is elicited automatically.

Most bird calls are seen to be automatic responses to environmental circumstances— such as events—or to the bird's mental state at the time, or both. But true communication is a two-way street: a noise that elicits no response is simply noise. The calls of birds, however, do contain meanings that affect others. The mother ptarmigan's call sends her

young scattering automatically for cover. The mother quail's call brings her brood swiftly and automatically into line. (How many human mothers well might envy the quail.) So the calls of birds—calls of distress, of hunger, of alarm, of location, of food, of assembly— can in fact be considered a kind of language, which is defined as (1) a vocabulary of meaningful sounds and (2) a way to use them.

The most noted and most delightful vocal achievement of birds is, of course, their songs. Not all birds sing, not even all passerines (the perching birds, also conventionally called songbirds), while many nonsongbirds, such as swifts, hummingbirds, and woodpeckers, do sing. Birdsong has delighted humankind throughout our time on the planet, and it has perplexed ornithologists since the science of bird study began. Because birds seem to sing most in the nesting and breeding season, it was originally and romantically thought that the males were putting on a show for the females: birdsong, mostly a male affair, was love songs. It then became clear that nesting birds tend to be highly territorial. Perhaps the singing was to announce to others of the species that a particular plot was taken and they should stay away. There is truth in both propositions, but, as ornithologists have been able to listen in with electronic ears and also have listened more carefully in tropical regions as well as their own temperate-zone territories with "their" birds, the matter of birdsong has become far more complex, and more and more questions have popped up.

How did birdsong evolve in the first place? Why do small songbirds exert so much energy singing at first light when they are half-starved from a night of not eating? Why, as is common in tropical birds, do the females sing? Is birdsong automatic—that is, are birds compelled to sing their song via genetic programming alone or is it learned? What is to be made of mimics like the mockingbird?

The answers tend to vary from species to species, even from individual to individual bird. One truth appears to apply universally: birdsong, as opposed to their many call notes, is exclusively intraspecific communication. It is advertisements of species identity. No matter how expertly a mockingbird imitates the local cardinals, the cardinals pay it no heed except presumably to be aware that there is a

The distinctive songs of birds, such as the "drink-your-tea" refrain of the rufous-sided towhee, opposite, arise from their syrinx, a unique vocal organ named for a nymph who escaped the seductive music of the woodland god Pan, above.

mockingbird in the vicinity. A good bird-watcher doesn't need to see a thing to know what birds are nearby: the songs are prescriptive. In fact, among certain *Empidonax* flycatchers and some other birds, song is the best way to make a field identification.

Life, it could be argued, is a never-ending tension between conservative pattern and revolutionary change and, as the great Yale ecologist G. Evelyn Hutchinson said, an evolutionary play performed on an ecological stage. It is only in such terms that birdsong can be understood. To us, with our comparatively impaired hearing and our naturally human-centered tendency to think in our own terms, the songs of birds seem beautiful and we almost instinctively regard them with our aesthetic sense. Philosopher and ornithologist Charles Hartshorne suggested some years back that certain virtuoso singers among the birds probably have an aesthetic appreciation of their own song production and may sometimes sing for the sheer pleasure of it. Repetition is boredom at a certain level of intelligence, he said, while variation is interest, one of the elements of aesthetic appreciation. Is the mockingbird, singing through the night of a full moon with such apparent musical playfulness, entertaining itself? Such a proposition, while almost impossible to prove or disprove, is not the sort of thing that appeals to most ornithologists, who proceed on the assumption that life for a bird is difficult, energy-consuming, and dangerous. Singing must serve a survival function, just as do the extravagant feathers of the bird of paradise. Birds do not have the liberty, it is believed, to fool around like people in a pickup jam session inventing jazz. (On the other hand, it would be hard to prove that those musicians in New Orleans who evidently did invent jazz were not influenced by riffs of local mockingbirds.)

Song, like other bird utterances, originates in the syrinx, but another vital organ is involved, of course—the brain, the seat of the bird's nervous system. Mediated by a sea of hormones and peptides and other chemical substances, the brain switches the syrinx on and off and specifies the message and the structure of the sound. This is true in infancy—even in some cases before hatching, when a chicken, for example, will begin to vocalize, registering its voice in its mother's mind. That

Contorted in energetic song, which in this species is harsh and nasal, a yellow-headed blackbird, opposite, proclaims his territory from the top of a cattail. More pleasing to the human ear are the sweet, musical songs of the yellow warbler, top, and those of that master mimic and virtuoso of North America, the mockingbird, above.

this is purely instinctive programmed behavior like that of an automaton does not mean that some learning is not going on, for the brain must grow and develop the necessary neuronal network to be able to produce a cheep, much less a song. Brain growth is a fundamental kind of learning.

It has been shown in zebra finches, those cheery, noisy favorites in aviaries, that a particular part of the hyperstriatum (the birds' substitute for our extra mammalian layers of cortex) grows by 50 percent during the 70-day maturing period when, among other things, the young zebra finch perfects its song. During the same period, another part of the brain, located in an area called the neostriatum, diminishes by half. This suggests that the young zebra finch is born with a wide capacity for learning possible notes, but once it has learned its own species song it sloughs off nerve cells that would permit it to use notes it no longer needs. This theory is supported by the finding that a zebra finch raised by a different species will learn the other species' song and will ignore another zebra finch's song for the rest of its life. At the same time, the diminishing neurons of the neostriatum play some role in learning song since, if this part of the brain is damaged early in youth, the finch's subsequent repertoire is retarded. Moreover, once a finch learns its song it doesn't learn any others, rather in the way that human beings tend to find learning a foreign language relatively easy in childhood (all languages are foreign to a newborn, of course) but considerably more difficult after puberty.

On the other hand, there are many species of birds such as canaries, which, if reared in draconian experimental isolation, eventually will sing their species song anyway—it is evidently hard-wired into such birds' genes—though perhaps the rendition may not be as elegant as that of a young bird that has had the benefit of overhearing its elders. And of course there are the virtuosos, which learn their species song patterns and, long into adulthood, continue to invent small or great variations on the theme—some wrens and warblers, for example, and that avian Mozart, the mockingbird. It shouldn't be surprising that much of birdsong is learned through mimicry of one's own kind. That among some advanced singers there is a continuing

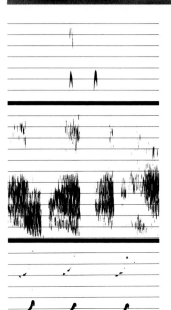

Symbols of the northern wilderness, common loons, above, warn intruders away from the chicks they are raising on a lake in Maine. While birdsong is species-specific, different calls can be understood across species lines. At left, spectrograms of Carolina wren vocalizations represent (from top) a chip or bark, a growl, and a whine. Above left, the gape of a young red-tailed hawk.

In an attempt to look and sound as fearsome—or at least as unafraid—as possible, a Canada goose uses hisses and outstretched wings to defend its eggs and itself against a potential predator, a skunk.

process of invention is not only a spectacular notion but, in some ways, the key to many questions about birdsong.

We must keep in mind that birdsong is, for the most part, long-distance communication, a device for sending important information over a large area, often to points beyond where the singer can be seen. And this brings us back to the realm of acoustics. A high-pitched song travels as short wavelengths, and an object such as a leaf or the branch of a tree or especially the trunk of a tree can cut it off. A low sound with its long wavelengths is better suited for getting around such obstacles. Thus the ovenbird and others such as the Kentucky warbler that tend to spend most of their time near the ground in woodlands have the lowest-pitched songs of the warblers, while a common yellowthroat, which prefers moist thickets and low trees, has a slightly higher song. The highest-pitched songs of all the warblers are from those such as blackpolls that sing from the tops of high trees where the song encounters little obstruction.

Most of this singing goes on during—as well as just before and just after—the breeding season and would appear to be closely associated with sex. Most familiar birds in North America follow this annual cycle, driven by a seasonal swelling of the gonads. For some reason that remains unclear, many songbirds experience a second, minor swelling of the sex organs in autumn, and this is accompanied by a renewed bout of singing.

Some birds stop singing once they have paired—these are often species of which the male has little to do with the rearing of young, such as hummingbirds. Other birds continue singing until the young have fledged and the need to defend a territory is past. Some, such as mockingbirds, sing throughout much of the year, even through the winter. While it is the male mockingbird who sings in the spring, at other times of the year both sexes sing, sometimes loudly, but often in what is called whisper song, a quieter, almost inward version of singing. It turns out that in winter mockingbirds continue to maintain territories—the female with one, the male with another—suggesting that the territorial function of song may be preeminent.

On the other hand it has been shown with European chiffchaffs, common Old World warblers named for the sound of their song, that the male song does make the female heartbeat grow faster, if not fonder. When mid-European chiffchaff females, rigged with electrodes, heard male songs, their heart rates rose as much as 12 percent. But if these same females heard songs from nonlocal males—those from Spain or the Canary Islands—they did not respond. Furthermore, chiffchaffs raised in isolation also responded to the local males' songs, suggesting that a genetic "scheme" of the song—their local variation or dialect—lies somewhere in their nervous system. Indeed, dialects are quite common among songbirds and others.

A number of tropical birds—shrikes, quail, rails, and wrens—perform duets. Describing the duet of the ovenbird (a funariid, not the New World warbler of the same common name), former Smithsonian Secretary Alexander Wetmore wrote: "One, presumably the male, with bill thrown up and wings drooped, gives vent to a series of shrieking, laughing calls, with distended, vibrating throat, and quivering wing tips. At about the middle of this strange song, its mate chimes in with shrill calls of a different pitch and the two continue in duet to terminate together."

Duetting occurs mainly in permanently paired species in which both sexes defend a joint territory year-round. Each pair member guards against others of the same sex; the female ignores a new male entering the territory, and vice versa. The song thus functions as a territorial defense mechanism in females in the same fashion as it does in males. (A kind of duetting may occur also in pair-bonded parrots to maintain contact during group foraging parties.)

One of the more difficult things to explain about birdsong is the value of variations on a species song in a bird's repertoire. Does a comparative virtuoso attract a better class of female? Swedish researchers found that, while the strikingly plumed and richly voiced pied flycatcher would suggest that such characteristics are paramount in a female's choice, it is clearly the quality of the territory that makes the difference. Male charisma has little to do with choice of mate. The researchers learned that the females preferred a new nest box with a small opening placed a bit less than

Seemingly lost in a crowd, a ring-billed gull chick calls for its parents. Seabirds, many of which breed in large colonies, are able to locate and identify their offspring by individual calls.

The melodious courtship songs of southeastern Australia's superb lyrebird, portrayed opposite in a 19th-century hand-colored lithograph by John and Elizabeth Gould, include perfect mimicry of other forest animals and even of manmade sounds, such as machinery.

two yards above ground in a big tree surrounded with birches. Then the Swedes played a trick: they provided just this kind of arrangement to males that, the previous year, had proven sexually unsuccessful. The females moved right in, ignoring the macho males of yesteryear.

Theories about song abound, and they vary depending on what birds in what region are being studied. One such theory, called the ranging hypothesis, predicts the range of singing behavior both in birds that have their song totally programmed in their genes and in those that have to learn the song from others. The theory places territoriality at the core of birdsong, although in a manner of considerable subtlety, as befits such complicated creatures as birds. Ranging, in this context, means assessing one's distance from a mate or family member. But its most complicated application is estimating one's distance from a competitor.

Birds, especially small birds, are on a parsimonious energy budget, and, while they can move about more widely than virtually any mammal, flying is expensive. And of course fights are all the more so. At the same time, for a creature so desperately dependent on an ample food supply for its own daily survival,

inhabiting a salubrious area, especially at breeding time, is of paramount importance. This makes long-distance communication also of paramount importance. With few exceptions (the sweet-singing lyrebird of Australia, for example, which is quite large), the most elaborate singers are the small passerines or perching birds, many of which spend a good deal of their time in places like forests and shrubbery that tend to inhibit and alter sound waves.

For a considerable time, ornithologists armed with arrays of electronic listening devices recorded bird songs and calls, analyzing their species-specific nature and also the distance over which they could be heard. But there is a factor involved in the production and hearing of sound that is far more subtle and, it turns out, more important in many kinds of birdsong than the mere distance over which it travels before it effectively fades below the threshold of the listener's ability to hear it. According to the nature of the song and the nature of the obstructions it must get past—trees, the sound of a stream, branches, leaves, wind—the song degrades. That is to say, with changes in frequency and other acoustical properties brought on by the environment in which it is sung, it changes

Brightly colored symbol of open grasslands, a western meadowlark, left, pours forth the loud, bubbling, flutelike song that has endeared it to so many people. In Jules Breton's The Song of the Lark *(1884), opposite, a peasant girl of the French countryside stands enraptured by the dawn arias of the skylark, characteristically singing on the wing.*

in structure. These changes in structure—or degradations—are a much more accurate measure of the distance a song has traveled than is the song's loudness or amplitude.

Now suppose that stored in their brains most singing birds have a knowledge of the basic pattern of their species song or songs. In that case, a bird can tell the difference between the ideal sound it has in its brain and what it hears from another member of its species inhabiting another territory, and thus it can get an accurate measure of how distant the singer is in those ecological circumstances. If the song is not degraded enough, then the bird knows it is too close and should move away.

In a situation such as those found in the tropics—a stable environment with food resources fairly evenly distributed—such information would be sufficient to avoid a lot of wasteful movement, fights, and other trouble. It would serve to keep intraspecific members well spaced. It is honest advertisement. And this, generally, is what ornithologists find in tropical songbirds, most of which, it turns out, produce little variety in a song once they have got it down.

What then would impel birds to be song-learners—birds that need to hear a conspecific song in order to reproduce it?

In an environment such as a temperate woodland, where resources may be more plentiful here than just over there, there would be an advantage to a bird whose song is confusing, that is, sounds closer than it actually is. In such a place, the acoustical properties of the area might differ within a single bird territory as well. A bird that could adjust its songs to slight variations in acoustical situations and make them sound closer to a listening competitor would gain because the listener would move away, thereby expending energy unnecessarily. Among the small, it is the energy-savers that tend to do best—those that use their resources only for important business. Another way to confuse a competitor is to jam the mechanisms by which he assesses his distance from the singer. It is useful to sing songs that do not quite fit the song pattern in the competitor's memory. Evolutionary advantage would thus be conferred upon the inventive bird: an arms race of sorts would ensue, with listeners developing better mechanisms for ranging a rival, and singers inventing yet other confusing variations.

Whichever bird is ahead in the arms race at any given time may aggrandize property and thus more food resources. In experiments with Carolina wrens, scientists found that a well-supplied wren, singing variously in response, not only brought neighboring wrens to silence but also evidently caused them to stop foraging altogether. If this disruption is brought about by vigorous, long bouts of singing, thereby keeping others both away and useless, one can begin to understand why a nearly starved small bird, upon waking up in the morning, might start singing like crazy to gain an advantage even though it is using up a precious reserve of energy to sing. Disrupting the neighbors is most advantageous at the time when they, too, are hungriest.

This ranging effect should apply to migrants as well. In red-winged blackbirds, for example, it does. The migratory ones that breed in the far northern parts of the range tend to have several song types (up to eight), while to the increasingly stable south the red-wings of Pennsylvania have five, those of Maryland two, and the nonmigratory red-wings of California and Cuba only one.

The ranging hypothesis also has something to say about duetting. This song strategy was thought to help coordinate learning between a pair, but then, in a contradictory finding, it was discovered that among certain wrens a complicated duetting song takes place spontaneously on a pair's first encounter. The ranging theory hypothesizes that duetting may serve to keep males and females from interfering with one another at the wrong time while they also are using the threat function of the song to keep interlopers at bay.

The ranging hypothesis pulls together into one framework a number of phenomena that had stood in uneasy isolation as scientists began to learn more details about the songs of birds. Uniquely, it puts birdsong into an evolutionary context, taking into account how natural selection pressures could have operated on so surprising a behavioral ability while also considering the ecological factors involved even at the refined level of acoustics. For now, the ranging hypothesis is a compelling union of the evolutionary play and the ecological theater.

Whether the hypothesis holds up to fur-

ther scrutiny—to additional information gleaned from the world of birds—remains to be seen. That is the way of good science. But it now sheds a new and coherent light on the welcoming sound of the birds at first light and offers an additional appreciation of the vespers of the thrush. It opens a new window on the meanings of birds. And, surely, though it lends a slightly lonely cast to these purposive little lives, it by no means diminishes the sense of beauty that the singing of birds conveys to us across the boundary between their universe and ours. 🕊

A sea gull alights on a roof-top, arranges its feathers, and stares implacably at its world. Another comes, and another. As each one arrives, there is a new and seemingly irritable jostling, so that the birds are always spaced equidistantly along the roofline. Such behavior led anthropologist Edward T. Hall to look at his fellow human beings much as an ornithologist looks at gulls, and he found much the same behavior among people waiting in line for a city bus or for the attention of a bank teller. He called this the "hidden dimension," the space around themselves that many creatures require, or at least prefer, the invasion of which is taken to be an act of aggression of one sort or another. The mating displays of birds—elaborate gestures and songs and even including the yellowing of a male goldfinch's plumage in season—can be thought of as ways to reduce this bubble of personal, psychological space.

And just as the size of this bubble varies among human cultures (the Italians often touch each other in

Preceding pages: A king penguin appears to get a nip and a nudge from its neighbors. The birds sometimes rub against each other for warmth; during the breeding season each pair defends a territory of about 5.4 square feet. Highly social, they live in groups and breed in huge colonies.

public; the British do not), it varies among bird species and almost certainly among bird individuals. Each has its tolerable limits, which depend on, among other things, the season, the needs of the moment, and the opaque psychology of a bird. For example, once the gulls are as close together on the rooftop as they can bear, the arrival of another brings about a testy departure, or even, in the murky motivations of gulls, the abandonment of the roof by all.

Sociability—be it human or avian—is a continuing affair of fine-tuning, of compromise between the needs to be among one's own and to be left alone: togetherness and privacy. Many humans, of course, though not all, have a clear choice in the matter. Some choose to live alone. Many Americans choose to live in suburban developments, often arrangements of houses equidistant from each other rather like sea gulls on the roof. Many others elect to live in the bustling and often anonymous crowd of an urban apartment building. Analogously, some birds are loners, pairing up only to mate, while others, such as starlings and blackbirds, go through that season in marital exclusivity but spend part of the year in the frantic proximity of great swarms. Some organize year-round communes. Still others, like some swallows and most oceanic birds, breed in vast, cacophonous colonies.

But unlike humans, birds have no choice in the matter as we think of it. Bird society is dictated by what has already worked for generations. Natural selection is intolerant of social experimentation at any given moment. It is only over long periods of time and many generations that aberrant behavior on the part of a few can lead to societal change. Along the way, many inadvertent oddballs—unknowing revolutionaries—perish. Bird society tends to conservatism, as do all purely subsistence cultures. By the same token, though, biological evolution has over time been extremely inventive.

In southwestern North America purple martins tend to breed in separate pairs in woodpecker holes in cacti. Each pair lives within the territory the birds somehow define as "their needs," the invasion of which by other martins they will not tolerate. Then how does one explain the urbanized behavior of purple martins in the East, populating crowded tenements on 15-foot poles, erected and often elaborately decorated in fine Victorian style by humans? Almost without question, martins evolved in the tropics and later came to migrate north where the bugs of spring abounded in breeding season. Presumably, then, the original "plan" of martins, as of many other songbirds, was that seen in southwestern martins: exclusive nesting territories. The eastern congregations, which

are so easy to anthropomorphize (a female martin leaning out her "window," for example, and seemingly commenting on tenement affairs at great length like any good grandmother in a brownstone) must be a relatively new arrangement in purple martin history.

The reason for the great groupings of purple martins in the East appears to lie in one of the most compelling biological urges: reproduction. And one way to unravel the complexity of these congregations is to wake up before dawn in the vicinity of a well-populated purple martin house and hear a male calling out from on high in a clear and especially loud and rhythmic voice. What on earth could such activity accomplish in his behalf? It is too dark to be catching insects, so the martin isn't warning others away from his feeding territory. In fact, purple martins don't defend feeding territories; as consumers of aerial plankton, they fly far and wide in search of floating spiders and flying insects whose whereabouts are unpredictable and therefore indefensible. The dawn song is not to attract a mate; it begins about a month after the males and females have come together. So why would a male fly off before it is light, singing its loudest song, and then return to the colony and keep up the serenade? Certainly not to defend his small nest compartment and those few empty ones that he also typically controls. After all, the males

most likely to intrude are only inches away. The dawn song, it turns out, is part and parcel of the evolution of colonial nesting, as are several related aspects of martin life.

Confronting purple martins long ago when they were extending their range eastward was a vast expanse of virgin forest, a great, green carpet interrupted here and there by a tracery of rivers and the occasional larger tree that by some form of good tree luck rose up above the rest. Many of these larger trees undoubtedly had dead tops riddled with woodpecker holes. Soon enough the martins took to these widely scattered natural apartment buildings, preferring them to single woodpecker holes. But why?

Typically, it is the dark-purple adult males that arrive first in the spring, having winged their way up from Brazil. They are soon followed by the adult females. Like most birds, martins tend to be monogamous for at least any given season. Before long a pair begins to build a nest (or several) out of mud, dead twigs, and stalks. Then, after about two weeks of this activity, the female flies up to the top of a tree and tugs off a green leaf, which she brings back to the nest. Soon the male takes over the task of bringing in green leaves. It seems that when the female brings in the first green leaf she is giving a precise signal to the male that the nest is complete, that she is committed to it and to him, and

A male purple martin, opposite top, retrieves a green leaf for its nest, an activity usually begun by the female as a sign that the nest is near completion and she is committed to her mate. Opposite bottom, a female martin collects nest material on the ground under the watchful eye of her mate, who is guarding her from any attempt at forcible copulation by another male. In the eastern United States, colonies of purple martins often live in apartment houses provided for them by humans, below. In these close quarters, a mated adult male may be able to cuckold a young male bird, who will then unknowingly raise the other's progeny.

that within three days she will begin to lay eggs. (An older female will lay a clutch of five or six; a yearling female only three or four.) Also, it is when the green leaves appear in the nest that dawn song commences.

The monogamous pattern is forced on the males by circumstances. The period from the time the eggs hatch until the post-fledged young are no longer dependent on their parents is a little over two months, during which it is all the parents can do to feed them. A second clutch could not fledge before it was time to migrate back to Brazil. And, while male martins have polygynous instincts and may seek more than one female mate at a time, it would not do them any good under the circumstances to fertilize a second female right after the first because the young would not survive in a single-parent home. Yet there is a certain amount of attempted cheating by adult male stragglers, so a male will vigorously defend his nest hole and the others he maintains in an empty state during early spring.

About a month after the first arrivals of adult purple martins comes another wave, this one mostly of younger males and females. The young males may have some purple splotches in their plumage, but for the most part they are a mottled gray—more like a female, in fact. An adult male martin is as tolerant of these young males as he is of the young females, and the strategy behind this tolerance evidently is this: if the adult male allows young couples to use his extra nest holes, he may get a chance to mate with the young females and fertilize another clutch of eggs, increasing his contribution to the purple martin gene pool over that of others. If he succeeds in his endeavors, the young males in all ignorance will do their accustomed share of feeding the chicks. The adult male, then, needs the young males around (otherwise the young females will stay only temporarily), and that may be the purpose of the dawn song.

Martins migrate by day or night but typically arrive at nest sites at dawn. Just before dawn an adult male flies up and broadcasts the excellence of his colony in his loudest voice over a range of an estimated 30 square miles, trying to attract the young birds. It is this slight competitive edge that long ago probably favored those martins that took up

Waiting for the male to return with food, a great gray owl guards her chicks. As with most raptors, the male hunts and the female incubates the eggs and feeds nestlings, though the male may feed older chicks.

residence in such colonies—first in tall snags above the canopy of the forest, later in the gourds and apartment buildings made especially for them by people.

To return to the perils of the ostensibly monogamous life of martins, a male is at greatest risk of being cuckolded when the female flies down to the ground to collect nesting material. At this point she is vulnerable to forcible copulation with another male lurking nearby. In part to combat such an action, apparently, many male martins guard their mates on these forays, flying down to the ground with them and standing guard until the females again are airborne. Then the male will collect some nesting material and follow her to the nest. Such behavior has been seen as a way the males can ensure their own paternity of whatever eggs result. But it is more complicated than that.

It has been shown that mate-guarding varies greatly among males in a given colony—some do and some don't. Furthermore, one would expect that a male who expended so much time and energy watching out for his mate in this manner also would spend more time feeding the subsequent young—protecting his investment, as it were. But this turns out not to be the case. It may be that mate-guarding has evolved to keep the females from being harassed, for if they are harassed they do not collect nesting material on that foray. And a brood that is born into a less well-constructed nest is likely to do less well in life.

Here again, in the question of how a martin ensures his patrimonial contribution, the green leaves may play a role. As we have seen, the female martin signals the completion of a proper nest by collecting green material, a job that the male soon takes over. It has been suggested that perhaps the leaves play a pharmacological role, helping to deter mites and other parasites. (Starlings usually reuse the previous year's nests, weaving various green plants into the old structures. They tend to choose seven specific plants, each of which deters one or another nest parasite.) It seems more likely, however, that among martins the green leaves serve chiefly as a stimulus for sex. A female is most fertile after the nest is built and egg-laying is about to commence. Taking a cue from the female, the male brings these stimulating green objects into the nest where the female is waiting, and there in privacy they can have unforced and frequent copulation, the better to ensure that the resident male wins the overall sperm competition.

To guard one's mate or not . . . for martins that appears to be a more complicated question than previously thought. Certainly, in species for which keeping an eye peeled is not possible, the paternity-security system of choice is frequent copulation. In birds of prey, for example, the females typically stay home during the crucial egg-laying period, while the males are off foraging for the better part of the day. It has been determined that a goshawk pair may copulate as many as 600 times for each clutch of eggs laid. Colonial nesting species such as oceanic birds also have high copulation rates: gannets may copulate 100 times per clutch. This behavior may be explained by the fact that it is possible for one clutch to contain eggs sired by different fathers; indeed, a female canary once produced three eggs fathered by a canary and one by a linnet, the latter being what could be thought of as a canary-linnet mule. In any event, the most efficacious way to assure one's patrimony in such matters is to flood the female with one's own sperm.

Sadly, for humans seeking moral examples from avian affairs, the marital habits of birds provide little except a kind of barely controlled licentiousness. As one ornithologist put it, a "tangled web of deceit, cuckoldry, and bigamy" is beginning to emerge from studies of presumed monogamy and polygamy among birds. Polygyny, or the taking of more than one female mate in a season, is not uncommon and is generally thought to occur in response to a situation in which resources, chief among them food, are patchily distributed. A male who establishes hegemony over an area with particularly rich resources would attract several mates, who would rather accept less help in child rearing from the male and better resources overall than mate with a second-rate male in a low-class locale, even if the latter offered more help in child rearing. Among honeyguides, which rely on beeswax for much of their diet, only a relatively few males control this scattered resource. Many males, therefore, go without mating, while a successful one may wind up mating with as many as 18 females. Similarly, the male marsh wren of North America establishes a territory in early spring and then proceeds to build nests—many of them. Evidently, the more abundant and easily caught food is, the more "dummy" nests the male builds. A bigamous male may build up to 25 nests, while most—those that settle for monogamy—generally build about half a dozen.

Polygyny is also the rule with such birds as sage grouse, in which the males gather together in mating season for a group display of their charms on common ground called a lek. Visiting females arrive periodically, select the male that most appeals to them, and mate, each subsequently going off to lay her eggs elsewhere and raise her precocial offspring alone. A female sage grouse copulates on the average once per clutch.

Rarer is polyandry, a reversal of sex roles in which the female normally mates with more than one male. Perhaps the most clear-cut example of such behavior is among the jacanas, tropical marsh birds whose amazingly long toes make them at home walking around on water hyacinths and water lilies. The female northern jacana is larger than the male and mates with up to four males, who then build nests of floating masses of vegetation. The female lays her eggs and leaves them entirely to the males to incubate and rear. Each male defends his own territory, while all the males' territories are under the protection of the female, who fends off other females and also breaks up squabbles between her males.

Just how polyandry arose is not clear. For jacanas, suitable nesting sites—ponds with plenty of lilies—are few and far between and do not provide much protection against predators. It is thus in the interest of the female to lay as many eggs as possible. And it is not difficult to see that, once the polyandrous mode of reproduction was established larger females would be selected over time. But what started certain birds on the path away from the uneasy monogamy typical of birds is hard to fathom.

With regard to monogamy in birds, it is becoming clear that it is often more honored in the breach. Also, its success usually depends on the nature of resources available—or so it was thought. That theory predicts that a secondary female, at some point called the polygyny threshold, gains by being second

The female American avocet, a long-legged wading bird, crouches low in the water as the male brushes past in a prenuptial display, top. He positions himself on her back to mate, center, then lays one wing over her as the two cross bills and run along the shore in a postnuptial dance, bottom.

A male blue bird of paradise hangs upside-down to display his gorgeous plumes, above. Over time, the males of many species of birds—peacocks and birds of paradise, most notably—have evolved exaggerated plumage to attract females. The greatly elongated tails of the Cape sugarbird of South Africa, opposite, and of several African widowbirds, right, also serve to turn females' heads. Such adaptations cease at the point where any increase creates a burden greater than the advantages it produces for the male.

fiddle—that is, she produces more young as a secondary mate in a rich habitat than as a single mate in a poor territory. Recent studies of two songbirds, however, cast doubt on the theory.

Swedish ornithologists turned to the pied flycatcher and found that a monogamous pair typically raises five young, while the second mate in a polygynous group rears three. The primary mate does better than the secondary one because the bigamist is more attentive to his first mate. But, in order to reject an already paired male, a female has to know that he is paired. The male pied flycatcher, upon attracting a female to his territory and mating with her, simply flies off and establishes a second territory, and usually not right next door. His first mate by then is committed to staying home to lay her eggs and tend them. The male promptly attracts a second mate and the process is complete. This appears to be more a case of male deceit than female compromise.

Another European species, the great reed warbler, accomplishes much the same deceit but by other means. The males establish large linear territories among the marsh grasses and reeds surrounding lakes. A hasty courter, the great reed warbler will attract a female to one end of his territory in part by singing a long, elaborate song—and the song appears

to be more intricate among polygynous than monogamous males. Once paired, the male turns to a much shorter and more economical song for territorial defense. Leaving before long for the other end of his territory, he resorts to the complicated sexual song to attract a second mate. As with the pied flycatchers, this arrangement is good for the male but not so good for the secondary female: the male great reed warbler's primary nest will produce three young, the other nest but one.

There is some evidence that female birds respond to being secondary females by producing fewer eggs, thus not wasting food that is difficult to come by on young that will not survive. This phenomenon also suggests that the males' deceits are not totally effective. And, of course, there are other forms of deceit: a male pied flycatcher that is too quick to leave his first mate to establish another family leaves that mate unguarded and subject to impregnation by a nearby male. Sex among birds appears, to a degree, to be war.

Lest there be any remaining sentimentality about monogamy in birds, recent studies of two classically territorial and supposedly monogamous species—white-crowned sparrows and indigo buntings—should settle the matter. Using the technique of electrophoresis to

measure genetic relatedness, researchers have found that a whopping 34 percent of white-crowned sparrow young were not the offspring of the putative father. About the same level of illicit conception was found in buntings. This was virtually all due to extra-pair copulations, not to females laying eggs in other birds' nests.

How do birds choose mates for the fray? Any number of ways, it seems, depending on the species. Charles Darwin suggested that among birds in which the males and females have very different plumage or other visual characteristics (that is, they are sexually dimorphic) it is the "excellence" of these secondary sex characteristics that attracts the female. The peacock's almost otherworldly tail is a special example. Another is the combined choreography and costume finery of the bird of paradise, crouching on a branch and waving its finery about: the Emperor of Germany bird of paradise starts off right side up but crouches farther and farther forward until he is upside down in a cascade of plumes. The blue bird of paradise starts off upside down, hanging from a branch, waving his feathers in what has been called "a lacy mist of blue spray around him."

But nowhere has the male's effort to attract females by what we would think of anthropomorphically as the elaboration of

A marsh wren, opposite, puts the finishing touches on its finely woven nest amid cattails and rushes. Male marsh wrens, such as the one above in courtship song, often build dummy nests to keep the site of the "real" one secret from other males, and may also mate with more than one female.

Under the majesty of the Grand Tetons, left, male sage grouse strut at a communal arena or lek, also known as a "booming ground." Tail feathers raised, top, a male heaves his ruff sharply upward, inflating air sacs, center. A second push completes inflation, above. Three seconds after the display begins, the air is expelled with a loud pop. Though all males "dance," females choose only a few to mate with, and then go off alone to lay eggs and raise the young.

Courtship display in the bowerbirds of Australia and New Guinea includes the construction of unique bowers and display grounds. As a female satin bowerbird of eastern Australia, below, visits the avenue-type bower that the iridescent, satiny-blue male has constructed, he grabs an ornament to hold during courtship. One end of the bower opens onto a display platform, opposite, which the male covers with natural and manmade objects, preferring those of a shiny blue color. Because females choose those males that build the best bowers and offer the best decorations, males steal objects from each other's bowers or even destroy them.

beauty become more baroque than among those cousins of the birds of paradise, the bowerbirds, which are themselves relatively dull in plumage. Indeed, the drabber the male of the species, the more ornate is the bower it builds—sticks and twigs woven around upright saplings or poles, decorated with an astonishing variety of colorful objects and even natural dyes. The bower is constructed solely to attract a female; once this is accomplished, the female abandons it and builds a nest elsewhere.

The satin bowerbird of New South Wales, Australia, prefers blue for decoration, especially blue parrot feathers, which are quite rare. The more blue parrot feathers the male collects and lays around his bower, the greater is his reproductive success. The result is a considerable amount of theft. Gerald Borgia of the University of Maryland marked the blue feathers found in a series of bowers made by this species and then tracked their whereabouts over time. He found that on the average theft occurred once every 10 days, that most thefts were from neighbors, and that a theft tended to bring on bouts of reciprocal stealing. Since females evidently use the blue feathers in a bower as their guide to male quality, the result—in the manner of disruptive birdsong—is that theft enhances a male's appeal while almost arithmetically reducing that of his neighbors.

Similarly precise are the females' judgments of plumage in some species. Recently scientists showed that, among widowbirds, if the males' tails were artificially elongated, they enjoyed greater mating success. But widowbirds, like peacocks, are polygynous, and it is not hard to understand that in such competition it would be greatly to a male's competitive advantage to be more "splendid" than his fellows. Such an edge would lead to an evolutionary escalation in such matters as plumage . . . but what would control it? Of course, the sheer physical requirements of daily life would preclude too enormous a tail. But there is a law of diminishing returns at work as well. If you put a lighted candle in a dark room, its effect is considerable; by the time you have added the 20th candle, its effect is negligible to the eye. Similarly, a fantastic, colorful tail at a certain level of splendor will take a great deal more by way of feather production to achieve even a small additional effect. There comes a point where the extra expenditure of "energy" simply isn't worth the small gain in advantage.

On the other hand, among birds that are essentially monogamous, theory suggests that over time female choice would have less of a runaway effect on the male's plumage. But Swedish ornithologists have shown that in a monogamous swallow species an artificially elongated tail confers a distinct advantage.

As with many other birds, appearance plays an important role in mate attraction in ducks. The female mallard at left was obviously successful in finding a suitable mate. A male hooded merganser, top, erects his fan-shaped crest during a courtship display. Above, a female wood duck assumes the mating position as her mate shows off his nuptial colors.

Males that have one attract females more easily and can mate earlier, thus giving them a better chance to produce a second brood in a short breeding season.

The question arises: why would a female prefer a male with extraordinary features? Presumably because such a mate would tend to produce young with similarly extraordinary features. But, again, what biological purpose does such a preference serve? What is the continuing advantage of such finery over generations?

Researchers from the University of Michigan have linked the dashing appearance of males to the matter of parasites. They surveyed blood parasites in 109 passerine species and found a link between the incidence of debilitating disease caused by the parasites and the status of a bird's secondary sex characteristics. Birds less resistant to parasites tend to display lethargically and to have ratty-looking plumage. The showier the male, the more likely he is to be resistant to parasites and disease, and that is advantageous to a female looking for a mate.

Variations on the plumage theme figure in the mate selection of some ducks, such as mallards. Pair formation takes place in late autumn at community display sites. The males arrive at a river or lake and immediately begin pushing, posturing, and shoving as they sort themselves into a seemingly disorderly but actually quite precise hierarchy. With the arrival of the females, the chaos intensifies as the males undertake various displays for the benefit of the females. The dominant males chase the more subordinate ones aside, so that the latter are at the edge of the females' field of vision and less likely to be noticed. Meanwhile the females swim about in the water, eyeing the changing lineup, and so the display is fluid (unlike a lek), with dominant males moving here and there to display before the females—a constant shoving match. In due course, a female selects a male from this melee and they copulate. The pair is formed—a monogamous pair, unlike the polygynous results of leks—and it will last until the nest is built and the eggs laid, at which point the male goes his own way and the female raises the ducklings.

What is a female mallard looking for in a mate? Evidently, status. She wants a domi-

nant male, one that can protect her from male harassment during her egg-forming period and thus allow her more time to feed at this crucial time.

Dominance hierarchies are common among animals from wolves to elephants to bees and are frequently found in groups of birds—indeed, the familiar term pecking order came from the first scientific study of such behavior in chickens, conducted in the 1920s. It was found that in an aggregation of hens there is always one that can peck all the others with impunity, a second one that can get away with pecking all but the first, and so on down the line—a linear hierarchy. Arguments are still carried out in scientific journals as to exactly how precise and linear these hierarchies actually are, and there is some evidence that they might be more fluid than they at first appear.

Understanding of what lies behind dominance hierarchies remains a bit up in the air as well: certainly hormones play a role, but they explain little. And it doesn't take long—often just several brief encounters—before two birds know which is boss. Just how they size each other up in these encounters and then adopt at least a semipermanent status role is also mysterious. But one criterion for low status is certainly youth. With the notable exception of many oceanic birds, such as white terns and penguins, which produce one egg a year (and even fewer among albatrosses), most birds overpopulate. A pair typically produces more than a pair of offspring each year. But in a world of limited resources, and with those resources allocated to territories under the control of experienced and dominant birds, where do all the young go? Many die in migration or in winter's cold; many will attempt to extend the species' range; many will simply hang around and do the best they can. Some turn out to be helpers.

Moorhens (also known as gallinules), for example, typically produce three broods in a season, but those that hatch first are stuck there: all around them are the fiercely defended territories of other moorhens. With no place to go, and if food is abundant enough that they can satisfy themselves, they will help their parents feed the next brood. A similar arrangement occurs among Florida scrub jays, which typically do not breed until

Conjugal relations in so-called monogamous birds are not always as we imagine them. A male indigo bunting stays close by his drab mate, opposite top, yet recent findings indicate that a third of their brood may result from her extra-pair copulations. A great reed warbler, below, may secure two mates by singing his courting song at opposite ends of his territory. Opposite bottom, monogamous blue-winged warblers remove a chick's fecal sac from the nest.

233

European cuckoos offer perhaps the best-known example of brood parasitism, a strategy in which birds build no nests of their own, but lay their eggs in the nests of other species, which then rear the young to the detriment of their own broods. A duped hedge sparrow, above, must stand on the back of its parasitic foster European cuckoo chick in order to feed it. Through a bizarre adaptation, the cuckoo undoubtedly ejected the sparrow's own eggs from the nest only hours after it hatched. Opposite, a brown-headed cowbird of North America has laid its speckled white egg in the nest of a wood thrush, which may well spot the alien egg and reject it.

their second year. Usually their habitat is fragmented as well as full of scrub jays, so yearlings will stay with their parents and help raise their close genetic kin, feeding hungry babies, defending a territory, and removing fecal sacs from the nest. As might be expected, a pair with helpers raises more offspring than a pair without. As for the helper, one advantage lies in the possibility that it could inherit the territory.

Helping at the nest occurs among some 100 bird species all told, and perhaps more. And it is predictably complex. Are the helpers inhibited from trying to breed by the dominance of the adults, or is there some sort of self-restraint involved? In studies of pied kingfishers, German scientists linked the social status of helpers with the birds' family relationships and hormone levels. These kingfishers receive help from both primary and secondary helpers. Primary helpers are the pair's unmated male offspring from the previous year. They stay on with their parents through the breeding season and behave submissively, with obeisant calls and posturing. The parents happily tolerate their presence and their assistance. Secondary helpers are other unmated males that arrive after the eggs have hatched, and, while the mated pair will let them bring food, they are not permitted anywhere near the female. On analysis, the primary helpers were found to be very low in testosterone, while the secondary helpers were at normal levels for males in the breeding season. Again, the primary helpers are furthering their own genetic stake and, at the same time, avoiding costly competition with adults. For the secondary helpers, with no relatives in the area, helping is a social compromise bearing with it the outside chance of cuckolding the old male.

Cooperative child-rearing has reached a kind of pinnacle in the most sociable of all North American woodpeckers, the acorn woodpecker. These birds live in year-round groups of up to 15, of all ages and both sexes. Two or three adult pairs may take turns digging out a hole in a tree or a telephone pole, where young and old all jointly share the tasks of incubation, defense, and feeding.

Clearly there is no avian deceit practiced in so open a community as that of the acorn woodpeckers, but deceit among other species is often the case. Cowbirds and Old World cuckoos are widely known for their habit of laying eggs in the nests of other species, but it has recently been found that cliff swallows typically engage in the surreptitious dumping of eggs in their fellows' nests, the better to produce more offspring with less work. Charles and Mary Brown came across this phenomenon when, studying a colony of cliff swallows in Nebraska, they occasionally noted the appearance of two eggs in a nest in one day, though the birds are capable of laying only one a day. They soon found that parasitic behavior was rampant in the colony (it also has been noted among starlings and moorhens). A swallow waits until a neighbor has gone, then flies into the nest, lays an egg in a mere 60 seconds, and leaves. Sometimes the parasite swallow kicks the other egg out of the nest, sometimes not. Any unguarded moment can invite trespass. On one occasion, while a nest owner was busy fighting off one intruder, a second one flew in and, in 15 seconds, laid an illicit egg and disappeared.

Probably all cliff swallows have the capacity to be parasitic, and success may depend only on luck and persistence. But can a swallow be a parasite and a host at the same time? If this were the case, it would be difficult to see the advantage in the frantic ruse. The task remains, then, to find out about individual birds in a vast colony: why is one a successful parasite and another not?

Such, in any event, are some of the risks of colonial life. You may derive from your fellows information about where an evanescent swarm of insects has just appeared, but you run a greater risk of infestation of parasites, and you also may wind up wasting parental effort on someone else's young.

Being in a crowd is both advertisement and concealment, and colonies and flocks also have much to do with predation. A predator has no difficulty spotting a cloud of flying prey, or a vast array of nesting birds on the ground. But many eyes provide an early warning system. Once spotted, a falcon may hesitate to fly straight into a suddenly more compact flock of starlings, and it may be easily chased away by a squadron peeling off to mob it. Such a group from a colony of Franklin's gulls in Minnesota was seen not only mobbing an approaching marsh hawk

but also "escorting" it away for nearly a third of a mile. Even an innocent intruder, a moose, got the bum's rush.

In the arithmetic of colonies and flocks, there is something called the swamping effect. Predators can get only to the fringes of such a group, and need to get only to the fringes. But in the interior one is relatively safe—thus the concept of the "selfish herd." Typically, the larger and more aggressive among a colony or roost are to be found in the center—the pecking order at work.

For breeding colonies of oceanic birds, there are two basic strategies besides the swamping effect to avoid predation. One is to breed on islands where there are no land predators; the other is to nest on precipices. The chief problem then is from other birds, such as the skuas that relentlessly raid the breeding grounds of penguins. Some species of island breeders nest in burrows and visit the nest only at night. One oceanic bird, the ancient murrelet, not only breeds in a burrow and visits the burrow at night, but also practically never visits it. The eggs, which are nearly one-fourth the weight of the mother at laying, need little incubation, and, the chicks, upon hatching, are programmed to head for the ocean; they automatically tend to run downhill, toward the sound of waves, and toward the strongest stimulus, which for them is light (the water is always brighter than the land). In a mad race, thousands of tiny murrelets, only two days after hatching, run a terrifying gauntlet of obstacles and predators, such as owls and deer mice, to hit the sea virtually running through the water. Once there, they head frantically out to sea past predatory fish, listening for the particular sound of their own parents' calls. Those that make it will spend the next year entirely at sea, feeding on planktonic creatures. These murrelets appear to be unique among oceanic birds in leaving the land so soon after hatching. Most such birds require a long period of parental care, and this, evidently, is one reason why colonies are so successful.

As in so many aspects of avian life, the availability of food seems to be the determining factor in social grouping, as in the awesome colonies of seabirds that congregate to breed in the hundreds of thousands on remote islands and on the faces of precipitous cliffs. In the Canadian Arctic, where the seas are clogged with shifting pack ice during the spring, biologist Tony Gaston studied colonies of thick-billed murres, large relatives of the auks and puffins. Murres, along with petrels and certain other seabirds, are among the most populous birds on Earth. Tens of thousands of murres may congregate to breed on a single, huge, sea-facing cliff, clinging face-in to narrow ledges where they lay generally only one pear-shaped egg on the bare rock. If an egg is disturbed, it tends to roll around its narrow end, remaining on the ledge. In summer there is no darkness, and the colony is active around the clock. The din is unrelenting. "Every avian arrival," Gaston has written, "warrants a comment from a neighbor—a grunt of surprise, an enthusiastic greeting, or a scream of disapproval."

And arrivals and departures are constant. Upon leaving its egg or chick, a parent will fly down to bathe in the sea, then head out for feeding grounds of cod, sand eels, and shrimplike plankton. As the birds fly off, they gather into groups that in turn merge into flocks of up to a hundred. Flock follows flock in a straight line to the horizon, separated from each other by about a half-minute, a long river of birds that, as Gaston has described it, dissolves "into the shimmer rising from drifting sea ice." They do not return until they have found food; then they fly low over the water in even larger flocks to within a mile of the cliff, at which point the individual birds climb and head for their nests.

Evidently, on the way out in long lines or V shapes, the flocks follow a leader that every now and then flies upward a few feet and then may change course. The lead bird is looking for the inbound flocks and the direction of success. And an inbound bird, arriving with a morsel for the young, may head back to sea for more, this time not joining an outbound flock but heading directly for the area where it previously found fish. Such a foraging strategy, so akin to that of swallows seeking insect swarms, would overcome the vagaries of changing feeding grounds and drifting pack ice.

Gaston suggests that a colony of fewer than 10,000 birds would not have sufficient outbound and inbound parties to provide the necessary information in the cold, ice-strewn oceans where feeding grounds can shift so abruptly. But, if there is an advantage in

Bird society is full of surprises. Acorn woodpeckers engage in communal nesting: a social group of up to 15 birds practices mate-sharing among adult breeders, who raise the group's offspring in one nest. Any chick could thus be the offspring of any given adult, so all adults incubate, feed, and guard all progeny.

The bill of the common puffin, right, is fine for fishing and also makes a good shovel. A pair digs a deep burrow in which to incubate the egg and hide the chick until fledging. To thwart predators, crested auklets, below, tuck their egg into a crevice high in a cliff or under a boulder on the shore.

Black-legged kittiwakes and murres perch precariously along a cliff in Alaska, left. The thick-billed murre, above left, like the common murre, lays its pear-shaped egg on bare rock ledges. If jostled, the egg will revolve around its pointed end rather than roll off the edge. Gannets, right, also nest in colonies on cliff ledges. A gannet pair may mate for life, maintaining their pair bond through such elaborate displays as bill fencing, above.

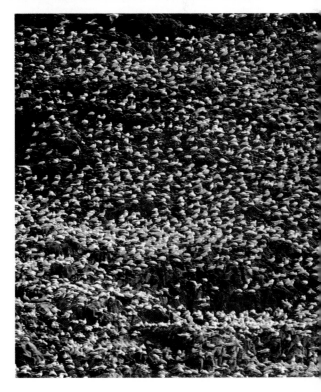

numbers, what keeps such colonies from growing indefinitely? All murres eat exactly the same thing; eventually a growing colony would deplete nearby supplies (up to 60 miles) to the point where the survival rate of chicks would begin to drop. As it turns out, the colony becomes stable in number at a population of around 250,000 birds. How did such colonies come about in the first place? Clearly, they had to have begun in warmer areas with smaller numbers (smaller murre colonies are the norm in fairer climates), which grew until they reached some critical size. Then, some 6,000 years ago, the Canadian Arctic turned far colder. Only those colonies of sufficient size endured. Gaston's prediction (and one he obviously would prefer to see untested) is that, if for one reason or another the vast northern citadels of murres were to be eliminated, they could not reconstitute themselves without a major warming of the Arctic.

Such spectaculars as breeding seabird colonies are seen only by the hardy and adventurous. But bird society is all about us in astonishing subtlety and variety. To understand it at all—even among birds so common as to be taken for granted—takes enormous patience. The black-capped chickadee, for example, is the quintessential birdfeeder bird— bold, perky, almost tame in its willingness to share one's backyard in fearless proximity, and somehow a gladdening source of optimism. Like most songbirds, black-capped chicadees breed in exclusive pairs, testily maintaining their territories (usually up to one-fourth of a square mile) with their sharp, eponymous call, feeding chiefly on caterpil-lars. But at summer's end they begin to gather in small flocks, including that year's young, and it is here, Susan Smith of Mount Holyoke College found, that social relations among chicadees become remarkably complex.

The flocks average about 10 birds, and each flock defends a territory through the winter—an area two or three times larger than a breeding territory. Of the 23 flocks Smith studied over five years, all had even numbers and were made up of equal numbers of males and females, suggesting that the flock consists only of birds that have paired up at summer's end. These are the

flock's "regulars." There are other black-capped chickadees about, but they do not lead solitary lives. Instead they are "floaters," ranging among three or four different flocks.

Within each flock there is a distinct pecking order among the regulars. Dominance is shown in several ways, as when chickadee A arrives and takes over the perch of B, or chases B, or takes the first seed from the birdfeeder even though both arrived simultaneously. The ranking extends to pairs: the mate of male A is female A in the pecking order. Meanwhile, the floaters—always young birds—rank below all of the regulars of their sex in whichever flock they happen to be visiting. Furthermore, there is a dominance hierarchy among floaters as well. If floater A dominates floater B in one flock, it will do so in any other flock they both visit.

The floaters seem utterly unnecessary— even to each other. They show no interest in pair-bonding like that of the regulars. What is the strategy of floating? The answer lies in the fact that the territory a flock defends in winter, only two or three times that of a breeding territory, will not provide enough room for all the pairs in the flock to breed the following spring. Only the highest-ranked pairs in the flock will be able to breed there; some of the others may find undefended territories elsewhere, but most simply will not get to breed at all. On first look, you would think that the least likely to breed would be the lowly floaters, but this is not entirely the case.

Winter is not kind to chickadees, and even those that enjoy a neighborhood birdfeeder are subject to mortality from predators and old age. If, say, the alpha (A) male dies, one might expect a shift in the hierarchy with the beta male moving up to pair with the alpha widow, but this rarely happens. Evidently, once a pair is bonded, the two tend to stick together till death parts them. Upon the death of the alpha male, the highest-ranking male floater present at the time leaves his role, moves in, and becomes the new alpha male regular. The same goes for females.

In Smith's study, 17 floaters obtained regular berths in flocks in this way—all in high-ranking slots—and all of these former floaters obtained breeding territories the following spring. (In two instances, it was more than a simple exchange: twice an older first-ranked bird died and was replaced by a member of the second-ranked pair. The floater then filled that vacancy.) In no case, however, did a floater move in to replace the deceased member of a pair that ranked lower than third in the flock. On 38 occasions, such lowly pairs were broken up by death and the widowed bird remained alone for the winter.

To add to the complexity of this kind of society, floaters will not form floater-floater pairs. If both members of the alpha pair died, their slot would not be filled by two floaters; instead, the other pairs would simply move up a notch in rank. And, if a newly inserted floater's mate dies, then that vacancy cannot be filled by a second floater. The first floater, now widowed, is doomed to leave the life of a regular and take up floating again, waiting for a new slot to open up.

All young chickadees must enter this system. The luckiest enter it as high-ranked pairs; they are the birds that begin first to form the flock. Even if a mate in a high-ranked pair doesn't make it through the winter, the widowed bird is assured of a new mate from the ranks of floaters. The other "choices" are to enter as a low-ranked pair, a high-ranked floater, or a low-ranked floater. Judging from the fact that floaters begin floating between flocks before the flocks are completely formed, one would deduce that being a high-ranked floater is the second choice. For a high-ranked floater, once inserted into the flock as a regular, the only risk is the death of its mate. Being a low-ranked floater is the most desperate choice, and often there are none.

Through this remarkably elaborate and rigid social system, the chickadees one sees darting back and forth between a tree and the birdfeeder are playing a dangerous game, the sweepstakes to see which ones will have the chance to remain in spring and perpetuate their kind. How many social schemes are there among birds? As many as there are bird species, and conceivably even more, from the complex to the simple, if indeed any society can be called simple. As naturalist Robert Finch wrote after spending one of many happy, if cold, mornings watching chickadees forage in a bog in winter: "Follow any animal carefully in the earnest pursuit of its living and it will show you a world you have never imagined."

A black-capped chickadee arrives at its nest hole with caterpillars to feed its young. When the breeding season is over, these chickadees enter into a complex social structure involving a regular breeding population and a floating, nonbreeding population. Interplay between members of the two groups determines which birds will rear the next generation of chickadees.

About 4,000 years ago, the progenitors of the people who would produce the great Mayan civilization in Central America hit upon a new way of making a living: swidden agriculture. Another name for it is slash-and-burn, wherein a patch of dense forest is cut down and burned and planted to crops for a year or so; then its exhausted soil is abandoned to become an area of brush until the forest in time reasserts itself. This move to an agricultural way of life was a step toward high civilization but also, it seems, a significant circumstance in the evolution of some other, more cosmopolitan, residents of the region—hooded warblers, which spent their winters there and bred far to the north in the forested eastern half of North America.

The male hooded warbler is something of a dandy, greenish on top, lemon-yellow below, with black eyes and a black cowl framing his yellow face. For the most part, the females of this species are duller and lack the black hood, but a very small number—maybe 6 percent—

Preceding pages: Martin Johnson Heade's Cattleya Orchid and Three Brazilian Hummingbirds *(1871) portrays the essential fecundity and variety of the South American tropical forest as it was before 20th-century human pressure began to erode its extent.*

Experiments and observations by National Zoological Park ornithologist Eugene S. Morton, above, and his colleagues suggest that habitat preferences of male and female hooded warblers, opposite, may be genetic, the result of human agricultural practices. Several thousand years of slash-and-burn agriculture in the birds' Central American wintering grounds may have exerted selective pressure on each sex's plumage and choice of habitat.

gain an incomplete hood of black. Until recently, it was thought that these melanin-tinged females were older birds. Like many migratory songbirds, hooded warbler pairs jointly defend a breeding territory but live in and defend separate territories in their southern wintering grounds. Since the females are smaller than the males, this would tend to put the females at a disadvantage in winter . . . if they shared the same habitat, but for the most part they don't. In Central America, the males repair to the forested areas, and their distinct (disruptive) coloration tends to make them invisible among the sun-dappled leaves; the females locate in the brushy areas, where their duller, more uniform feathers are harder to spot. Thus is competition between males and females in the wintering grounds avoided.

It is a matter of sheer instinct, not learning. Hand-reared hooded warblers—birds with no adults around to provide any kind of example, and no foliage whatsoever in their cages—have been shown to have innate preferences for habitat based only on gender. Ornithologists at the National Zoo in Washington, D.C., took hooded warblers from their cages and placed them one at a time in a room, one end of which was decorated with vertical stripes of black crepe paper, the other adorned with *diagonal* stripes. Almost invariably, the young males would stay near the vertical stripes (the geometric essence of tree trunks) while the females preferred the diagonal stripes (brush).

But this instinctive preference among the females could not always have been the case, for, before the advent of swidden agriculture, their wintering grounds consisted of miles and miles of unbroken forest. Presumably, in those earlier times, most females developed black near-hoods after their first molt and competed with the larger (and evidently more numerous) males for territory, probably to their general disadvantage. But some females —a small percentage—would retain their duller, immature plumage after the first molt, again probably to *their* disadvantage until the Mayas came along and created areas where such coloration would work in the females' behalf, as well as eliminating male competition for resources. (It is interesting to note that hooded warblers get together to breed in areas where there is forest underlain by brush—both vertical and diagonal lines.) Gradually,

over thousands of hooded warbler generations, females with dull, immature-type plumage did better than their darker sisters in the woods and thus became by far the more numerous form. And so, over 4,000 years a new instinctive habitat preference became prevalent, to the evident advantage of a bird species—a harmless, one might even say benevolent, shift in evolution brought about however unwittingly by the hand of man.

Today, as always, evolution proceeds, but people have so sped up the change in the habitats of the planet that there is not enough time for such delicate matters as the instincts of most birds to keep up the pace. (However, some species, such as European starlings, seem preadapted to handle rapid changes, much like weed plants.) For thousands and thousands of years, the great rain forest of the Amazon Basin went through two seasons a year, the wet and the dry, and the life the forests supported and that supported the forests adapted and emerged in such great diversity that this area has been called the most complex ecosystem in the world. Today there is a third season, the *queimadas*, the burnings, which takes place in the interval between the rains and the dry times. During this period slash-and-burn agriculture is practiced on such a scale that 4 percent of the Amazon rain forest is destroyed each summer. Some 5,000 fires are set each day between July and October, the result being the annual loss of enough forest to cover nearly the entire state of Idaho. The smoke from these fires blankets the region, closing airports, turning the sun into a dim bruise of light, and almost certainly providing a major impulse to the greenhouse effect, the overall warming trend of the global climate. Many reasonable people wonder if even the clever brain and other computers of humankind, much less the instincts of birds, will have time to adapt to such wholesale change.

On the other hand, pessimism is not a useful mindset for those faced with a challenge, and a surprising number of people are coming to the realization that, in order to save ourselves, we must save the kinds of places that are inhabited by birds. Indeed, virtually every bird species is now a canary in the mine, alerting us to one human error or another. More than a quarter of a century ago, Rachel Carson's alarming image of the

arrival of spring without the sounds of birds led to the realization that toxic pesticides were not only bad for the likes of peregrine falcons, ospreys, and other birds at the top of the food chain, but quite likely dangerous to us and our children. With DDT banned, and by virtue of a series of what might be called heroic interventions—rearing and releasing birds into the wild and not so wild—ospreys have dramatically extended their range and numbers in recent years; and the peregrine is recapturing its range, as well as finding a usable niche in the man-made crags of such cities as New York and Baltimore, and a bountiful food supply in the pigeons urbanites attract.

When seabirds by the thousands were found on beaches, covered with oil from sea-borne slicks, people who might never have paid much attention (such as the mystery-book writer Ross MacDonald, whose private eye, Lew Archer, patrolled the seamy side of Los Angeles society for years) volunteered their help and became conservationists overnight. The tragic and dramatic photographs of the petroleum-blackened birds began to awaken the nation to the immensity of the insult to the world's oceans and of the threat both to wildlife and to the commercial fishing industry.

It was the imminent loss of the snowy egret and other birds to the fashions of the millinery trade that led to the founding in the 1890s of the first conservation organization devoted to birds—the Massachusetts Audubon Society, today the largest statewide group of this sort and an organization whose concerns have expanded from purely avian affairs to the ecological health of the globe itself.

Birds, indeed, are among the most useful information sources for conservationists, since they have been so much more thoroughly studied than other animals. Also, the distribution of birds has been all but totally pinpointed, even in the more remote regions of the planet, and their finely tuned ecological preferences are *relatively* well understood. Scientists from the International Council on Bird Preservation and the International Union for the Conservation of Nature and Natural Resources recently identified 172 species of birds in Africa in imminent danger of extinction and another 122 that are threatened. This is, of course, terrible news. Most of the birds so identified are forest birds, and most of these—88 percent—have ranges that are centered in five areas of sub-Saharan Africa and eastern Madagascar. Three of the areas—Cameroon, the Albertine rift, and eastern Kenya and Tanzania—are probably the main African forest areas that survived the drying up of the continent that accompanied the Ice Ages, and that now support a great diversity of birds and other life forms. Destruction of a relatively small amount of forest in these five critical areas would extin-

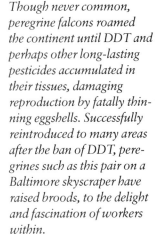

Though never common, peregrine falcons roamed the continent until DDT and perhaps other long-lasting pesticides accumulated in their tissues, damaging reproduction by fatally thinning eggshells. Successfully reintroduced to many areas after the ban of DDT, peregrines such as this pair on a Baltimore skyscraper have raised broods, to the delight and fascination of workers within.

guish a large proportion of the endangered and threatened species.

But a cup that is half empty is also half full. The scientists have pinpointed 75 forest tracts that, if preserved, would save a large number of the species in question and the diversity of habitat and life in those tracts, of which the birds are notable emblems. Whether those tracts will in fact be set aside is an entirely different question, but in a world often faced with the implementation of triage—in this case, of concentrating limited resources where they may do the most good and allowing other areas to go by the board—it is of paramount importance to recognize those sites most worthy of being saved.

Such choices and the management practices required can lead reasonable and informed people into disagreement. The story of the whooping crane is an example. Few argued

with the notion of setting aside as a reserve the area along the southern coast of Texas now known as Aransas National Wildlife Refuge, the last remaining wintering grounds of these majestic birds, whose population had dwindled to a paltry 16. And there was no argument about preserving the birds' breeding grounds in northern Canada (once the area was discovered). But controversy swirled around the decision to remove some eggs from whooping crane nests in the wild in order to develop a captive population for safe-keeping, as it were. Today some 46 whoopers live at the U.S. Fish and Wildlife Service's Patuxent installation in Laurel, Maryland. Recently, biologists have proposed dividing the Patuxent flock in order to combat the risks inherent in keeping these birds together. The plan calls for sending half the flock to a new home at the International Crane

Since DDT and some other pesticides were banned from use in the United States in 1972, fish-eating ospreys and other birds of prey have once again become a common sight along our coasts and rivers.

Foundation in Baraboo, Wisconsin.

In the early 1970s, biologists identified another suitable wintering ground for whoopers—or so it seemed—on the Rio Grande south of Albuquerque, New Mexico, where thousands of smaller sandhill cranes winter after flying down from breeding grounds in Idaho and other Rocky Mountain states. The trick (again controversial) was to take whooper eggs from the Canadian nesting grounds and put them in the nests of the sandhills in Idaho, in the hope that the sandhills would become unwitting parents for young whoopers. In 1984, between 30 and 34 whoopers were numbered among the teeming sandhills. By 1989, however, this project's outcome was uncertain because of excessive mortality primarily due to avian tuberculosis and collisions with powerlines as well as to the wide dispersal of the birds, especially females, and the fact that no permanent pair bonds had formed among these whoopers.

The jury—and the judgment—also remain out in the matter of the California condor, whose wingspan—which may exceed nine feet—is the greatest of any North American

Beginning in the 1970s, wildlife managers attempted to increase the numbers and diversify the range of critically endangered whooping cranes. Taking whooper eggs from nests in northwestern Canada, biologists put them into the nests, top, of sandhill crane "foster parents" in Idaho. If the sandhill-raised whooping-crane chicks, such as the diminutive one swimming above, survived to maturity, they might add numbers and new nesting and wintering territories to the tiny whooper population. Opposite, a white whooping crane stands amid sandhill crane foster parents on the Rio Grande in New Mexico.

land bird. The condor is a direct and little-changed holdover from Pleistocene times, when huge, now-extinct mammals such as mammoths, gigantic bison, and ground sloths roamed the land, all eventually becoming large carcasses for a large scavenger. Controversy has attended virtually every effort to save the remaining condors; in the latest, they have all been captured from the wild and placed in captivity at the San Diego Wild Animal Park and the Los Angeles zoo. The condors produced two chicks by mid-1989, and biologists hope to reintroduce this species into the wild in 1992.

Time seems to work against the life of the world. Each day, somewhere, a biologist tells an audience that species are disappearing at a rate of one a week, maybe one a day, soon one an hour. Most of the species vanishing in such a stunning cascade of extinction are insects and plants, and most of them are unknown to science, utterly unheralded denizens of the tropics that so quickly and devastatingly are being denuded for farming and cattle ranching and a lucrative trade in teak and mahogany.

But also, according to the International Council on Bird Preservation, by 1988 more than one in 10 of all bird species faced extinction—some 1,029 in all. Only 10 years ago, 290 species faced their doom. In Brazil alone, the figure rose from 29 endangered species in 1978 to 121 a decade later. In Indonesia, the number grew from 14 to 126. Habitat destruction is the major cause, although not the only one: the Bali myna declined in that same decade from some 500 individuals to about 60, a victim of poaching as well as habitat loss.

So the urgency increases daily, but another sense of time also is involved—a commitment over periods that are hard to imagine, especially for people given to thinking in fiscal years. It has been estimated that, left largely to its present devices, the human population will stabilize agonizingly at some unimaginable number of billions within 500 years. No computer can suggest what will be left of the natural world then. How long does it take, say, for a rain forest to regenerate itself? No one today can say with any certainty how large a rain forest reserve or any other reserve must be to avoid decay or to retain its own biological integrity, which

Legendary Thunderbird of California Indians, the California condor, opposite and below, may spread its wings 10 feet or more. With numbers reduced to nine wild birds in 1985, the last free-flying condors were captured and placed in zoos. Molloko, above, born in 1988, was the first captive-bred California condor chick successfully hatched. Here he is fed and cared for by unseen humans through a realistic hand-puppet "parent." Today zoos house about 30 condors.

includes a natural loss of species diversity. The answers to these questions will be forthcoming, as a result of the largest single ecological study ever undertaken, but they are years, maybe decades, away.

In the late 1970s, ornithologist Thomas Lovejoy, then of the World Wildlife Fund and now the Smithsonian's Assistant Secretary for External Affairs, saw a unique opportunity for a tropical forest reserve study in the passage of a Brazilian law that, while encouraging cattle ranchers to cut down large tracts of rain forest in Amazonia, also required them to leave half the forest intact. If, Lovejoy reasoned, the ranchers could be persuaded to leave the intact half in the form of variously sized, isolated, islandlike tracts, it would be possible to observe the natural process of species diminution and to determine the minimal critical size for tropical forest reserves—to make ecology in this quintessentially complex life system a predictive science.

By the early 1980s, a small band of American and Brazilian scientists had begun to take a census of the life forms—trees, mammals, birds, and insects—in a series of areas ranging from one to 1,000 hectares (a hectare is about 2.5 acres). Once a census was complete, the tract was isolated and the forest surrounding it cut down. Then, in order for the scientists to see which animal species

abandoned a tract and when, the scientists began taking the census again. The first phenomenon they noted was that the number of species in an isolated tract increased rapidly as creatures from the former forest flocked to the remnant habitat. This increase lasted only temporarily, however; soon the number of species of birds and other animals fell drastically.

The scientists found also that the remnants created an edge habitat that was subject to the direct sun as well as to wind. Soil, which in tropical forests is poor and thin, dried up, and winds blew down trees. Second-growth shrubs and trees quickly appeared in this drier and brighter edge habitat, and, along with them, animal species adapted to the conditions. A one-hectare forest tract soon became all edge, and both the overall number of birds and the number of bird species in the tract diminished. As the edge penetrated deeper into the remaining forest in larger tracts, other events took place. Army ants, those awesome raiders of the forest floor, found insufficient territory for their forays, and with their disappearance so went the birds known as obligate ant followers that foraged in their wake. Wild pigs also departed these tracts, and with them the frogs that used their wallows as breeding places.

In the publish-or-perish atmosphere of much of science, there has been some criti-

In a long-term project begun by Thomas E. Lovejoy, today a Smithsonian Assistant Secretary, biologists in Brazil study "islands" of tropical forest remaining in deforested areas. They hope to learn the minimum and optimum sizes of forest area required for the survival of various plants and animals. Opposite left, World Wildlife Fund project director Rob Bierregaard removes a dove from an ultrafine mist nest as part of a census of bird species in a patch of forest. Opposite right, graduate student Rita Mesquite studies seed dispersal of rain forest plant species. Left, a Brazilian researcher records data.

cism of the project to the effect that it has produced relatively few scientific papers or hoped-for guidelines for policy-makers. But science, too, can become captive to the fiscal-year mentality, which is hardly useful when looking at long-term processes. Will the answers, whenever they do emerge, be too late? Lovejoy points out that even if by the turn of the century half the forest is gone, much will remain, and by then we may know how to regenerate such complex systems. By then, new techniques may have been developed to log rain forests selectively for the likes of teak and mahogany, leaving the less economically desirable trees standing, rather than burning them. By then, governments of tropical nations may have learned to use the wisdom of those who for thousands of years made the forests agriculturally productive.

In southern Mexico, a group of only a few hundred Lacandon Mayas live by ancient practices that have worked for more generations than anyone can remember. They slash and burn a forest patch of about one hectare and plant fast-growing crops that thrive in the ash and protect the soil. The next year they plant such crops as corn and onions. Wild species such as pineapple and corkwood are permitted to take hold, and the diverse mix of forest and domestic plants attracts deer and other animals that can be hunted, and protects against plant disease as

well. After about five years, the Indians leave rubber and cacao trees behind; about 15 years later the forest begins to take over. A single Lacandon farmer's family thus may need to clear no more than 10 hectares of virgin forest over a period of 50 years.

Throughout the tropical world, remnants of such land-wise people remain, often scorned as savages and dismissed as living at a mere subsistence level. But the vast majority of other people living in those parts—dispossessed, thrown into cities and the burgeoning shantytowns around them—are below subsistence. The urgent need is to confront and alleviate the nearly unimaginable poverty and overpopulation of those cities, thereby relieving at least some of the pressure to destroy the world's tropical forests and perhaps restoring a kind of natural equilibrium.

Today the bird enthusiast, finding fewer birds in his area during the nationwide spring bird count, thereby finds himself caught up in international economics and politics. He is witnessing one of the results of the desperate problems of overpopulation in lands he has never seen and may not even be able to find readily on a map—part of a series of interlocking problems of people in faraway places who even within the borders of their country speak utterly different languages and whose universe is almost as different from the bird counter's as is the universe of the birds he so

Philippine eagles, top, among the largest raptors in the world, may number only about 300. Loggers, above, sometimes kill the eagles while felling trees. Such habitat destruction, exemplified by the denuded, eroded hills of Madagascar, opposite, is a threat to wildlife worldwide.

admires. It is certain that the World Bank is as important to bird preservation as are those organizations with "bird" or "nature" in their names.

It is hypocritical, however, to scorn desperate people trying to survive or even to scorn less desperate people seeking a higher standard of living by fulfilling an insatiable foreign market demand, thereby also improving their country's balance of payments. The demand for the likes of teak, bananas, beef, and sugar in such enlightened nations as Japan and the United States is a major part of the reason tropical forests and their avian inhabitants are vanishing at so great a rate. Ours is, as the migrant birds have shown, one world.

And how are the migrants faring in North America? From 1979 to 1986, there was a continuous drop in the numbers of long-distance migrant songbirds, a trend spotted by the national Breeding Birds Survey, which has been conducted for more than two decades by Chandler Robbins, a wildlife biolo-

gist with the U.S. Fish and Wildlife Service. Each year the survey employs some 2,000 ornithologists (both professional and amateur) to sample population numbers at strategic points along various routes. This is a purely statistical survey, subject to happenstances including weather and the ornithological experience of its participants. But all in all the routes cover some 50,000 miles, and over long periods happenstance is not an important factor. According to the survey, whole groups of birds that winter in the tropics—thrushes, vireos, warblers, and tanagers—suffered population declines in the 1980s, some species as much as 30 percent.

"Some of the birds we're talking about," says Robbins, who is perhaps best known as one of the authors of the popular *Golden Guide to North American Birds*, "are among the best-known backyard birds in North America—the wood thrush, the red-eyed vireo, the scarlet tanager. Those and others seem to be having serious problems now and are probably headed for worse."

Before the Breeding Bird Survey began seeing declines in migrant bird populations in the '80s, an older counter of birds, the Breeding Bird Censuses, sponsored by the National Audubon Society, showed declines beginning about 1965. These censuses count the number of breeding pairs of each species within a given block of habitat, and the results are presented as the number of breeding pairs per 100 hectares. A number of breeding bird censuses date back to the 1940s, including one still being conducted in Rock Creek Park in Washington, D.C., by Shirley Briggs, formerly a colleague of the late Rachel Carson. Recently, David Johnston and Steven Taub of George Mason University in suburban Washington, D.C., looked at trends in breeding bird numbers using only the long-term censuses and only those in locations that had not been changed by suburbanization. They noted a striking concordance. In places where the neotropical migrants outnumbered nonmigrant species before 1965, the line showing neotropical migrant numbers subsequently dipped below that depicting the numbers of breeding residents. Chickadees, blue jays, cardinals, and other resident birds did not increase to cause the population lines to cross: the neotropical migrants declined. .

Further evidence for an earlier widespread decline appears in an unlikely source. Weather radar blips of birds migrating at night across the Gulf of Mexico decreased radically after 1965 until, in the mid-'80s, those expert at identifying birds from radar could find few.

John Terborgh of Duke University points to the loss of habitat in South and especially Central America as the leading cause for the reduction in songbird numbers. Songbird populations are far more densely packed in their southern wintering grounds than they are in the north, where a decline becomes apparent only through such comprehensive censuses as Robbins's. A casual backyard observer would be hard put to realize that the vireos that nested on his property declined to three one year, or even two. "As far as our migrants are concerned," Terborgh says, "the area that is especially crucial is what I call the near tropics. Half of all the landbirds that breed in North America winter in just five countries—the Bahamas, Cuba, Mexico, Haiti, and the Dominican Republic." He estimates that clearing one acre of forest in those areas is equivalent in loss of bird habitat to clearing five to eight acres in the north. The Bachman's warbler, he notes, is most likely now extinct, not having been seen in 15 years. Much of what was probably its primary winter habitat in Cuba is now largely given over to the growing of sugar cane.

Russ Greenberg of the National Zoo also theorizes that it is tropical deforestation that has taken the toll in songbird numbers. He has studied the wintering habitats of many warblers and other neotropical migrants, some of which change their habitats between breeding and wintering from forest to shrubland and vice versa. According to his research, only those species that winter in tropical forests have declined, and not those that breed in temperate forests but winter in tropical shrublands and fields.

The problem for these songbirds, however, is not confined to the tropics. Forests in North America are mostly fragments now, and the fragmentation continues with the growth of suburbs. Here, as in the tropics, when a forest is fragmented the edge effect takes over. Even a forest tract of hundreds of acres may offer certain songbirds no true forest interior. Predators such as raccoons and opossums thrive on the margins of for-

In North America, changing land-use patterns pose a threat to some familiar species. Still-numerous flickers, opposite, compete for nest holes with aggressive starlings, which accompany suburban sprawl, above. Below, breeding over much of the eastern half of the United States, the American woodcock may find some new habitat in old farms left to return to woodland, while losing ground to shopping malls and other manifestations of human population pressure.

ests. Suburban cats and dogs—which from the standpoint of birds and many ornithologists are nothing more than subsidized predators—join in causing songbird nest failure. And one of the worst problems for nesting songbirds is another bird—the brown-headed cowbird. Originally a bird of open lands in the Great Plains, it now occurs in all of the lower 48 states and up into Canada as a result of the clearing and breaking up of large tracts of forests. Many birds that live within the cowbird's new, expanded range have not evolved adequate defenses against the cowbird's parasitic tactics—laying eggs in other birds' nests—and are generally helpless. Often more than half of the nests built near a forest edge or along roads penetrating a forest are parasitized during the May-to-mid-June period of the nesting season.

By contrast, studies of the vast and still largely continuous tracts of Great Smoky National Park in Tennessee and North Carolina show that in many instances migrant songbird populations are holding their own. This, of course, suggests that the great tracts of wooded lands under the management of the U.S. Department of Agriculture's Forest Service might provide viable northern strongholds for such migrants.

U.S. forestry practice, however, is to manage the forests for multiple use, a major one being logging. It is common for logging roads to penetrate deep into wildernesses and near-wildernesses, with various tracts being clear-cut—a more economical tech-

Toxic industrial wastes poured into streams and rivers, above; solid-waste landfills such as this Alaskan one, top, frequented by bald eagles; and irrigation waste water contaminated with leached salts threaten bird populations in almost every corner of the continent. On the other hand, the greening of suburban lawns has helped American robins, opposite, extend their range into the South.

nique than selective cutting. To be sure, such tracts usually are replanted, but often with only one or two types of tree, thus assuring a continuing loss of forest diversity. Also, the roads and the clear-cut tracts produce vast reaches of edge in the midst of what appears to be plentiful, continuous forest.

But another legal requirement under which the Forest Service operates is that no resident species shall become endangered. New plans call for extensive wilderness areas to remain roadless. In the George Washington National Forest in Virginia, for example, half the trees will never be cut. It may be, too, that as the edge effect becomes more clearly understood and appreciated even fewer holes will be punched into these crucial songbird population centers.

In the summer of 1988, the Forest Service took a step that outraged logging interests but delighted conservationists: it allowed an owl to put a stop to logging in some of the United States' oldest and largest stands of original forest. The northern spotted owl, about which little was known until recently, will nest only in trees that generally are older than the U.S. Constitution. Most of these—Douglas firs, cedars, hemlocks, and spruces as many as 1,200 years old, some with trunks eight feet in diameter—are to be found in the wet coastal forests of the Pacific.

The national forests of the Pacific Northwest are home to some 1,600 pairs of spotted owls, and arguments continue as to whether that number gives the bird endangered species status or not. In any event, the Forest Service decided to reverse earlier plans that called for increased logging in such original-forest areas and instead to reserve 2,700 acres of old-growth forest for each pair of owls. Arguments may well continue on the adequacy of even this step, but it must be seen as salutary that an obscure owl became a flagship for the attempt to save a unique habitat, and one that supports hundreds of other wildlife species as well as the owl. In response to this decision, made amid howls of protest by timber interests, the *New York Times* announced flatly that the emphasis of U.S. national forest policy is "now tilting toward wildlife and recreational use."

It is not merely habitat destruction by changing land-use patterns—the building of shopping malls and highways, timbering, or turning marshland to farmland, seashores to condominiums—that threatens birds. So does habitat poisoning. Here again, it was birds that signaled to humankind that something was awry and potentially dangerous to human life.

In the early 1980s thousands of dead and deformed aquatic birds started turning up at Kesterson National Wildlife Refuge, south of San Francisco. The wings and legs of many were stubs, and others suffered corkscrew beaks, open skulls, loss of eyes: it was as if an avian thalidomide had been put into the water. This alarming scene was repeated throughout other wildlife areas in California, Nevada, Utah, and Montana. It is generally believed that the culprit behind the birds' suffering is irrigation waters from agricultural lands draining into ponds and other bodies of water and producing vast buildups of potentially toxic trace elements such as selenium, cadmium, mercury, and arsenic. These elements not only cause deformities in young birds but also weaken the immune systems of adults, making them more susceptible to such diseases as avian cholera. Ducks, grebes, herons, coots, and pelicans all have been found to have high concentrations of these elements.

In 1987 efforts began to clean up the Kesterson refuge—at a probable cost of $50 million—by scraping off the top 15 centimeters of soil in the area into a waste dump. No one knows if the procedure will work. A soil specialist at the University of California at Riverside pointed out: "We must find a solution to what is happening, not only to save wildlife but to save agriculture as well. If we don't have anywhere to put our irrigation water, we may have to convert to dry land farming." In this regard, it is notable that no human civilization that depended on intensive irrigation has lasted for much more than 500 years.

The litany of bird endangerment could go on and on and fill an encyclopedia of many volumes; meanwhile, the linkage between the viability of bird habitat and other wildlife habitat and the long-term viability of human habitat becomes clearer. The ominous tear in the ozone layer has scared the human race with threats of skin cancer and worse; but the ultraviolet light it lets through also interferes with the ocean's production of krill, a main

source of food not only for many whales but also for many fish and seabirds, including penguins. The overfishing of krill and sand eels in the northern seas is also a potential threat to certain seabird populations—as well as to the animal-feed industries that rely on these catches even as they use them up. Oceans that cannot support oceanic birds cannot support humans either; oceans that are toxic to fish and birds will poison us as well. All of this is slowly but perhaps increasingly becoming clear: we are all in it together. Public acceptance of the notion that we can continue so profligately will soon, perforce, change. As the late physicist Richard Feynman said in another context, "Reality must take precedence over public relations, for nature cannot be fooled."

Still, a certain kind of public relations—used in behalf of biological reality—shows signs of working: it is called education. In Mali, one of the poorer nations of Africa, the desperately hungry populace might not be considered a likely seedbed for the conservation ethic. But local people along the Niger Delta look upon the Abdim's stork as a bird of good luck, since its annual arrival signals the onset of the rainy season. Taking advantage of this regard, a team led by Monique Trudel of the International Council for Bird Preservation a few years ago undertook the task of visiting every secondary school in the delta region at least twice, bearing posters showing that the Abdim's stork and also the white stork are valuable because they help control the locusts that attack the local crops of rice. Before long, the students were asking insightful questions about bird ecology, presenting Trudel and her colleagues an opportunity to talk about habitat destruction and the role humans have played in bringing it

The Exxon Valdez *oil spill was just the worst of such disasters to afflict Alaska's once-pristine coastal waters. Opposite, a fisherman in Cordova Bay holds an oiled harlequin duck; above, an oil-mucked beach in Prince William Sound. After light fractions evaporate, tarry oil residue, top left, may sink to the bottom where its toxic effects will linger for years.*

about. The presentations also attracted friends and parents, who began to see the role they could play in habitat *protection* in order to maintain the auspicious birds. Both teenagers and adults also learned of the migrations of the storks and other birds, and thus were better able to envision their own small village in a global context. All this might seem a modest step, but even in advanced industrialized nations the conservationist's cry boils down to little more than "think globally, act locally." And there is nothing like children to influence their parents.

At the same time, all those children soon will be of parenting age; in developing countries it is not atypical to find that some 50 percent of the entire population is under 15 years. The figure in Kenya, for example, is about 55 percent. The greater than twofold increase in human population that such a demographic profile almost guarantees for Kenya will be accompanied by a catastrophic strain on that nation's natural resources, including its parks and reserves. The grim fact is that in such places there will be much starvation, many malnourished brains, and many extinctions of species at least at the local level as desperate governments try to feed their teeming cities. Such a tide of need has led many wildlife and park managers to realize that it simply won't do to establish a reserve and put a fence around it. It is necessary instead to see to it that the local population around a reserve has a stake in the protection of the reserve's flora and fauna and receives more from its continuation than merely a few tourism jobs.

In Nepal's Chitwan National Park—which was set aside by Nepal's king specifically for tigers but which also encompasses a major habitat for rhinoceros and a host of other species—it became clear that giving local populations the right to obtain thatch for roofs not only would influence the people to look more kindly on the park but also would give them a better chance of survival themselves. And so tree plantations—with the promise of renewable sources of firewood—were set up around the park.

Norman Myers, for long an outspoken wildlife conservationist in Africa for the United Nations, has upset many saviors of wildlife by proposing that culling 10 percent each year of the great herds of wildebeest, zebras, giraffes, and other animals, putting their meat "into cans, and [having] the cans distributed around the countryside in local African markets," might be the only way to ensure African people a sufficient stake in their spectacular wildlife to save it. At that rate of culling, Myers says, the herds would be self-sustaining. He proposes such measures with great reluctance: "A dreadful response to a dreadful problem. . . . I advocate it only because I do not see what other options we have." Considering such a gloomy assessment, one is reminded of *The Plague*, the existentialist novel by Albert Camus, in which the (anti)hero doctor goes about the daily and hopeless business of relieving the suffering of the afflicted as each day more and more are afflicted. What else is there to do, after all?

In the face of such prospects, it is rapidly becoming clear to wildlife managers that there is really nothing left of wilderness. "A wildlife reserve and a zoo," says Christen Wemmer, director of the National Zoo's Conservation and Research Center in Front Royal, Virginia, "have to be managed in the same manner."

Less than a generation ago, zoos often were perceived as an extractive industry, taking animals from the wild for display to a public that otherwise would never see such creatures. But during the 1970s it became widely understood in zoo circles that the time for such extraction was for the most part over. If they could cooperate rather than compete, zoos could become one of the last remaining arks for wildlife. At the same time, a burgeoning understanding of population genetics began to reveal another arm of the grim reaper of wildlife, be it in zoos or in the wild. Small zoo populations, or small wild

populations, were subject to inbreeding, which usually meant lowered fertility and less viable offspring. With this understanding began what may one day be called the heroic era of zoos, which can be summed up in three words: Species Survival Plans (SSPs).

As a part of the Smithsonian Institution, the National Zoo had long shared a research-oriented organization's finicky regard for keeping records, and in the late 1970s the Zoo's records of births and deaths and parentage provided zoologist Katherine Ralls with the information needed to show the debilitating effects of inbreeding on a zoo population. It became clear that, henceforth, as many zoo populations of a given species as possible had to be considered a single population, with "founders"—that is, sires and

dams—not allowed to dominate the gene pool. This in turn meant that zoos would have to ship good breeders back and forth among themselves and retire some animals from breeding once their contribution was at the point of becoming too widespread. Such an organized effort necessitated a great deal of record-keeping, including the creation of studbooks, as among racehorse breeders. The beginnings of such a record bank existed at the time; it is now called the International Species Inventory System (ISIS) and is under the management of the American Association of Zoological Parks and Aquariums. Hundreds of zoos worldwide contribute information to ISIS, and, from this computerized captive-animal data file, breeding plans for 46 endangered species had been devel-

CES OISEAUX PROTEGENT LES RECOLTES
CAR ILS SE NOURRISSENT DES CRIQUETS
QUI RAVAGENT LES CULTURES

Critically endangered Guam rails, above, and Micronesian kingfishers, below, were nearly eradicated by brown tree snakes accidentally introduced to Guam in the 1940s. Captive breeding programs at the Smithsonian's National Zoological Park and other zoos have raised the numbers of these birds, but their future remains in doubt. The snakes, which have wiped out three other bird species native to Guam, must be eliminated completely before the captive-bred birds can be reintroduced.

oped by 1989 and new animals are being added all the time. For such a plan to come into being, the species must be endangered in the wild and breedable in captivity. Futhermore, a number of zoos must have the necessary genealogical data for the species, as well as the personnel to implement whatever scheme is produced. The system is a kind of triage based on very practical considerations indeed.

Among species that now are being bred under such plans are at least 11 kinds of birds. One of these is a snowy white bird with blue-black wingtips, dark legs, and bright blue skin around the eyes—the rarest and most fabulous bird known to the equally fabulous island of Bali in Indonesia. It is alternately known as the Bali myna, Bali starling, Rothchild's myna, and locally as the Jalak Bali. In 1988 there were only about 60 wild individuals left on the island. A popular zoo bird since its discovery in 1911, the Bali myna had not been actively bred in American or other zoos (insect- and fruit-eaters are harder to breed in captivity than seed-eaters). Well before the advent of species survival plans, however, Guy Greenwell, then curator of birds at the National Zoo, had begun keeping a registry of captive Bali myna births and encouraging other zoos to breed them. In late 1987, after an SSP had been developed,

it was possible to take 39 captive-bred individuals from North American zoos and ship them to Indonesia. There, in the Surabaja zoo, they produced more offspring, three of which were released into Bali Barat National Park (two of these birds have since disappeared, and the status of the third is not certain).

The North American-bred birds were kept in the zoo as a hedge against the accidents and vagaries of reintroduction, which, as with the mynas, can be many and mysterious. For, in putting a captive population back into the wild, one is reintroducing not a species but a number of individuals of a species. Evolution and adaptation and natural selection work at the level of the individual, and it is the sum total of those individual experiences that speaks of the destiny of the species. The evolutionary forces of captivity on a group of birds are not understood very well. Furthermore, by the time captive-bred birds are released into the wild, the wild itself may have changed in subtle as well as obvious ways.

When the Panama Canal was dug in 1913, it formed a considerable inland body of water called Gatun Lake, in which a former forested hilltop became an island now known as Barro Colorado. The island soon became a major site for the intensive study of tropical biology, and for decades it has been adminis-

Captive-bred Jalak Balis, or Bali mynas, above, have been reintroduced into the wild in their native Indonesia. After habitat destruction nearly extirpated them in the wild, numbers of the mynas were bred at the National Zoological Park and other North American zoos. Meticulous record-keeping helped to minimize the incidence of problems related to inbreeding.

tered by the Smithsonian Institution. As with any island, its size dictated that a certain number of species would not continue to live there—theory in practice, but the theory did not explain why any particular species would vanish from its precincts, nor what would happen if species that once lived there were reintroduced. In the late 1970s, ornithologists sought to reintroduce to the island two species of wrens from the mainland—one of them the song wren. During the period of the song wren's absence from the island, other birds known as antwrens had become populous there, and it was thought that in the new island environment perhaps the antwrens had driven the song wrens off. It turned out, however, that the song wren's disappearance from Barro Colorado was a result of its nesting habits.

Song wrens tend to build nests just below human-eye level in saplings growing next to sluggish streams. The nests, messy affairs that resemble the kind of plant detritus that gets washed up and caught in branches during spring runoff, offer the song wrens a reasonable amount of camouflage from predators. Two pairs of reintroduced song wrens found relatively sluggish streams for nesting, but Barro Colorado, being an island and a former hilltop, provided few such habitats.

Instead, thanks to the presence of generations of biologists, the island provided foot trails that evidently reminded the wrens of streams, and along these they built their just-below-eye-level nests. But along the trails the nests were easily discovered by predators, and the song wrens survived only a few years before once again vanishing from Barro Colorado. Those that had lived there before it became an island were probably those that had been forced out of their good habitat as the lake formed. Similarly, before reintroducing a group of captive animals to a place where they have become extinct or where their numbers are seriously dwindling, it is wise to know the causes of that animal's population reduction in the wild.

The cause of the extinction of most of the birdlife on the Pacific island of Guam is generally believed to be the brown tree snake, which is endemic to the Solomon Islands, the lowlands of New Guinea, and northern Australia. Inadvertently introduced to Guam after the ravages of World War II, the snake was a grand herpetological success, its population on the island rapidly exploding to an estimated seven per acre. One-third of its diet consists of birds and bird eggs, and, not long after its arrival, it became apparent that the snake—an active nocturnal hunter and an agile climber—was wreaking havoc on the local bird fauna, with incubating females and their eggs disappearing first and at an accelerating rate.

By the beginning of 1983, three endemic bird species of Guam had become extinct. Another two—a striking flightless rail and a small, bright, land-feeding kingfisher—also appeared doomed. That same year, the remaining Guam rails and Micronesian kingfishers were collected and their fate placed in the hands of several American zoos and breeding facilities on Guam. By the beginning of 1989, the captive population of Guam rails had increased to approximately 140 birds, the kingfisher's to about 50. Plans are now afoot to introduce offspring from these populations to an island north of Guam that has similar habitat but as yet no snakes. But, warns Scott Derrickson, curator of birds at the National Zoo, "there is a wild card in the deck. With 26 potential breeders at the outset, the kingfisher may do all right—if we can keep them nesting. A problem for the rails

Kuna Indians of Panama's San Blas Islands created this colorful reverse appliqué mola, *a needlework portrait of parrots of the dwindling forest of their coastal home. Opposite, the thick-billed parrot, exterminated in the southwestern United States by the 1930s, has been reintroduced from Mexico to the Chiricahua Mountains of southern Arizona. There these northernmost American parrots seem to be holding their own.*

may be the small number of founders: just nine birds. We don't know if the species will hold up through the inevitable inbreeding."

Such are the choices facing those who would preserve some of the diversity of the world's birds—a role not unlike that most often attributed to God. But in the absence of divine omniscience, and as the French philosopher Montaigne pointed out, one needs to be ignorant of many things in order to act. And, like Camus's doctor, act we must. Is the potential of saving a flightless rail on a distant and remote island—a secretive bird that practically no one will ever see anyway—worth such an effort? Would saving one more bird species be just a drop in the bucket? Not for the rail, certainly.

But there are more than 1,000 bird species now in considerable danger, and all the zoos in the world would fit into the borough of Brooklyn, New York. As one ornithologist has pointed out, "it would be an arrogant assumption on the part of humans to believe they can maintain, through captive breeding, entire functioning communities, entire ecosystems. Surely the best answer is to maintain throughout the world habitats of adequate size and diversity so that nature can take care of itself."

That is clearly the challenge, the key to survival—the survival of birds, and the survival also of a dignified existence for humanity on the only planet known to support life. Surely, somehow, we are up to it.

The stars still shone in the predawn sky as we walked quietly across the prairie towards the river. A chorus of crickets and frogs sang softly in the dark, but mostly all was still hushed. Then, as we drew nearer the river, strange, guttural sounds met our ears—the soft murmurings of thousands of sandhill cranes waking from their nighttime roost in the Platte River.

Only gradually as dawn dispelled the dark did the tall, graceful cranes become visible. They stirred, stalking about in the shallow water, prancing in little dance steps, testing their wings in the cold dawn air. Their voices grew louder and louder as the morning brightened. Then, their calls filling the air, they rose up in small groups and headed out to the surrounding fields and wet meadows to feed.

The gathering of up to half a million lesser sandhill cranes along the Platte in south-central Nebraska is surely one of the most spectacular rites of spring on Earth. It is the largest congregation of cranes anywhere in the world. Following migration patterns evolved since the end of the last Ice Age, the birds fly in from their widely scattered wintering grounds

Silhouetted against the sunset, opposite, sandhill cranes congregate at dusk in the shallow Platte River in south-central Nebraska. Hundreds of thousands of these long-legged, long-lived birds, below, gather here each spring on their northern migration, roosting in the river at night and feeding in wet meadows and cornfields during the day.

in the American Southwest and Mexico, arriving in early March.

Here on the Platte they have always found the wide river channel, shallow waters, and submerged sandbars that provide safe roosting from predators during the night. And here they have always found food. The native prairie grasslands and wet meadows have provided abundant tubers, invertebrates, and small vertebrates, important sources of the protein and calcium stores needed for egg production in the north. Today the cranes also glean tons of waste corn from agricultural fields. Food is particularly crucial to them at this juncture: the Platte River Valley is the only place on their 2,500-mile journey where they actually can put on weight, building up a reserve of fat that will help them complete the last leg of their migration to nesting grounds in Canada, Alaska, and Siberia.

Despite the huge numbers of sandhill cranes that continue to congregate at these staging grounds each spring, alterations to the river's flow and to much of the surrounding land threaten the future of the

An aerial view of a stretch of the Platte River, above, reveals the shallow, broad channel and open sandbars that have provided safe roosting sites for sandhill cranes for thousands of years. The diversion of increasing amounts of the Platte's water in recent years, however, has al- *lowed the encroachment of woody vegetation into the channel and greatly reduced the amount of this vital riverine habitat that can be used by the cranes. In some areas, right, people now use machinery to clear vegetation, a task once accomplished by the Platte's strong spring flows.*

majestic birds—and that of others as well, including the endangered whooping crane. The Platte—the old "mile-wide-and-an-inch-deep" river of western pioneers—has had increasing amounts of water diverted from it for agricultural and hydropower purposes. The river channel has been greatly narrowed, and the powerful spring flows that kept the channel and sandbars scoured of vegetation—and thus suitable for the cranes—are no longer strong or swift enough to do the job.

The cranes, which 100 years ago spread themselves out along 300 miles of river during their stay here, are now confined to a stretch of only about 70 miles. In some areas people and machinery have been employed to do what the river once did, uprooting rank vegetation and small trees and shrubs that have colonized the river's sandy islands. The concentration of cranes into such a small area has biologists worried, for it renders the birds much more vulnerable to a catastrophic storm or toxic spill or to a potentially devastating epidemic such as fowl cholera (in fact, the first cranes to be diagnosed

as having this disease turned up in March 1988).

The cranes have also lost much of the wet-meadow habitat surrounding the river; hundreds of thousands of acres of these wetlands have been drained for row crops. The cranes must now fly farther and farther afield to find this habitat—an inefficient feeding strategy for large birds in need of fat reserves. Wet meadows are also places of crane courtship and thus are crucial to the annual renewal of the lifelong pair bond between male and female cranes.

So far the cranes are for the most part faring well; another spring has seen hundreds of thousands of them converge once again on the Platte. So far this short stretch of river in the region known as the big bend and the now mostly agricultural

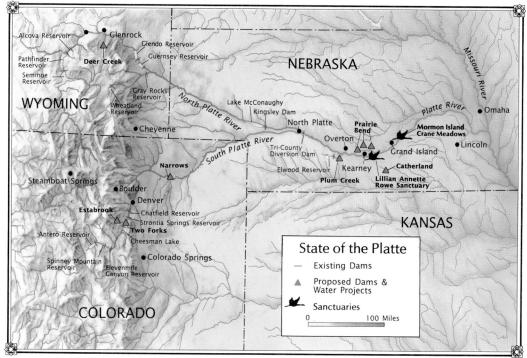

A distinctive, bright-red cap of bare skin covers the forehead of an adult sandhill crane, above. Today these birds crowd into only about 70 miles of the Platte River, left, in the region known as the big bend, roughly between Overton and Grand Island.

State of the Platte
— Existing Dams
▲ Proposed Dams & Water Projects
🦢 Sanctuaries
0   100 Miles

Sandhill cranes at left forage in a field of corn stubble along the Platte. Native wet meadows, below, also provide crucial food for the cranes and serve as areas for dancing and courtship. At right, hundreds of cranes fill the air at dawn over a roost on the river. After about a six-week stay on the river, from early March to mid-April, the cranes set off for breeding grounds in Canada, Alaska, and Siberia.

land around it continue to sustain them. And so far, in a sense, the cranes continue to sustain us, offering us an unmatched spectacle of the wildness and inexorable rhythms of nature. Surely there is something restorative in watching wave after wave of these great, long-lived birds, silhouetted against the sunset, flying in to roost in the shallow, blue river, their calls gradually becoming muted in the twilight. The society of the cranes is wondrous.

Soon enough their visit ends. On a certain morning in early April, a large roost of cranes stirs restlessly in the river, and then, in the usual flurry of wings and trumpeting calls, heads out to the cornfields to feed. They seem too distracted to eat, however, and the intensity of their calls increases considerably as the morning warms. Then they are off, once again gaining the air with their characteristically slow, deliberate wing beats. Spring thermals carry them ever higher; finally they form into long, wavering lines and set off on the final leg of their northern journey. It is a leave-taking that has marked the turn of the seasons here for thousands of years. As they disappear into the distance, their calls faint on the wind, we are reminded that it is up to us to ensure that the cranes return to the Platte next year and for many years to come.

After watching the 20th century arrive in a maelstrom of new values and new ways of evaluating the world, the historian Henry Adams wrote in dour protest that "the practical value of the universe has never been stated in dollars." How, then, are we, nearing the end of the 20th century and almost absent-mindedly engaged in the most deadly war of all time—a war against the rest of nature—how are we to appraise the value of the likes of nature's jewelry, the sparkling diversity of birds?

A diamond has value. It is made up of carbon atoms, each of which consists of a known number of protons and electrons. Its weight can be expressed in carats, its brilliance described by other numerical scales. Armed with such numbers, experts can compute a monetary value for the diamond, and it can even be insured at replacement cost. If, by accident, madam flushes the diamond down the toilet, the insurance company can be persuaded to buy her another one that—in numerical character—matches the one she lost. The lost diamond, however, may have been a romantically tendered gift, and the insurance company replacement, though much like the old one, cannot carry with it precisely the original connotations. The new one satisfies the numbers but in some sense is inert, with what might be called the heart of it gone.

In 1988, editorial writers in many major newspapers noted the death of a single bird. This bird—a dusky seaside sparrow—simply did what all creatures do: it died. But it was the last remaining dusky seaside sparrow—the last of its race—in the world. It was gone, extinct forever. This passing of the bird and its race was duly lamented, and then the editorial writers went on to more pressing matters, matters more easily expressed in numbers—the cost of living, for example.

Numbers are colorless, odorless, disembodied. They express relationships among things that seem to be real and thus take on their own kind of reality. Modern science is, for the most part, a matter of numbers. No cosmologist actually can sense in his mind's eye the explosion that may have created the universe—the so-called Big Bang. It is known only by means of numbers—unimaginably large numbers of degrees of heat, unimaginably small fractions of seconds. The dance of subatomic particles that make up madam's diamond is understandable to physicists today only by means of statistics. That such numerical understandings are valuable, that they yield practical results, is inarguable. Even the journals of ecology are sprinkled with numbers, with formulas; and one day, if we are lucky, these formulas may help us to understand—perhaps even to save and replenish—the natural world.

Worthiness is another matter altogether. There is no such thing as a priceless diamond, or a priceless work of art. Dollar values can be assigned to such things and *are* assigned routinely in museums and auction houses and stores. Like science, economics is an attempt to understand the world by means of numbers. And, like scientists, economists are given Nobel prizes for coming up with formulas that explain how things work. They often deal in replacement costs: the formula may include a particular commodity or resource with an assigned value. If, for some reason or another, the commodity or resource is unavailable or exhausted, another commodity can be inserted in the formula with perhaps a slightly different assigned cost, and all is well. This, of course, is a kind of alchemy, resting on the notion that there are no laws of nature.

Its plumage changing with the season, a willow ptarmigan, opposite, peers over the richly colored tundra vegetation in Alaska's Denali National Park and Preserve. Below, a plate featuring several species of wood warblers, painted by Smithsonian bird curator Robert Ridgway and published in A History of North American Birds (1874), *on which he collaborated with Spencer Baird and Thomas Brewer, hints at the diversity of these jewels of the bird world.*

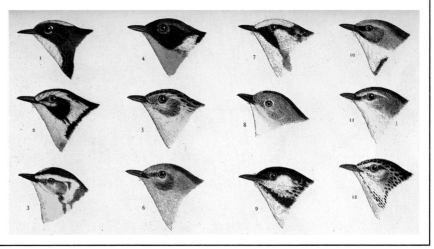

Even so, economic arguments can be—and are—used by conservationists to persuade people that it is in their self-interest to preserve such things as the habitats of birds. Such strategies as selective logging and small-scale farming are intertwined with the harvesting of thatch for roofs and with tourism to provide potential long-term benefits to people. The number of binoculars purchased and motel rooms rented by people who want to see the spotted owl, for example, can be computed against the shifting value of board feet of old Douglas fir. People with little interest in the natural world *per se* can be convinced that certain actions are necessary because of economic and other benefits to one's compatriots or even to the human race at large.

But many biologists, faced with other concerns, including an aesthetic and empathetic feeling for the great cathedral of life, look at the burgeoning rate of extinctions and conclude that something more is needed than economic arguments. Yet all of the potentially valuable pharmaceutical plants that remain unknown and undescribed in the tropical rain forests seem not to be of sufficient value to stem the tide of devastation. In September 1986, at a Smithsonian symposium on biodiversity, Paul Erlich of Stanford University said, "We must, if we are going to solve this problem in any permanent way, create a feeling for other organisms that goes beyond what they might or might not do for Homo sapiens."

It may be too late in the development of human civilization to invest the natural world and its creatures with a spiritual dimension—the animism that is prevalent in so many cultures we like to think of as primitive or pagan. It may be that the relentless reasoning of science precludes that. But science is practiced by human beings, and it can provide us with more than mere knowledge or ethically neutral facts. It can—whether it is groping toward an understanding of the extent of the universe or of the motivations of a house wren—provide a sense of awe and respect that is the fundament of humanity's ineradicable religious urge. To hear the purple martin's dawn

song and have an understanding of its meaning; to glimpse however dimly that other universe in which birds live, uniquely perceived by them but linked so directly with our own; to realize that the great forces of nature, such as evolution, are not grand abstractions but play themselves out on the level of the individual creature, on each red knot among the hundreds of thousands that alight on the shores of Delaware Bay, precisely attuned to the timing of the mating of horseshoe crabs—to gain such intimate understandings from the auspicious science may, one can hope, be a step in the greater understanding that all of life is a gift—a truly priceless gift from the universe—and should joyously, *in excelsis*, be treated as such.

Asian relative of the North American wood duck, a male mandarin duck, opposite, fluffs his feathers as he preens. Above, a boy and a blue grouse fascinate each other in Yellowstone National Park.

INDEX

Illustrations and caption references appear in *italic*.

Central America, 99, 100, 122, *137*, 242, 244, *244*

Chat, 191

Chickadee, 135, 144, 257; black-capped, *165*, 240-41, *241*

Chicken, 32, 36, 63, 80-81, 107, 121, 131, 144, 205, 233

Chiffchaff, European, 208

China, 30, 31, *33*, 36, 40

Chiricahua Mountains (Arizona), *268*

Chitwan National Park (Nepal), 263-64

Christmas Island, 104-7, *129*

Cincinnati Acclimatization Society, 107

Cleveland Museum of Natural History, 63

Climate. *See* Habitat

Coelurosaur, *65*

Color, birds and, 13

Communication, 192-213; calls, 195-97, 199-203, *206*, *209*; long-distance, 208; motivation-structural rules model, 195, 197-99, *206*; nonvocal, 193-94, *197*, *198*, *199*, *201. See also* Displays

Compsognathus, 54, *54*, 55, 62

Condor, 77, 100; Andean, 100; California, 75, 100, 248-51, *251*; La Brea, 77

Conservation, 246-69

Cook, Captain James, 111

Coot, 65, 86, 260; American, *10*

Cormorant, 80, 132, 151; double-crested, 159

Cortés, Hernán, 32

Corvidae, 92

Cowbird, 234; brown-headed, *234*, 258

Crabs, horseshoe, shorebirds and, *183*, 187-88

Crane, 24, 32, 65, 68, 72, 77, *139*, 191; crowned, *197*; red-crowned, *197*; sandhill, *139*, 248, *248*, 270-75; sarus, *21*; whooping, 194, 247-48, *248*, 273

Cretaceous Period, 63, 64, 67-69, 89, 99

Crocodilian, 63; Crocodile, 13

Crossbill, red, *152*

Crow, 30, 92, 131, 144, 163, 194; Hawaiian, 113; Indian house, colonization by, 108-9

Cuckoldry, *217*, 218, 234

Cuckoo, 32, 75, 138, 194; European, *234*; Old World, 179, 234; shining bronze, 179

Curlew, Eskimo, 188

D

Daedalus, *26*

Daly, Jim, *181*

Damselfly, *19*, *121*

Darling, J.N. "Ding," *45*

Darwin, Charles, 47, 84, 86

DDT, 246, *246*, 247

Decoys, *44*

Deforestation, 251

Delaware Bay, *183*, 187, 279

DeLeon, Jennifer, *181*

Derrickson, Scott, 268

Diatryma, 78, 81

Diet. *See* Food

Digestion, 121

Dinosaurs, 54, *54*, 60, 62-63, 64, *65*, 68, 78, 81

Dipper, American, 97

Dispersal of bird species, *84*, 86

Displays, *201*, 214, *221*; courtship, *129*, 194, *194*, *198*, *199*, *214*, *227*, *228*, *228*, *231*, 232-33, *239*; postnuptial, *221*; prenuptial, *221*; territorial, 194, *197*, *199*; threat, 197-98, *201*, 207

Distribution. *See* Habitat

Dodo, 76, 79, 80

Domestic pigeon, 97

Domestication, 32-36

Dominance hierarchies, 233, 240

Donovan, Amy, 58, *271*

Dove, *35*, 80, 131, 135, *253*; mourning, 144; Polynesian, 89

Dovekie, 92

Dowitcher, long-billed, *122*

Duck, 68, 70, 78, 80, 92, 111, 122, 138, 144, 176, 260; evolution of, 69-70; harlequin, *95*, *96*, *262*; mandarin, *279*; Muscovy, 32; wood, *231*, *279*

Duck stamps, *45*

Dummy nests, 221, *225*

Dunlin, *155*, *183*

E

Eagle, 75, 100, 112, 135, *139*, *180*; bald, 112, 159; Daggett, 77; golden, 26, *131*, *181*; Philippine, 145, *151*, *254*

Ear, evolution of, 75

Echolocation, *121*

Edge effect, 257

Egg dumping, 234

Egret: cattle, *106*, 108; great, 130, *137*; snowy, 246

El Niño, 104-7

Elephant bird, 77, 79

Elliott, Daniel Giraud: *A Monograph of the Pittadae*, *50*

Embryology, 63

Emlen, Stephen, 184

Emu, 79, 80

Enaliornis, 67

Endangered species, 246-51, *251*, 258, *266*, *267*, *268*, 273; Atlantic coastal lands and, 188; captive breeding, 264-69; predators, *266. See also* individual species

Endothermy (warm-bloodedness), 62

England, 38, 45, 67

Environmental degradation, 21-23. *See also* Habitat destruction

Eocene Epoch, 68, 69, 70, 72, 75, 78

Erlich, Paul, 279

Europe, 32, 36, 78, 107

Everglades, Florida, *13*, *95*, *96*, *118*

Evolution, 53-81, *65*; adaptation to seed diet, 146; angiosperms, 68; gymnosperms, 68; mammals, 68; reptile-bird transition, 54-81; study of, 92. *See also* individual species

Evolutionary theory, 60

Extinct species, 90, *201*, *258*

Extinction of species, 107, 277, 279; Cretaceous Period, 68-69; in Hawaiian Islands, 90, 111-14; species distribution and, 100

F

Falconry, *36*, 38, 116

Falcon, 75, 100, *130*, 132, *180*, 234; peregrine, 132, 144, 194, 246, *246*; wings, *130*

Fantail, rufous-fronted, *201*

Feathers, 26, 125, 126, 137-38; barbules, 59; care of, *135*, 137-38; contour, 138; evolution of, 54, 55, 56, 60-62; fossil, *56*; identification of, 58-59; millinery trade and, *137*, 138, 246; primary, 126; secondary, 125

Feduccia, Alan, 62, 68, 72

Feeding strategies, 122, *125*, 237-38, 241; aerial, 176; filter-feeding, 70-72; habitat and, *95*, 96-97; herbivorous birds, 79; of cedar waxwings, 190; of eastern kingbirds, 190; of Hawaiian finches, 86-89; of orchard orioles, 190; of vultures, 100

Feynman, Richard, 262

Field Guide to the Birds, A (Peterson), *46*

Fieldfare, 89

Filoplume, 138, 139

Finch, *46*, 113, 138, 175, 191; California house, 108; eastern house, 108; Galápagos woodpecker, 160; Laysan, 113; Nihoa, 113; sharp-billed ground, 159; woodpecker, *159*; zebra, 205

Finch, Hawaiian, *90*, *91*, 111; evolution of, 86-89; extinction of, 90

Finch, Robert, 240

Fitzpatrick, John W., 188

Flamingo, 68, 72, 138, 145; evolution of, 69-70; greater, *70*; lesser, 145

Flicker, 107, *257*

Flight, 116-39; adaptations for, 125; adaptations to, 118-22, *119*; aerodynamics, 60; evolution of 60-62, 118; modes of, *118*, 122, 124, *125*, 126, *126*, *128*, 135-37, *139*; soaring in migration, 176; symbolic, 24, 30-31

Flightless birds, 145; diet, 145; extinction of, 111, 114

Flightlessness, 90, 124; evolution of, 67, 78, 80-81

Flocks. *See* Troupial birds

Florida, 79, 96, 97, *106*, *118*, 135; Everglades National Park, *13*

Flycatcher, 99, 100; *Empidonax*, 188, 190; evolution of, *186*; Hawaiian, 86; migration of, *186*; pied, 208, 224; tyrant, *187*; tyrant, migration of, 188-89; vermilion, *100*; willow, *100*

Food: aerial insectivores, 217; competition for, 159; consumption related to body weight, 144-45; foraging behavior, 159-63; hoarding, 142-44, *143*, 144; seasonal variation, 151; specialists versus generalists 146-51; starvation, 164-65. *See also* Habitat; Insectivorous birds; Predatory birds; Raptors

Forbush, Edward Howe, 107

Legend: B Bottom; C Center; L Left; R Right; T Top.

Abbreviation: SI Smithsonian Institution

FRONT MATTER & INTRODUCTION: p. 1 James R. Fisher/DRK Photo; 2-3 Chip Clark; 4-5 Sharon Cummings; 6-7 Chip Clark; 11 Chuck Gordon; 12 Sharon Cummings; 14 National Museum of Natural History/SI, photo by Ed Castle; 15T SI; 15B from Harper's Weekly, June 1, 1878, after original sketches and photographs by Henry W. Elliott; 16 art by Walter A. Weber, photo by Mark Gulezian/ QuickSilver; 17 SI; 18 Townsend P. Dickinson/ Comstock; 19T Michael Fogden; 19BL Townsend P. Dickinson/Comstock; 19BR Townsend P. Dickinson/Comstock; 20 Belinda Wright/ DRK Photo; 21T Richard Howard; 21B Spencer Baird, Thomas M. Brewer, Robert Ridgway. *A History of North American Birds.* vol.II. Little, Brown & Co., 1877. SI Libraries, photo by Mark Gulezian/QuickSilver; 22-23 James D. Young; 23 SI.

ENCHANTMENT: pp. 24-25 Wolfgang Bayer; 26T Jean Vertut; 26B Chuck O'Rear/West Light; 27 *Victoire de Samothrace,* Louvre, © Reunion des Musées Nationaux; 28 MS. Douce 211, fol. 13r Bodleian Library, Oxford; 28-29 The British Museum, photo by Michael Holford; 29 Metropolitan Museum of Art, Chapman Fund, 1958 (58.125.4); 30 National Museum of American History/SI, photo by Kjell Sandved; 31T Ed Castle; 31B The White House; 33 "The Phoenix," from *Ten Album Leaves* by Hua Yen, (60.25A), Freer Gallery of Art/SI; 34 *Kakubha Ragini* c. 1770? Victoria & Albert Museum (IS 158)1952; 35T Henri Cartier-Bresson/Magnum; 35B MS. Ald. 42130. fol. 169v. by permission of the British Library; 36T,36B Ulisse Aldrovandi. *Ornithologiae hoc est de avibus historiae libri XII,* vol. 1-3. Bologna, 1599-1603. SI Libraries, photos by Mark Gulezian/QuickSilver; 37 from the Manesse MS. at Heidelberg, Universitäts Bibliothek Heidelberg, by permission of Inse-Verlag, Leipzig; 38T Conrad Gesner, *Historiae animalium liber III, qui est de avium natura.* 1585. SI Libraries, photo by Mark Gulezian/ QuickSilver; 38B, 39 Mark Catesby. *The Natural History of Carolina, Florida and the Bahama Islands.* 1731. SI Libraries, photo by Mark Gulezian/QuickSilver; 40 Edward Lear. *Illustrations of the Family of Psittacidae or Parrots.* 1832. SI Libraries, photo by Mark Gulezian/QuickSilver; 41 John Gould. *A Monograph of the Trogonidae, or family of trogons.* 1836-1838. SI Libraries, photo by Mark Gulezian/QuickSilver; 42 Alexander Wilson.

American Ornithology, vol. III. SI Libraries, photo by Mark Gulezian/QuickSilver; 43 John James Audubon. *The Great American Cock.* National Gallery of Art, gift of Mrs. Walter B James; 44,45B Kenneth L. Garrett; 45T Copyright Department of the Interior. Artists: top, John S. Wilson, 1981, center Neal R. Anderson 1989, bottom Arthur M. Cook, 1972; 46 © Roger Tory Peterson. *A Field Guide to the Birds East of the Rockies.* 1980. Reprinted by permission of Houghton Mifflin Company and courtesy of the artist and Mill Pond Press, Fla. 47 Budd Titlow-f/stop.

RARE BOOKS, RARE BIRDS: ORNITHOLOGY AND ITS ILLUSTRATION 1450-1900: pp. 48L Eleazar Albin. *A Natural History of Birds.* 1731-1738. SI Libraries, photo by Mark Gulezian/QuickSilver; 48R Hartmann Schedel. *Liber chronicarum.* 1493. SI Libraries, photo by Mark Gulezian/QuickSilver; 49T Conrad Gesner. *Historiae animalium liber III, qui est de avium natura.* 1585. SI Libraries, photo by Mark Gulezian/QuickSilver; 49L Francis Willughby. *Ornithologiae libri tres.* 1676. SI Libraries, photo by Mark Gulezian/QuickSilver; 49R George Louis Leclerc Buffon. *Histoire naturelle des oiseaux.* 1770-1783. SI Libraries, photo by Mark Gulezian/QuickSilver; 50T John Latham, MD. *General History of Birds,* vol. VII. 1823. SI Libraries, photo by Mark Gulezian/QuickSilver; 50B Mathurin-Jacques Brisson. *Ornithologia.* 1760. SI Libraries, photo Mark Gulezian/QuickSilver; 51 Daniel G. Elliot. *Monograph of the Pittidae.* 1893-1895. SI Libraries, photo by Mark Gulezian/Quick-Silver.

ORIGINS: pp. 52-53 James A. Kern; 54 art by Charles Knight, Field Museum of Natural History, Chicago (neg. #CK39T); 55 Chip Clark; 56L Peabody Museum of Natural History, Yale University; 56R art by Rudolf Freund, courtesy of The Carnegie Museum of Natural History; 57, 58, 59 Chip Clark; 60 art by John Anderton; 61 Frans Lanting/Photo Researchers Inc.; 62T art by O.C. Marsh, Peabody Museum of Natural History, Yale University; 62B David Smart/DRK Photo; 63T art by O.C. Marsh, Peabody Museum of Natural History, Yale University; 63B John H. Ostrom & Peabody Museum of Natural History, Yale University; 65T Field Museum of Natural History, Chicago; 65B based on pg. 29, *The Age of Birds.* Alan Feduccia. Harvard University Press, 1980; 66 Eric Horan/Photo Researchers Inc.; 68 Michael Fogden; 69 Stephen J. Krasemann/DRK Photo; 70T Erwin & Peggy Bauer; 70B T.W. Wienwandt/DRK Photo; 70-71 Stephen J. Krasemann/DRK Photo; 72

Ed Castle; 73 art by Bonnie Dalzell, photo by Mark Gulezian/QuickSilver; 74 D.P. Whistler & Natural History Museum, Los Angeles County; 75 art by Charles Knight, Field Museum of Natural History, Chicago (neg. #CK8T); 76T Henrik Gronvold, *The Dodo and Given,* National Museum of American Art/SI, (transfer from National Museum of Natural History, Division of Birds); 76B Karen Petersen; 77 art by Charles Knight, Field Museum of Natural History, Chicago, (neg. #CK32T); 78, 79 Stuart Strahl; 80 painting by J. Fenwick Lansdowne. From *Rails of the World: A Monograph of the Family Rallidae* by S. Dillon Ripley. 1984. © Feheley Fine Arts Inc., Toronto; 81 E.R. Degginger.

WHEREABOUTS: pp. 82-83, 84 William Burt; 85 painting by J. Fenwick Lansdowne. From *Rails of the World: A Monograph of the Family Rallidae* by S. Dillion Ripley. 1984. © Feheley Fine Arts Inc. Toronto; 86 Grant Heilman/ Grant Heilman Photography; 87T Roger B. Clapp; 87B Eric Curry: Maps/West Light; 88 Stan Osolinski; 90T Ian C. Tait; 90B by permission of Kamehameha Schools/Bernice Pauahi Bishop Estate, Honolulu; 91 painting by H. Douglas Pratt, Bishop Museum, Honolulu; 93 Cassin. *Mammalogy and Ornitholgy Atlas.* plate 31. SI Libraries; 94-95 Wolfgang Kaehler; 95T James A. Kern; 95B Jack A. Barrie; 96T Karen Petersen; 96B Michael Fogden; 97 Dr. H. Barnett/Peter Arnold, Inc.; 98 Jamie Quintero; 99 Bob & Elsie Boggs/Photo Researchers, Inc.; 100 Tom J. Ulrich/TSW-CLICK/ Chicago; 101 Raymond G. Barnes/TSW-CLICK/Chicago; 102-103 Stan Osolinski; 103T Leonard Lee Rue III/DRK Photo; 103B Wayne Lynch/DRK Photo; 104, 105 Ralph W. & Elizabeth A. Schreiber; 106T Margarette Mead; 106B Chuck O'Rear/West Light; 107T Roger Wilmshurst/Bruce Coleman Inc.; 109 David Cavagnaro/DRK Photo.

FRAGILE OUTPOSTS: pp. 110 painting by H. Douglas Pratt, Bishop Museum, Honolulu; 111 R. Michael Severns; 112 Carol Pearson Ralph; 113T, 113B Victor Krantz/SI; 114L, 114R Lionel Walter Rothschild. *Avifauna of Laysan.* 1893-1900. SI Libraries, photo by Mark Gulezian/QuickSilver; 115 Scott B. Wilson assisted by A.H. Evans. *Aves Hawaiienses—The Birds of the Sandwich Islands.* 1890-1899. SI Libraries, photo by Mark Gulezian/QuickSilver.

FLIGHT: pp. 116-117 Gordon Langsbury/ Bruce Coleman Inc.; 118 M.P. Kahl/DRK Photo; 119 art by John Anderton; 120 Mik Dakin/Bruce Coleman Inc.; 121 Merlin D.

Tuttle; 122 Gary R. Zahm/DRK Photo; 123T, 123C art by John Anderton; 123B Andreas Feininger, LIFE Magazine © Time Inc.; 124-125 Dwight Kuhn; 125 Neal Smith; 126 Frans Lanting; 126-127 Tom & Pat Leeson; 128TL from Scientific American, *Birds*, "Birds as Flying Machines," by Carl Welty; 128BL Jack D. Swenson; 128R Frans Lanting; 129TL Roger B. Clapp; 129TR Tui De Roy; 129B E.R. Degginger; 130T Alan & Sandy Carey; 130B art by John Anderton; 131 Thomas D. Mangelsen/Images of Nature; 132 David Cavagnaro/DRK Photo; 133 John W. Warden; 134 Lynn M. Stone; 135 Stan Osolinski/TSW-CLICK/Chicago; 136 Jeff Foott; 137 Michael Fogden; 139 James Tallon/Outdoor Exposures.

SUBSISTENCE: pp. 140-141 Thomas D. Mangelsen/Images of Nature; 142T Carter Johnson; 142B David Neil Parks; 143 Sharon Cummings; 144 Jeff Foott; 145L Harold Hoffman; 145R Tom Brakefield/Bruce Coleman, Inc.; 147T Paul E. Meyers; 147B Robert Carlyle Day/National Audubon Society-Photo Researchers, Inc.; 148T Bob & Clara Calhoun/Bruce Coleman, Inc.; 148BL G.K. Brown/Ardea, London Ltd.; 148BR Jeff Lepore; 149T J.L.G. Grande; 149BL Jeff Foott; 149BR E.R. Degginger/Bruce Coleman, Inc.; 150 Dr. Robert Kennedy; 151 Michael Fogden; 152L Wayne Lankinen/DRK Photo; 152R Frans Lanting; 153TL Steve Kaufman; 153TR E.R. Degginger; 153B Margarette Mead 154 James R. Fisher/DRK Photo; 155T Tom McHugh/National Audubon Society-Photo Researchers, Inc.; 155B Jack A. Barrie; 156 Tui De Roy; 157T Wolfgang Kaehler; 157BL, 157BR Tui De Roy; 158 John Shaw/Tom Stack & Assocs.; 159T, 159B Tui De Roy; 160 Glenn Van Nimwegen; 161 M. Danegger/Peter Arnold, Inc.; 162 George H. Harrison; 163 Jeff Foott; 164 J.C. Carton/Bruce Coleman, Inc.; 165 Tom A. Schneider/DRK Photo.

MIGRATION: pp. 166-167 Jeff Foott; 168T James F. Parnell; 168B Stephen J. Krasemann/Photo Researchers Inc.; 169 Dwight R. Kuhn; 171 Stephen J. Krasemann/DRK Photo; 172 Stephen J. Krasemann/DRK Photo; 173 Lynn M. Stone; 174 Gregory K. Scott; 174-175 Tom & Pat Leeson; 176 Jonathan Blair/Woodfin Camp Inc. 177 M.P. Kahl/DRK Photo; 178T Tom & Pat Leeson/Photo Researchers Inc.; 178B Paul E. Meyers; 179 Gary R. Zahm/DRK Photo; 180, 181 George H.H. Huey; 182T, 182-183 Jeff Lepore; 183 Michael Fogden; 184-185 John W. Warden; 186 Leonard Lee Rue III; 187T Gregory K. Scott/Photo Researchers Inc.; 187B T.W. Wiendandt/DRK Photo; 188 Paul E. Meyers; 189 James D.

Young; 191 Stephen J. Krasemann/DRK Photo.

COMMUNICATION: pp. 192-193 Keith A. Szafranski; 194 Steve Maslowski/Photo Researchers, Inc.; 195 Spencer Baird, Thomas M. Brewer and Robert Ridgway. *A History of North American Birds.* vol.I. Little, Brown, & Co., 1874, SI Libraries, photo by Mark Gulezian/QuickSilver; 196 Steve Kaufman/Peter Arnold, Inc.; 197 M.P. Kahl/DRK Photo; 198T Wolfgang Kaehler; 198B M.P. Kahl/DRK Photo; 199T Jeff Foott; 199B Nell Bolen/National Audubon Society-Photo Researchers, Inc.; 200T Michael Fogden; 200B Heather Davidson; 201 Nick & Gidge Dramos; 202 Sharon Cummings; 203 The Bettmann Archive; 204 Tom & Pat Leeson; 205T James D. Young; 205B Thomas D. Mangelsen/Images of Nature; 206L Margarette Mead; 206B Eugene S. Morton; 206-207 Lynn Rogers; 207B Thomas Kitchin/Tom Stack & Assocs.; 209 Nick & Gidge Dramos; 210 art by John Anderton; 211 John Gould. *The Birds of Australia.* vol.III. 1840-1848. SI Libraries, photo by Mark Gulezian/QuickSilver; 212 Steve Kaufman/Peter Arnold, Inc.; 213 Jules Breton. "The Song of the Lark." 1884. Henry Field Memorial Collection (1894.1033) © 1989 The Art Institute of Chicago.

SOCIETY: pp. 214-215 Frans Lanting; 216, 217 Eugene S. Morton; 218-219 Jeff Foott; 221 Keith A. Szafranski; 222 Michael Fogden; 223T Brian J. Coates/Bruce Coleman Inc.; 223B Stan Osolinski; 224 Stephen J. Krasemann/DRK Photo; 225 Keith A. Szafranski; 226-227 Glenn Van Nimwegen; 227 Jeff Foott; 228, 229 Jean-Paul Ferrero/Ardea, London Ltd.; 230 Tom J. Ulrich/TSW-CLICK/Chicago; 231T Tom & Pat Leeson; 231B Stephen J. Krasemann/DRK Photo; 232 Nick Bergkessel/Photo Researchers Inc.; 232-233 Barth Schorr/Bruce Coleman Inc.; 233 Dennis Avon/Ardea, London Ltd.; 234 Stephen Dalton/NHPA; 235 Jeff Lepore; 236 Vernon E. Grove; 238T Paul Meyers; 238B Art Wolfe; 239TL Steve Kaufman; 239TR Nick & Gidge Drahos; 239BL Hope Alexander; 239BR Kevin Schafer/Tom Stack & Assocs.; 241 James D. Young.

CHALLENGE: pp. 242-243 Martin Johnson Heade. "Cattleya Orchid and Three Brazilian Hummingbirds." 1871. National Gallery of Art, Washington, D.C. Gift of the Morris and Gwendolyn Cafritz Foundation; 244 Jessie Cohen/National Zoological Park/SI; 245 Alvin E. Staffan/Photo Researchers, Inc.; 246 Michael Ventura/Folio Inc; 247 Tom & Pat Leeson; 248T Thomas D. Mangelsen/Images of Nature; 248B Roderick C. Drewien ©

National Geographic Society; 248-249 Art Wolfe; 250 Tom McHugh/Photo Researchers, Inc.; 251T © Zoological Society of San Diego, photo by Ron Garrison; 251B John Borneman/Photo Researchers, Inc.; 253, 254 Stephanie Maze/Woodfin Camp, Inc.; 254T F.R.E.E. Ltd./Neil Rettig; 254B F.R.E.E. Ltd./Wolfgang Salb; 255 Frans Lanting; 256 Wayne Lankinen/DRK; 257T George Rockwin/Bruce Coleman, Inc.; 257B William Burt; 258T Art Wolfe; 258B The Bettmann Archive; 258-259 Jack D. Swenson/Tom Stack & Assocs.; 260T Stephen J. Krasemann/DRK; 260B Eric H. Poggenpohl/Folio Inc.; 261 Laura Riley; 262 Bill Nation/Sygma; 262-263 Richard Hartmier/First Light, Toronto; 263 Bill Nation/Sygma; 264-265 M.P. Kahl/Photo Researchers, Inc.; 265 I.C.B.P., Paris; 266T Joseph Van Wormer/Bruce Coleman, Inc.; 266B Jessie Cohen/National Zoological Park/SI; 267 Kenneth W. Fink/Ardea, London Ltd; 268 David Cavagnaro; 269 Fulvio Eccardi.

CRANES ALONG THE PLATTE: pp. 270-271 Ron Spomer; 271, 272L Thomas D. Mangelsen/Images of Nature; 272B Stephen J. Krasemann/DRK Photo; 273T James Tallon/Outdoor Exposures; 273B *Audubon* Magazine, Joe LeMonnier; 274, 275 Ron Spomer.

EPILOGUE: pp. 276 Sharon Cummings; 277 Spencer Baird, Thomas M. Brewer, Robert Ridgway. *A History of North American Birds.* vol.I. Little, Brown & Co., 1874. SI Libraries, photo by Mark Gulezian/QuickSilver; 278 Sharon Cummings; 279 Jeff Foott.

Engravings and Woodcuts:
p. 10 Spencer Baird, Thomas M. Brewer, Robert Ridgway. *A History of North American Birds.* vol.I. Little, Brown and Co., 1874. SI Libraries; 13 Thomas Nuttall. *A Popular Handbook of the Ornithology of Eastern North America.* vol.I. Little, Brown & Co., 1896, SI Libraries; 24 Baird, vol. II; 30 Ulisse Aldrovandi. *Ornithologiae hoc est de avibus historiae libri XII.* vol.I. Bologna, 1599-1603. SI Libraries; 32 Ibid.; 52 Baird, vol.II; 64 Baird, vol.III; 67 Baird, vol.II; 83 Thomas Nuttall. *A Manual of the Ornithology of the United States and of Canada.* 2nd ed. Hillard, Gray and Co., 1834. SI Libraries; 89 Baird, vol. I; 116 Baird, vol. III; 138 Nuttall, *Handbook*; 141 Baird, vol. II; 154 Nuttall, *Handbook*; 166 Ibid.; 193 Ibid.; 208 Baird, vol.I; 214 Baird, vol.III; 240 Ibid.; 242 Nuttall, *Handbook*.

ACKNOWLEDGMENTS

Jake Page would like to express his gratitude to a Mrs. Moore who taught grade school in Chappaqua, N.Y., in the 1940s and who appreciated Page's watercolor of a recognizable robin unecologically juxtaposed with a rose; his wife, Susanne, who (among other things) showed him his first prothonotary warbler; Amy Donovan and Alexis Doster and the other people at Smithsonian Books who had faith in this project; E.G. Buxton, a Latin teacher who made the mystery of sentences a bit more clear; David Brower, the only successful fusion experiment in this century; S. Dillon Ripley, who allowed Page to play in his fields for a time and gave advice on raising pekin robins; a countless array of other ornithologists, who freely share their data and insights and leaven our lives in doing so; and Letty Morton, who sees to Gene when he fetches up on the banks of the Severn River in Maryland at their comforting center of good fellowship, informal science, and, what may save us all, good humor.

Gene Morton wishes to thank the following students and colleagues for their contributions to and support for this project: Steve Bissinger, Cathy and Chuck Blohowiak, Priya Davidar, Kim Derrickson, Scott Derrickson, Russ Greenberg, Guy Greenwell, Mike Erwin, Susan Farabaugh, Sheri Lynn Gish, Sue Haig, Judith Hand, Tom Lovejoy, Jim Lynch, Sarah Mabey, Vicky McDonald, Doug Mock, Martin Moynihan, Charles Pickett, Mario Ramos, John Rappole, Eyal Shy, Cindy Smith, Neal G. Smith, Stanley Rand, Martha Van der Voort, Dennis Whigham, and Kim Young. Last but not least, I extend heartfelt thanks to my wife, Letty, and my parents, Gene and Jane Morton, all of whom have shown great patience with me in the production of this book and otherwise.

The Editors of Smithsonian Books would like to thank the following people for their assistance in the preparation of this book:

The curators and other members of the staff of the Division of Birds, National Museum of Natural History/SI; Leslie K. Overstreet and Ellen Wells, Special Collections, Smithsonian Institution Libraries; Bruce M. Beehler and Mary T. Pacaro, Office of the Secretary Emeritus; Roger B. Clapp, U. S. Fish and Wildlife Service; Hans-Dieter Sues, Department of Paleobiology, National Museum of Natural History/SI; Neal G. Smith, Smithsonian Tropical Research Institute; Peter F. Cannell, Smithsonian Institution Press; Philip Herron, Library technician, National Museum of Natural History/SI; Ed Castle; Mrs. Alexander Wetmore; James H. Bruns, Curator, National Philatelic Collection, National Museum of American History/SI; Thomas Lawton, Senior Research Scholar, Freer Gallery of Art and Arthur M. Sackler Gallery/SI; Martin P. Amt, Special Assistant to the Director, Freer Gallery of Art and Arthur M. Sackler Gallery/SI; Milo C. Beach, Director, Freer Gallery of Art and Arthur M. Sackler Gallery/SI; Kay Zakariasen, Picture Editor, *Natural History* magazine; Mark Gulezian/QuickSilver Photography; Robert W. Skelton, O.B.E.; Gerald C. Pustorino and Walter Thompson, Ringier America; Lou Jordan, Westvaco; Ronald Harlowe, Steve Smith and Joe Vicino, Harlowe Typography, Inc.; Bruce Cunningham, Harry Knapman and Dale Freeman, The Lanman Companies; John Quill and Charles A. Sicard, Ecological Fibers, Inc.; Bob Jillson, Holliston Mills, Inc.; Lynne Komai, Don Komai, Lynn Umemoto, Don Wheeler, Janie Koussis and Steve Blackwood, The Watermark Design Office.